BEGINNING DATA STRUCTURES USING

C

By:

YOGISH SACHDEVA

1

PREFACE

Friends, when I was doing MCA from Panjab University, Chandigarh, I had to search books on Data Structures through C for making preparation for examinations. Though this search led me to the selection of some good books on this subject, yet I could not find any book, which might have dealt with the Programming in such a manner, so that the students like me could do the same with ease. Thus it gave me an idea of writing a book on this subject, so that a learner of this subject may find the programming interesting. It is with this object in view, that an effort has been made to give proper explanations of the programs. I hope you will find this book very helpful in your studies. However if you find any mistake, or want to give some suggestions for the improvement of this book, then the same may be sent to the publishers, so that the mistakes may be rectified and the suggestions may be incorporated in the next edition. I consider it my duty to convey my hearty thanks to the various authors, whose books have made me competent enough to write this book. In the end, I would like to thank the publishers, who have taken keen interest and rendered me their full cooperation in the publication of this book.

YOGISH SACHDEVA

Table of Contents

6

Introduction to Data Structures

A **data type** is an instance of data that may be native to the language or defined by the user. And a composition of data types, which forms some kind of systematic organization, is called **Data Structure.**

Data structure = Organized data + Allowed operations

Simple Data structure can be used as building blocks of complex data structure. Array is a simple type of Data structure by using which we can build more complex data structure. Data structure can be classified according to the following four types.

1. Linear & Non-linear: The data stored in a sequence is called Linear, while the other is called Non-linear e.g. Array is Linear & Tree is Non-linear.

2. Homogenous & Non-homogenous: The data structure, which contains single type of data, is known as Homogenous whereas others are Non-homogenous. For example, Array is an ordered set of homogenous elements stored in a contiguous memory location. And Record (structure) is a Non-Homogenous.

3. Static & Dynamic: This means the allocation of memory, either Static or Dynamic.

4. Direct access & Sequential access: The ability of directly referring to an item without having access to any other is called Direct access. Sequential access is searching through a number of items before finding a specific item i.e. an item, which is not accessible. For

example, arrays provide a direct access to any element within the array by means of an index (direct access). But in linked lists, we must traverse through the list to locate a specific node (sequential access).

Some of the data structures, which will be discussed in detail later in the book, are given below.

1.1   Arrays

This is a simplest type of linear data structure (one dimensional array), by means of which a set of finite number say n of similar data elements can be referenced by a set of n consecutive numbers 1, 2, 3, …….. n. For example, consider the following list of elements:

5, 6, 8, 4, 3, 1, 2, 56, 67, 78

This list of 10 elements can be stored in an array of size 10 as follows:

A[1]	A[2]	A[3]	A[4]	A[5]	A[6]	A[7]	A[8]	A[9]	A[10]
5	6	8	4	3	1	2	56	67	78

Array 'A'

Note: Arrays will not be discussed hereafter in this book. It will be presumed that the reader is familiar with arrays.

1.2   Stacks

Stack is a linear data structure of dynamic height, all components of which are of same data type (Homogenous components). A stack is also called a Last-In-First-Out (LIFO) system, in which insertion and deletion of any component can take place only at the top of the stack, where 'top' is an end of the stack. That is, at any given time, the only item, which can be accessed to, is on the top of the stack (sequential access). A common example of a stack is a dish or a coin stacker. Dishes are "pushed" onto the top and "popped" off the top.

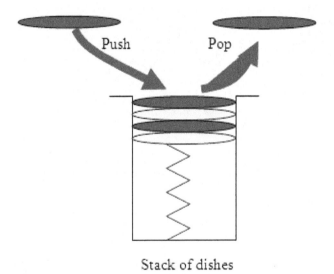

Stack of dishes

1.3   Queues

Queue is also a linear data structure of dynamic height, which contains single type of data. Thus it is a homogenous data structure, all components of which are of same data type. A queue is, also, called a First-In-First-Out (FIFO) system, in which insertion of a component can take place only at one end, called "rear" end of the queue and deletion of a component can take place only at other end, called "front" end of the queue (Sequential access). The word "queue" is thus like the queue at a counter for service, in which customers are dealt with in the order in which they arrive.

1.4   Linked Lists

Linked list is again a linear data structure of dynamic length. All components within the list are of same data type stored in nodes. Thus it is also a homogenous data structure. To locate a specific node in the list, we must sequentially traverse through the list (Sequential access). In a linked list, each item is allocated a space in memory as it is added to the list. A link is kept between each item with the next item in the list. Each node of the list has following two elements:
- The item being stored in the list and
- A pointer to the next item in the list

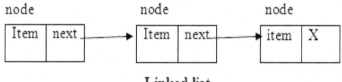

Linked list

The last node in the list contains a NULL pointer to indicate that it is the end or tail of the list. As items are added to a list, memory for a node is dynamically allocated. Thus the number of items that may be added to a list is limited only by the amount of memory available.

Note: Above shown example of linked list is a Linear Linked List. There are two more variations of linked lists: Doubly Linked List and Circular Linked List. These lists will be discussed later in the book.

1.5   <u>Trees</u>

A tree is a non-empty finite set of vertices & edges, which satisfy a certain criterion. A vertex is a simple entity (node) that can have a name and contains some other associated information. An edge is a connection between two vertices.

In a tree, there is one specially designated vertex called root and the remaining vertices are partitioned into a collection of sub-sets, each of which is also a tree. The nodes emerging from a particular node are called children of that node and the node itself is named as the parent of all those nodes. A node may or may not have children. The line from parent to a child is called an edge.

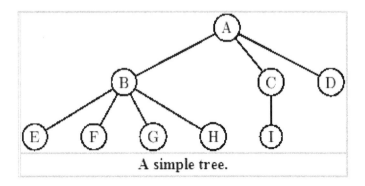

A simple tree.

It is a non-linear data structure of dynamic height, in which each node contains single type of data (Homogenous Components). To locate a specific node in the tree, we have to traverse through a number of nodes in the tree (Sequential access).

1.6 **Graphs**

A graph is, also, a non-empty finite set (V, E) of vertices & edges, where V shows the set of vertices and E is a set of edges connecting the vertices. Each element e in set E is associated with an unordered pair (V_i, V_j), where V_i and V_j are elements of set V, which are connected through 'e' (edge). A tree is a graph, but a graph may not necessarily be a tree.

EXAMPLE:

V = {1,2,3,4,5}
E = {(1,2), (1,3), (1,4), (1,5), (2,3), (2,5), (3,4), (4,5)}

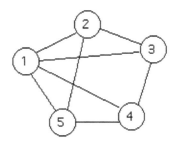

1.7 Data Structure Operations:

The data visible in the data structures is processed by means of some specified operations. These operations are called data structure operations. The following operations play a major role in the processing of data:

Traversing: To visit each and every node of data structure exactly once is called traversing.

Insertion: To insert (add) a new record into the data structure.

Deletion: To delete (remove) a record from the data structure.

Searching: To find the location of a specific record in the data structure.

The following two operations are, also, a part of data structure operations, but these two are used in some special situations.

Sorting: Sorting means the arranging of the records of a data structure in some logical manner. (e.g. to arrange a list of alphabetical numbers in a dictionary order or arranging a list of numerical numbers in an increasing or decreasing manner).

Merging: Merging means the combining of the records of two sorted files into a third sorted file.

STACKS

A Stack is a linear list of elements in which an element may be inserted or deleted only at one end, called the top of the stack. This means that the element, which has been lastly inserted onto the stack, will be the first to come out. In view of this a stack is also called a Last-In-First-Out(LIFO) system, in which insertions and deletions can take place only at one end, called the top.

Special terminology is used for two basic operations associated with the stacks:

"Push" is the term used to insert an element onto a stack.
"Pop" is the term used to delete an element from a stack.

The following figure illustrates a stack, which can accommodate a maximum of 10 elements:

(a) Empty stack

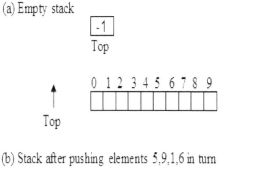

(b) Stack after pushing elements 5,9,1,6 in turn

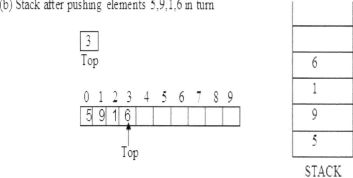

(c) Stack after popping top two elements i.e. 6 and 1 in turn

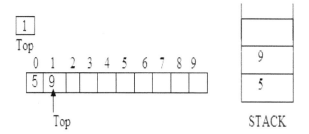

Sometimes it is required to access the top element of the stack without removing it from the stack, so a special term 'Peek' is used for performing this operation.

16

```
************************************************

/*      Implementing a stack using an array       */

#include<stdio.h>
#define MAX 100

typedef enum Boolean { False, True }Boolean;

typedef struct Stack
{
    int Top;   /* Variable 'Top' is used to denote the top position of stack */
    int S[MAX];   /* Array of integer elements */
}Stack;

void Push(Stack *, int), Display(Stack *);
int Pop(Stack *), Peek(Stack *);
Boolean IsEmpty(Stack *), IsFull(Stack *);

void main()
{
    int x, Item;
    Stack St;

    St.Top = -1;   /* Initializing top */

    while(1)   /* Infinite loop */
    {
        printf("Enter choice \n");
        printf("1. Push\n");
        printf("2. Pop\n");
        printf("3. Peek\n");
        printf("4. Display\n");
        printf("5. Exit\n");
        scanf("%d", &x);
        switch(x)
```

```c
{
    case 1:
        if(IsFull(&St))
        {
            printf("Overflow\n");
            break;
        }
        printf("Input the element\n");
        scanf("%d", &Item);

        Push(&St, Item);
        break;
/* Invoke Push function and break the switch statement */
    case 2:
        if(IsEmpty(&St))
        {
            printf("Underflow\n");
            break;
        }

        Item=Pop(&St);
        printf("Popped element: %d\n", Item);

        break;
/* Invoke Pop function and break the switch statement */
    case 3:
        if(IsEmpty(&St))
        {
            printf("Stack is empty\n");
            break;
        }

        Item=Peek(&St);
        printf("Top element: %d\n", Item);
```

18

```
                        break;
        /* Invoke Peep function and break the switch statement   */
                case 4:
                        if(IsEmpty(&St))
                        {
                                printf("Stack is empty\n");
                                break;
                        }

                        Display(&St);
                        break;
                        /* Display the Stack */
                case 5:
                        exit();     /* Exit the program */
        }  /* end switch */
    }  /* end while */
}  /* end main */

Boolean IsFull(Stack *St)
{
        if(St->Top==MAX-1)
        return True;    /* Stack cannot store more than 'MAX' elements */
        else
        return False;

}  /* end IsFull */

Boolean IsEmpty(Stack *St)
{
        if(St->Top == -1)
        return True;        /* No element in Stack */
        else
        return False;
```
19

} /* end IsFull */

```c
void Push(Stack *St, int Item)
{
        St->S[++St->Top]=Item;  /* Push the element in array 's' */
}    /* end Push */

int Pop(Stack *St)
{
        int Item;
        Item=St->S[St->Top--];   /* Pop the top element of array 's' */
        return Item;
} /* end Pop */

int Peek(Stack * St)
{
      int Item;
      Item=St->S[St->Top]; /* Assign top element of the stack to Item */
      return Item;
}

void Display(Stack *St)
{
        int I;
        for(I=St->Top;I>=0;I--)
        printf("      %d\n", St->S[I]);
} /* end Display */

/*
```

After executing:

Enter choice
1. Push
2. Pop
3. Peek
4. Display
5. Exit
1
Input the element
1
Enter choice
1. Push
2. Pop
3. Peek
4. Display
5. Exit
1
Input the element
2
Enter choice
1. Push
2. Pop
3. Peek
4. Display
5. Exit
1
Input the element
3
Enter choice
1. Push
2. Pop
3. Peek
4. Display
5. Exit
3
Top element: 3
Enter choice
1. Push
2. Pop
3. Peek
4. Display
5. Exit
4
   3

```
2
1
Enter choice
1. Push
2. Pop
3. Peek
4. Display
5. Exit
2
Popped element: 3
Enter choice
1. Push
2. Pop
3. Peek
4. Display
5. Exit
2
Popped element: 2
Enter choice
1. Push
2. Pop
3. Peek
4. Display
5. Exit
2
Popped element: 1
Enter choice
1. Push
2. Pop
3. Peek
4. Display
5. Exit
2
Underflow
Enter choice
1. Push
2. Pop
3. Peek
4. Display
5. Exit
5 … … … … … … … … … … … … … (Terminated)

*/
```

****

Steps of the program:

In this program, a structure 'Stack' has been declared, which contains a variable 'Top', used to denote the top position of the stack, and an array 'S' of integer elements to capture the elements of the stack.

```
typedef struct Stack
{
    int Top;
    int S[MAX];
}Stack;
```

In addition to this, an enumerated data type 'Boolean' has been declared, which can take value False or True.

```
typedef enum Boolean { False, True }Boolean;
```

When an enumerated data type is declared, its members are automatically assigned integer values 0, 1, 2, 3... in succession, beginning with 0 for the first member.

So internally members 'False' and 'True' of enumerated data type 'Boolean' are assigned values 0 and 1 respectively.

void main()

This function invokes different functions, which are used to perform desired operations entered by user.

1) Here variable 'St' of type Stack has been declared, which contains a variable 'Top' and an array 'S' of integer elements.

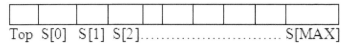

Top S[0] S[1] S[2]............................ S[MAX]

Here 'Top' will point to the topmost element in array 'S'.

2) Option 1 is used to push an element onto the stack. But before pushing an element, it is to be verified that stack should not be full i.e. it must have some space to grab an element. So 'IsFull' function is invoked, which returns either True or False, depending upon whether stack is full or not.

3) Option 2 is used to pop an element from the stack. But before popping an element, it is necessary to verify that stack should not be empty i.e. it should have some element, which can be popped out. So 'IsEmpty' function is invoked, which returns True or False, depending upon whether the stack is empty or not.

4) Option 3 is used to display all the elements of the stack.

5) Option 4 is used to terminate the program.

In functions 'Push' & 'Pop', pointer to structure variable 'St' has been passed so that changes made in this structure variable can be reflected in function 'main'.

void Push(Stack *St, int Item)

1) Value of 'Top' is incremented by 1.

2) Item is inserted at position 'Top' in array 'S'.

24

*int Pop(Stack *St)*

1) Top element of the stack is popped out and collected in variable Item.
2) Value of 'Top' is decremented by 1.
3) Variable 'Item' is returned to function 'main'.

*int Peek(Stack *St)*

1) Value of top element of the stack is assigned to Item.
2) This variable 'Item' is returned to function 'main'.

*Boolean IsFull(Stack *St)*

If value of variable 'Top' is 'MAX-1', then it means that the stack is full, so Boolean value True is returned; otherwise this function returns False.

*Boolean IsEmpty(Stack *St)*

If variable 'Top' is at position -1, then it shows that the stack is empty, so Boolean value True is returned; otherwise this function returns False.

*void Display(Stack *St)*

In this function, loop 'for(I=St->Top;I>=0;I--)' will display all the elements of the   stack in a vertical line e.g. if elements inserted in stack are 1, 2 & 3 respectively then this function will give the following output:

```
3
2
1
```

2.1   Polish Notation:

Normally, in an arithmetic expression, the operator symbol is placed between its two operands. For example,

$$A / B, \quad X * Y, \quad C - D$$

This is called infix notation.

A notation in which the operator symbol is placed before its two operands is called "Polish Notation". For example,

$$/ A B, * X Y, - C D$$

Prefix notation is the other term used for Polish Notation.

Similarly, a notation in which the operator symbol is placed after its two operands is called "Reverse Polish Notation":

$$A B /, X Y *, C D -$$

This notation is also called **postfix** (or suffix) notation.

2.2   Transforming an infix expression into a postfix expression:

Usually, there are five binary operations, which are used in an arithmetic expression, as given below:

Addition, Subtraction, Multiplication, Division and Exponentiation.

Out of these, first four are available in C and are denoted by usual operators +, -, * and /. The fifth operator,

26

exponentiation, is not available in C, so in our discussion, we will represent this operator by symbol '^'. The value of expression A^B will be A raised to the B power, so that 3^2 is 9. For these operators, the order of precedence (highest to lowest) is as under:

Exponentiation
Multiplication / Division
Addition / Subtraction.

Let us take the following examples of transforming infix to postfix expressions.

Infix	Postfix
A + B	A B +
A + B - C	A B + C -
(A + B) * (C - D)	A B + C D - *
((A + B) * C - (D - E)) ^ (F + G)	A B + C * D E - - F G + ^

Consider an arithmetic expression Q, written in infix notation, which may contain operators, operands and left & right parentheses. The following algorithm converts the infix expression Q into its equivalent postfix expression presuming that the operators in Q consist only of exponentiations (^), multiplications (*), divisions (/), additions (+), and subtractions (-), and they have the usual three levels of precedence as given above.

(1) push '(' onto STACK and add ')' to the end of Q.

(2) Scan Q from left to right and repeat this step until all the elements of Q are processed.

   a) If a left parenthesis is encountered, push it onto the stack.

   b) If an operand is encountered, then append it to the postfix expression.

   c) If an operator, say O is encountered, then :

   Repeat
   {

       (i)   If there is no operator at the top of the stack, then push O onto the stack.

       (ii)   Else, if precedence of the operator, which is at the top of the stack, is higher than or equal to the precedence of O, then pop that operator from the stack and append it to the postfix expression.

       (iii)   Else, push O onto the stack.

   } Until operator O is pushed onto the stack.

   d) If a right parenthesis ')' is encountered, then :

       (i) Pop off all the operators from the stack and append these to postfix expression, until you reach a left parenthesis '('.

(ii) Remove left parenthesis '(' from the stack.

(3) EXIT.

We will simulate the above algorithm to transform an infix expression into its equivalent postfix expression. Consider the following infix expression:

Q: (A + B) * C + (D – E) ^ F

First push '(' onto the stack, and add ')' to the end of Q.

Now Q is: (A + B)*C + (D - E)^F).

Following figure shows the status of STACK and of the resulting postfix expression as each element of Q is scanned.

	Symbol Scanned	STACK	Postfix Expression
1.	(	((	
2.	A	((	A
3.	+	((+	A
4.	B	((+	A B
5.	)	(	A B +
6.	*	(*	A B +
7.	C	(*	A B + C
8.	+	(+	A B + C *
9.	(	(+ (	A B + C *
10.	D	(+ (	A B + C * D

11.	-	(+ (-	A B + C * D
12.	E	(+ (-	A B + C * D E
13.	)	(+	A B + C * D E -
14.	^	(+ ^	A B + C * D E -
15.	F	(+ ^	A B + C * D E –F
16.	)		A B + C * D E – F ^ +

The following program converts an arithmetic expression from infix to postfix notation, presuming that the input given by the user for infix expression is correct. This program will not work correctly, if the entered string is an invalid infix expression.

****

/*   *Program to convert an expression from infix notation to postfix notation*   */

```
#include<stdio.h>
#include<string.h>
#define MAX 80

typedef enum Boolean {False, True} Boolean;

typedef struct Stack
{
     int Top;
     char S[MAX];
}Stack;

int Priority(char);
void ConvertInfixToPostfix(char *, Stack *, Stack *);
Boolean IsDigit(char);
void Push(Stack *, char Item);
```

```c
char Pop(Stack *);
char Peek(Stack *);
Boolean IsHigherOrEqual(int, int);

void main()
{
        char Infix[MAX];
        Stack St, Postfix;

        St.Top = Postfix.Top = -1;       /* Initialize top */

        printf("Input the infix expression\n");
        gets(Infix);

        ConvertInfixToPostfix(Infix, &St, &Postfix);

        printf("Postfix Expression: %s \n", Postfix.S);
}

void ConvertInfixToPostfix(char Infix[], Stack *St, Stack *Postfix)
{
        int I, Len;
        char Item;

        Len = strlen(Infix);
        Infix[Len] = ')';    /* Insert ')' at the end of expression 'Infix' */
        Infix[Len+1] = 0;        /* NULL Character */

        Push(St, '(');         /* Push '(' onto the stack */

        for(I=0; Infix[I]!=0; I++)
        {
            switch(Infix[I])
            {
                case ' ':
                        break;
```

31

```
                    case '+':
                    case '-':
                    case '*':
                    case '/':
                    case '^':
        while(IsHigherOrEqual(Priority(Peek(St)), Priority(Infix[I])))
                            {
                                    Item = Pop(St);
                                    Push(Postfix, Item);
                                    Push(Postfix, ' ');
                            }
```
/ Above 'while' loop will pop all the operators from the stack, which have
priority higher than or equal to Infix[I] */*

```
                    Push(St, Infix[I]);  /* Push Infix[I] onto the stack */
                            break;
                    case '(':
                            Push(St, Infix[I]);
                            break;
                    case ')':
                            while( (Item = Pop(St)) != '(' )
                            {
                                Push(Postfix, Item);
                                Push(Postfix, ' ');
                            }    /*  Pop off all the operators from the
                                     stack and append these to the postfix
                                     expression, until a left parenthesis
                                     '(' is encountered  */
                            break;
                    default:
                            if(IsDigit(Infix[I]))
                            {
                                    while(IsDigit(Infix[I]))
                                    {
                                            Push(Postfix, Infix[I]);
```

```
                                        I++;
                                    }   /* Append all the consecutive
                                        character digits to the postfix
                                        expression */
                                    Push(Postfix, ' ');
                                    I--;
                                }
                                else
                                {
printf("Incorrect character encountered in Infix expression");
                                exit();
                                }
                            break;

                        }   /* end switch */

                    }   /* end for */

                Push(Postfix, 0);
            }   /* end ConvertInfixToPostfix */

void Push(Stack *Temp, char Item)
{
                Temp->S[++Temp->Top] = Item;
}   /* end Push */

char Pop(Stack *Temp)
{
                char Item;
                Item = Temp->S[Temp->Top--];
                return Item;
}   /* end Pop */
```

33

```
char Peek(Stack *Temp)
{
            char Item;
            Item = Temp->S[Temp->Top];
            return Item;
}    /* end Peek */

int Priority(char Item)
{
            switch(Item)
            {
                  case '^':
                              return 3;
                  case '*':
                  case '/':
                              return 2;
                  case '+':
                  case '-':
                              return 1;
                  default:
                              return 0;
            }    /* end switch */
}  /* end Priority */

Boolean IsHigherOrEqual(int A, int B)
{
            if(A>=B)
            return True;
            else
            return False;
```
34

```
}   /* end IsHigherOrEqual */

Boolean IsDigit(char Item)
{
        if(Item>='0' && Item<='9')
        return True;
        else
        return False;
}   /* end IsDigit */
```

```
/*

After executing:

Input the infix expression
(2 + 3) * 4 + (5 - 3) ^ 2
Postfix Expression: 2 3 + 4 * 5 3 - 2 ^ +   ............... (output)

*/
```

****

Steps of the program:

In function main, two variables 'St' and 'Postfix' have been declared of type Stack. Variable 'St' will hold the elements of the stack, which will be created during the execution of the program and 'Postfix' will contain the actual postfix expression after the execution of the program.

void ConvertInfixToPostfix(char Infix[], Stack *St, Stack *Postfix):

1) Append right parenthesis ')' to the Infix expression.

2) Push left parenthesis '(' onto the stack.

3) Loop 'for(I=0; Infix[I]!=0; I++)' is executed until all the elements of array 'Infix' are scanned. The following steps are executed at each iteration of this loop.

   (a) If an operator is encountered in array 'Infix', then all the operators are popped out from the stack and appended to the postfix expression, which have priority higher than or equal to that operator. After that the operator is pushed onto the stack.

   (b) If a left parenthesis ('(') is found, then it is pushed onto the stack.

   (c) If a right parenthesis (')') is encountered, then all the operators from the stack are popped out and appended to the postfix expression, until a left parenthesis ('(') is found in the stack.

   (d) If a number is seen in array 'infix', then it is appended to the postfix expression.

void Push(Stack *Temp, char Item):

Character 'Item' is inserted at position 'Top+1' in array 'S' and value of 'Top' is incremented by 1.

char Pop(Stack *Temp):

Top element of the stack is popped out and the value of variable 'Top' is decremented by 1.

int Priority(char Item):

As discussed earlier, the order of precedence for the operators are as following:

^	(Exponentiation)
*, /	(Multiplication, Division)
+, -	(Addition, Subtraction)

So this function returns 3, 2 or 1 depending upon whether ('^'), ('*', '/') or ('+', '-') has been passed in character 'Item' or not. In the default case (In case of left parenthesis), this function returns 0.

Boolean IsHigherOrEqual(int A, int B):

This function returns True, if A is greater than or equal to B; otherwise it returns False.

Boolean IsDigit(char Item):

This function returns True, if the character passed in this function is a digit; otherwise it returns False.

2.3   Evaluation of a Postfix Expression

The procedure for evaluating a postfix expression is as follows:

1) Scan the postfix expression from left to right and repeat this step until all the elements of the expression are processed.

(a) If an operand is encountered, push it onto the operand stack.

(b) If an operator is found, then its operands will be the top two elements of the stack. So pop these two elements and perform the indicated operation on them. Push the result back onto the operand stack, so that it will be available for use as an operand of the next operator.

2) After all characters are scanned, we will have only one element in the stack. That is the result of the postfix expression.

We take an example. Suppose we have to evaluate the following postfix expression:

5 4 2 - +

So according to our procedure, following steps are executed to evaluate the postfix expression " 5 4 2 - + ".

➤ Numbers '5', '4' and '2' will be pushed onto the stack.

➤ Now operator '-' is encountered, so this operator is applied onto the top two elements of the stack and result is put back onto the stack.

    Now stack elements are:

    5 and (4-2) = 5 and 2.

➤ '+' will be encountered in the last. So this operator is applied on '5' and '2' and the result: '5+2 = 7', is pushed back onto the stack.

➢ In the last, top value of the stack, which is the result of the postfix expression, is printed.

In our program, postfix expression will be stored in the form of a string of digits and operator symbols.

Note: Postfix expression should contain non-negative numbers.

****

```
/*        Program for evaluation of a postfix expression        */

#include<stdio.h>
#include<math.h>
#define MAX 100

typedef struct Stack
{
        int Top;
        int S[MAX];
}Stack;

typedef enum Boolean {False, True}Boolean;

void Push(Stack *, int);
int Pop(Stack *);
Boolean IsDigit(char);
int EvaluatePostfixExpresion(char *);
void GetNumber(char *, int *, char *);
void main()
{
        char Postfix[MAX];
        int Result;
```

```c
        printf("Enter the postfix expression\n");
        gets(Postfix);

        Result = EvaluatePostfixExpression(Postfix);

        printf("Result:%d ", Result);
}   /* end main */

int EvaluatePostfixExpression(char Postfix[MAX])
{
        Stack St;
        int number, Result, op1, op2, I;
        char Number[MAX];

        St.Top = -1;        /* Initialize Top */
        for(I=0; Postfix[I]!=0; I++)    /* Loop until 'NULL' character
                                           is encountered */
        {
                if(Postfix[I]==' ' || Postfix[I]==',')
                continue;

                if(IsDigit(Postfix[I]))
                {
                        GetNumber(Postfix, &I, Number);
        /* Copy all the consecutive character digits in string 'Number' */

                        number = atoi(Number);
                        Push(&St, number);
                        I--;
                }
                        /* Above steps are used to convert all the consecutive
                           character digits into an integer, which is pushed onto
                           the stack */

                else
                {
```

40

```
                op2 = Pop(&St);
                op1 = Pop(&St);
                            /* Pop the top two operands */
            switch(Postfix[I])
            {
              case '+':  Result = op1 + op2;  break;
              case '-':  Result = op1 – op2;  break;
              case '/':  Result = op1 / op2;  break;
              case '*':  Result = op1 * op2;  break;
              case '^':  Result = pow(op1,op2);  break;
              default:   printf("Illegal operation\n");
                         exit();
            }

              Push(&St, Result);
          }

      }   /* end for */

      Result = Pop(&St);
      return Result;

}   /* end EvaluatePostfixExpression */

void GetNumber(char Postfix[MAX], int *Index, char
Number[MAX])
{
      int J=0;

      while(IsDigit(Postfix[*Index]))
              Number[J++] = Postfix[*Index++];
      Number[J]=0;

}   /* end GetNumber */
```

```
Boolean IsDigit(char Item)
{
                if(Item>='0' && Item<='9')
                return True;
                else
                return False;
}    /* end IsDigit */

void Push(Stack *Temp, int Item)
{
                Temp->S[++Temp->Top] = Item;
}    /* end Push */

int Pop(Stack *Temp)
{
                int Item;
                Item = Temp->S[Temp->Top--];
                return Item;
}    /* end Pop */

/*

After executing:

Enter the postfix expression
6 7 + 9 -
4 ……………………………… Output

*/
```

****

Steps of the program:

int EvaluatePostfixExpression(char Postfix[MAX]):

1) If a ' ' (space) or ',' (comma) is encountered in the postfix expression, then execution of 'for' loop is continued for scanning the next character of the expression.

2) If a digit is encountered, then all the consecutive character digits are copied in string 'Number' and this string is converted into an integer variable 'number', which is pushed onto the stack.

3) Or if an operator is encountered, then that operator is applied onto the top two elements of the stack and result is pushed back onto the stack. (See switch statement)

4) In the last, top value of the stack, which is the result of the postfix expression, is returned to function 'main'.

Boolean IsDigit(char Item):

This function returns True, if the character passed in this function is a digit; otherwise it returns False.

void Push(Stack *Temp, int Item):

Integer 'Item' is inserted at position 'Top+1' in array 'S' and value of 'Top' is incremented by 1.

int Pop(Stack *Temp):

Top element of the stack is popped out and the value of variable 'Top' is decremented by 1.

void GetNumber(char Postfix[MAX], int *Index, char Number[MAX]):

This function copies all the consecutive character digits starting from position '*Index' to string 'Number'.

QUEUES

A queue is defined as a "First-In-First-Out" system, briefly called as "FIFO" system, in which deletions can take place only at one end, called the front, and insertions can take place only at the other end, called the rear. To represent a queue, we need two variables- one pointing to the front element of the queue and the second pointing to the last (rear) element of the queue.

EXAMPLE:

The following figure illustrates a linear queue, which can accommodate maximum of 10 elements.

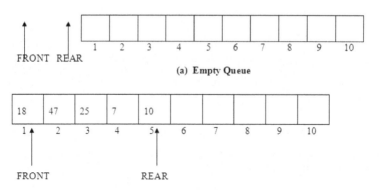

(a) Empty Queue

(b) Linear Queue after inserting elements 18, 47, 25, 7, 10 in turn.

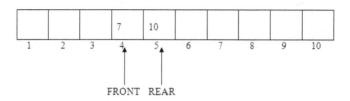

(c) Linear Queue after deleting elements 18, 47, 25 in turn.

45

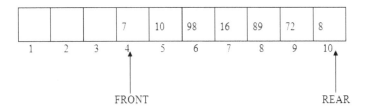

(d) **Linear Queue after inserting elements 98, 16, 89, 72, 8 in turn.**

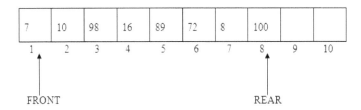

(e) **Linear Queue after inserting element 100.**

One limitation of the linear queue is that if the last room of the queue is occupied, then we cannot insert more elements in the queue, though there are vacant positions in the starting. As shown in above figure: (d), there are vacant rooms in the queue, but it is not possible to insert more elements, because the vacant positions are towards the front side, whereas insertion can take place from the rear side. To overcome this problem, the elements of the queue are moved forward, so that the vacant positions are shifted towards rear end of the linear queue. After shifting, front and rear are adjusted properly, and then further insertions can be carried out as usual.

****

/*   *Array implementation of Linear Queue*   */

```c
#include<stdio.h>
#define MAX 5

struct queue
{
        int front;
        char elements[MAX];
        int rear;
}q;

void insert(), del(), disp();

void main()
{
        int x;

        q.rear=q.front=0;    /* Initially queue is empty, so initialize
                                'rear' and 'front' with 0    */
        while(1)
        {
                printf("enter choice\n");
                printf("1. Insert an element\n");
                printf("2. Delete an element\n");
                printf("3. Display\n");
                printf("4. Exit\n");
                scanf("%d", &x);

                switch(x)
                {

                        case 1:     insert();       break;
                        case 2:     del();          break;
                        case 3:     disp();         break;
                        case 4:     exit();
```

```
                    }       /*    end switch  */
            }     /*   end  while   */
}      /*   end main   */

void insert()
{
            char ch;
            int i;

            if(q.front==0 && q.rear==MAX)
            {
                    printf("queue is full\n");
                    return;
            }

            if(q.rear==MAX)
            {

                    for(i=q.front; i<q.rear; i++)
                    q.elements[i-q.front]=q.elements[i];
                    q.rear=q.rear-q.front;
                    q.front=0;
            }
                       /*   if there is no space at rear side, then move all the
                            elements towards front side of the queue   */

            printf("Input the element\n");
            fflush(stdin);
            scanf("%c", &ch);

            q.elements[q.rear++]=ch;

}    /*  end  insert  */
```

```c
void del()
{
        if(q.rear==q.front)
        {
                printf("Queue is empty\n");
                return;
        }

        q.elements[q.front++]=NULL;   /* delete the front element
                                         of the queue */
        printf("item deleted\n");

}   /* end del */

void disp()
{
        int i;

        if(q.rear==q.front)
        {
                printf("queue is empty\n");
                return;
        }

        printf("elements in queue are:\n");

        for(i=q.front; i<q.rear; i++)
        printf("%c ", q.elements[i]);

}   /* end disp */

/*
After executing:

enter choice
1. Insert an element
```

49

2. Delete an element
3. Display
4. Exit
1
Input the element
1
enter choice
1. Insert an element
2. Delete an element
3. Display
4. Exit
1
Input the element
2
enter choice
1. Insert an element
2. Delete an element
3. Display
4. Exit
1
Input the element
3
enter choice
1. Insert an element
2. Delete an element
3. Display
4. Exit
3
elements in queue are:
1 2 3 enter choice
1. Insert an element
2. Delete an element
3. Display
4. Exit
2
item deleted
enter choice
1. Insert an element
2. Delete an element
3. Display
4. Exit
3
elements in queue are:
2 3 enter choice
1. Insert an element
2. Delete an element

50

Steps of the Program:

void insert():

1) If 'front' is pointing to the first location of the queue and 'rear' is pointing to the last location of the queue, then print: "queue is full" and return.

2) If only 'rear' is pointing to the last location of the queue, then there is no space at rear side, but there are vacant positions at the starting, so move first element at the 0th position, second element at first position,............. and so on. And adjust 'front' and 'rear' positions accordingly.

3) Now insert the new element in the queue, and increment 'rear' by 1.

void del():

1)   If 'front' and 'rear' are pointing to the same location in the queue, then print:
"queue is empty". And go back to the previous function.

2)   Else, delete the front element of the queue. And increment 'front' by 1.

51

void disp():

Starting from the front element of the queue, print each and every element upto the rear end of the queue.

3.1   <u>Circular Queue</u>

Let us have an array A that contains n elements in which A[1] comes after A[N]. When this technique is applied to construct a queue then the queue is called a circular queue. In other words, a queue is called a circular queue when first room comes just after the last room.

In a circular queue A, if A[N] is occupied and we have to insert an element, then instead of moving all the elements forward, we insert this element at position A[1]. This operation takes less time than that of moving all the elements forward.

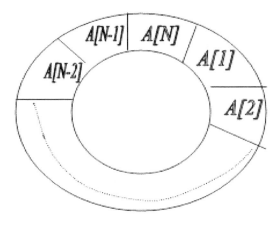

Circular Queue

EXAMPLE:

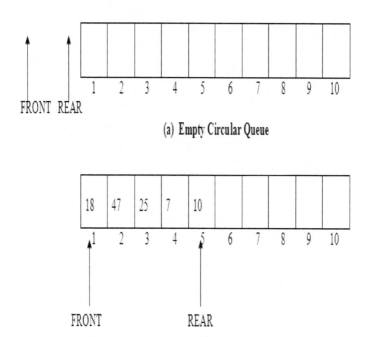

(a) Empty Circular Queue

(b) Circular Queue after inserting elements 18, 47, 25, 7, 10 in turn

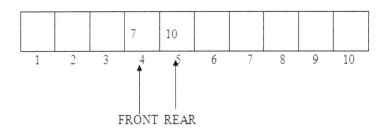

(c) Circular Queue after deleting elements 18, 47, 25 in turn

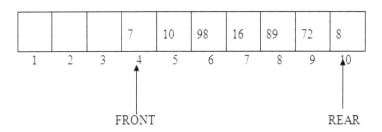

(d) Circular Queue after inserting elements 98, 16, 89, 72, 8 in turn

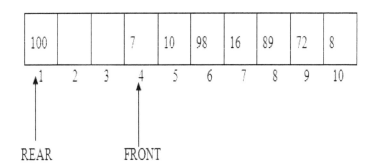

(e) Circular Queue after inserting element 100

```
*********************************************

/*    Implementation of Circular Queue    */

#include<stdio.h>
#define MAX  5
struct queue
{
        int count;
        int front;
        char elements[MAX];
        int rear;
}q;

void insert(), del(), disp();

void main()
{
        int x;

        q.count=q.rear=q.front=0;

        while(1)
        {
                printf("enter choice\n");
                printf("1. Insert an element\n");
                printf("2. Delete an element\n");
                printf("3. Display\n");
                printf("4. Exit\n");
                scanf("%d", &x);

                switch(x)
                {
```

```
                case 1:     insert();     break;
                case 2:     del();        break;
                case 3:     disp();       break;
                case 4:     exit();
```

} /* end switch */

} /* end while */

} /* end main */

```c
void insert()
{
        char ch;

        if(q.count==MAX)
        {

                printf("overflow\n");
                return;
        } /* If there are MAX elements in queue, then queue is full.
             Here 'count' represents the total number of elements in
             the queue. */

        if(q.rear==MAX)
        q.rear=0;

        printf("Input the element\n");
        fflush(stdin);
        scanf("%c", &ch);

        q.elements[q.rear++]=ch;
        q.count++;

} /* end insert */
```

```
void del()
{
        if(q.count<=0)
        {
                printf("Underflow\n");
                return;
        }    /* 'count' shows the total number of elements in the queue   */

        if(q.front==MAX)
        q.front=0;

        q.elements[q.front++]=NULL;   /* delete the front
                                         element of the queue   */
        q.count--;

        printf("item deleted\n");

}  /* end del */

void disp()
{
        int i;
        if(q.count<=0)
        {
                printf("no element in queue\n");
                return;
        }

        if(q.rear>q.front)
        for(i=q.front;i<q.rear;i++)
        printf("%c ", q.elements[i]);
        else
        {
                for(i=q.front;i<MAX;i++)
```

57

```
                    printf("%c ", q.elements[i]);

                    for(i=0;i<q.rear;i++)
                    printf("%c ", q.elements[i]);
            }

}   /* end disp */
```

/

After executing:

enter choice
1. Insert an element
2. Delete an element
3. Display
4. Exit
1
Input the element
1
enter choice
1. Insert an element
2. Delete an element
3. Display
4. Exit
1
Input the element
2
enter choice
1. Insert an element
2. Delete an element
3. Display
4. Exit
1
Input the element
3
enter choice
1. Insert an element
2. Delete an element
3. Display
4. Exit
1
Input the element
4

enter choice
1. Insert an element
2. Delete an element
3. Display
4. Exit
1
Input the element
5
enter choice
1. Insert an element
2. Delete an element
3. Display
4. Exit
1
overflow
enter choice
1. Insert an element
2. Delete an element
3. Display
4. Exit
2
item deleted
enter choice
1. Insert an element
2. Delete an element
3. Display
4. Exit
1
Input the element
6
enter choice
1. Insert an element
2. Delete an element
3. Display
4. Exit
3
2 3 4 5 6 enter choice
1. Insert an element
2. Delete an element
3. Display
4. Exit
4 ... ...(terminated)

*/

****

Steps of the Program:

void insert():

1) If 'count' reaches MAX, then print: "queue is full" and do return the control.

2) If 'rear' is pointing to MAX, then adjust its value so that it points to the first room of the queue.

3) Now insert the element in the queue, and increment 'count' by 1.

void del():

1) If 'count' is 0, then print: " No element in queue" and return the control.

2) If 'front' is pointing to MAX, then assign 0 to 'front', because, in a circular queue, first element comes just after the last element.

3) Now delete the front element of the queue, and decrement 'count' by 1.

void disp():

If queue is not empty, then there are following possibilities:

(a) If 'rear>front' :

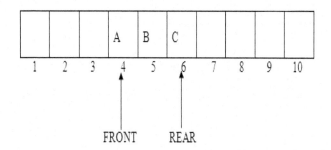

Then, starting from the front element, print all the elements upto the rear element.

(b) Else, if 'front>=rear' :

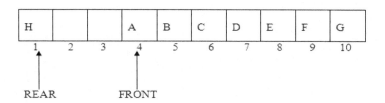

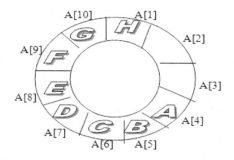

Circular Queue

Then, starting from the element, pointed by variable 'FRONT', print all the elements upto the end of array. And after that, starting from the first element, print upto the element pointed by variable 'REAR'.

3.2   **Priority Queues:**

A priority queue may be defined as a queue, in which each element has a priority associated with it; this priority determines the order in which they exit the queue. Highest priority items are removed first. In a priority queue, the order in which the elements are deleted and processed may be summed up as under:

1) An element of higher priority is processed before any element of lower priority.

2) Two elements with the same priority are processed according to the order in which they were added to the queue.

EXAMPLE:

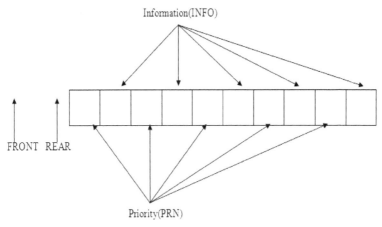

(a) **Empty Priority Queue**

62

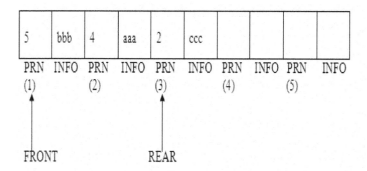

5	bbb	4	aaa	2	ccc				
PRN	INFO	PRN	INFO	PRN	INFO	PRN	INFO	PRN	INFO
(1)		(2)		(3)		(4)		(5)	

FRONT   REAR

(b) Priority Queue after inserting elements aaa, bbb, ccc in turn, with priorities 4, 5, 2 respectively.

Note: To insert an element of higher priority, shift all the elements of lower priority to one position backward in the queue and then insert the element.

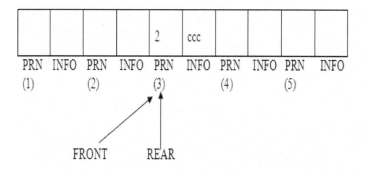

				2	ccc				
PRN	INFO	PRN	INFO	PRN	INFO	PRN	INFO	PRN	INFO
(1)		(2)		(3)		(4)		(5)	

FRONT   REAR

(c) Priority Queue after deleting elements bbb and aaa in turn.

63

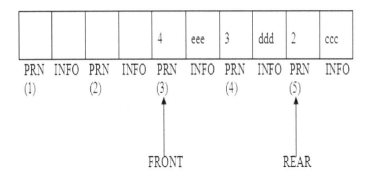

(d) Priority Queue after inserting elements ddd, eee with priorities 3 and 4 respectively.

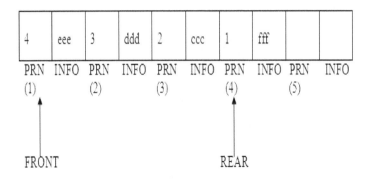

(e) Priority Queue after inserting element fff with priority 1

Note: To implement priority queues, two arrays are used. One stores the priority of each element and second stores the information part of the elements.

****

/*   *Array implementation of priority queue*   */

```c
#include<stdio.h>
#define MAX 5
#define NIL  -1

struct queue
{
        int front;
        int priority[MAX];
        char info[MAX];
        int rear;
}pq;

void insert(), del(), disp();

void main()
{
        int x;

        pq.rear=pq.front=0;

        while(1)
        {
                printf("enter choice\n");
                printf("1. Insert an element\n");
                printf("2. Delete an element\n");
                printf("3. Display\n");
                printf("4. Exit\n");
                scanf("%d", &x);

                switch(x)
                {
                        case 1:     insert();       break;
                        case 2:     del();          break;
                        case 3:     disp();         break;
```

```
                    case 4:        exit();

            }       /*    end switch  */

      }    /*    end while   */

}    /*   end main  */

void insert()
{
            char element;
            int prn, i, j;

            if(pq.front==0 && pq.rear==MAX)
            {
                   printf("queue is full\n");
                   return;
            }

            if(pq.rear==MAX)
            {
                   for(i=pq.front; i<pq.rear; i++)
                   {
                        pq.info[i-pq.front]=pq.info[i];
                        pq.priority[i-pq.front]=pq.priority[i];
                   }

                   pq.rear=pq.rear-pq.front;
                   pq.front=0;

            }  /* end if */
                /*   if there is no space at the back side of the queue, then
                     move all the elements of the queue forward   */

            printf("enter priority of the element\n");
            scanf("%d",&prn);
```

```c
        printf("Input the element\n");
        fflush(stdin);
        scanf("%c",&element);

    for(i=pq.front; i<pq.rear && prn<=pq.priority[i]; i++)
                ;
        for(j=pq.rear-1; j>=i; j--)
        {
                pq.priority[j+1]=pq.priority[j];
                pq.info[j+1]=pq.info[j];
        }

        pq.priority[j+1]=prn;
        pq.info[j+1]=element;    /* Insert 'element' at ith
                                    position */

        pq.rear++;

}    /* end insert */

void del()
{

        if(pq.rear==pq.front)
        {

                printf("Queue is empty\n");
                return;
        }

        pq.priority[pq.front]=NIL;
        pq.info[pq.front]=NULL;   /* delete the front element of
                                     the queue */
        pq.front++;
```

67

```
}  /* end del */

void disp()
{
        int i;

        if(pq.rear==pq.front)
        {
                printf("queue is empty\n");
                return;
        }

        printf("elements in queue are:\n");

        for(i=pq.front;i<pq.rear;i++)
printf("priority:%d element:%c\n", pq.priority[i], pq.info[i]);

}  /* end disp */

/*

After executing:

enter choice
1. Insert an element
2. Delete an element
3. Display
4. Exit
1
enter priority of the element
4
Input the element
A
enter choice
1. Insert an element
2. Delete an element
3. Display
```

4. Exit
1
enter priority of the element
5
Input the element
B
enter choice
1. Insert an element
2. Delete an element
3. Display
4. Exit
1
enter priority of the element
2
Input the element
C
enter choice
1. Insert an element
2. Delete an element
3. Display
4. Exit
3
elements in queue are:
priority:5 element:B
priority:4 element:A
priority:2 element:C
enter choice
1. Insert an element
2. Delete an element
3. Display
4. Exit
2
enter choice
1. Insert an element
2. Delete an element
3. Display
4. Exit
3
elements in queue are:
priority:4 element:A
priority:2 element:C
enter choice
1. Insert an element
2. Delete an element
3. Display
4. Exit

4............................(terminated)

*/

****

Steps of the Program:

void insert():

1) If 'front' is pointing to the first room, and 'rear' is pointing to the last room, then print: "queue is full" and do return the control.

2) If only 'rear' is pointing to the last room, then it means that there is no space at the end of the queue, but there are vacant rooms in the beginning. So move front element of the queue at 0th position, second element of the queue at 1st position, and so on. Adjust 'front' and 'rear' positions accordingly.

3) Insert the priority 'prn' of the element, which is to be inserted, in 'priority' array, such that all the elements of 'priority' array are in descending order. Suppose 'prn' is inserted at i$_{th}$ position in 'priority' array, then insert 'info' part of the element at i$_{th}$ position in 'info' array. And increment 'rear' by 1.

void del():

1) If 'front' and 'rear' are pointing to the same location in the queue, then print:
"queue is empty", and return the control.

2) Else, delete the front element of 'info' and 'priority' array, and increment 'front' by 1.

void disp():

Starting from the front element of the queue, print each and every element upto the rear end of the queue.

3.3 **DEQUES**

A Deque may be defined as a linear list in which insertions and deletions are possible at either end but not in the middle.

It may be represented by different ways in computer's memory. We assume that our deque is maintained by circular array 'elements' with pointers LEFT and RIGHT, initially pointing to the two ends of the deque. Insertion and deletion of an element can take place at either of these two locations, pointed by LEFT and RIGHT pointers. Since our deque is maintained by a circular array, so we will insert the elements with the LEFT pointer in the clockwise direction and delete the elements in the anticlockwise direction. In the case of insertions and deletions with the RIGHT pointer, the vice-versa procedure will be adopted. The following example shows the insertions and deletions in a deque:

EXAMPLE

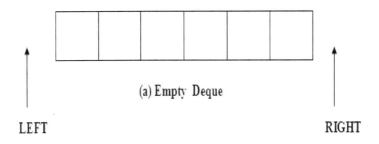

(a) Empty Deque

LEFT   RIGHT

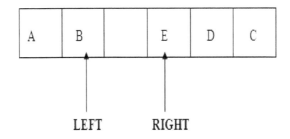

LEFT   RIGHT

(b) Deque after inserting A, B at the left and C, D
    and E at the right.

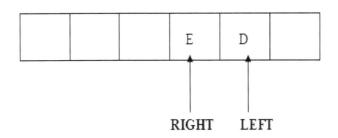

RIGHT   LEFT

(c) Deque after deleting 3 elements from the left in turn.

Note: As shown above, in figure (c), the third element deleted is the first element from right side. This is because our deque is maintained by a circular array.

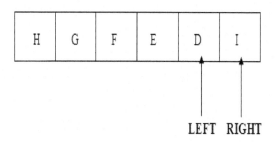

LEFT   RIGHT

(d) Deque after inserting F, G, H and I in turn, at the right.

****

```
/*        Implementation of Deque        */

#include<stdio.h>
#define MAX 5

struct deque
{

        int count;
        int left;
        char elements[MAX];
        int right;
}dq;

void insert(), del(), disp();
void leftinsert(), rightinsert(), leftdelete(), rightdelete();

void main()
{
```

73

```
        int x;

    dq.left=0;


    dq.right=MAX;
    dq.count=0;
    while(1)
    {
                printf("enter choice\n");
                printf("1. Insert an element\n");
                printf("2. Delete an element\n");
                printf("3. Display\n");
                printf("4. Exit\n");
                scanf("%d",&x);

                switch(x)
                {
                            case 1:     insert();     break;
                            case 2:     del();        break;
                            case 3:      disp();      break;
                            case 4:      exit();

                }  /* end switch */

        }  /* end while */
}  /* end main */

void insert()
{
        int x;

        printf("1. Insertion at left\n");
        printf("2. Insertion at right\n");
         scanf("%d",&x);
```
74

```
        switch(x)
        {
                case 1:  leftinsert();          break;
                case 2:  rightinsert();         break;
        }

}   /* end insert */

void del()
{
        int x;

        printf("1. Deletion at left\n");
        printf("2. Deletion at right\n");
        scanf("%d",&x);

        switch(x)
        {
                case 1:  leftdelete();          break;
                case 2:  rightdelete();         break;
        }
}   /* end del */

void leftinsert()
{
            char item;

            if(dq.count==MAX)
            {

                    printf("deque is full\n");
                    return;
            }   /* Here 'count' denotes the total number of elements in
                    the deque   */
```

```c
        if(dq.left==MAX)
        dq.left=0;

        printf("enter element\n");
        fflush(stdin);
        scanf("%c",&item);

        dq.elements[dq.left++]=item;
        dq.count++;

}  /* end leftinsert */

void rightinsert()
{
        char item;
        if(dq.count ==MAX)
        {
                printf("deque is full\n");
                return;
        }
        if(dq.right==0)
        dq.right=MAX;

        printf("enter element\n");
        fflush(stdin);
        scanf("%c",&item);

        dq.elements[--dq.right]=item;
        dq.count++;
}  /* end rightinsert */

void leftdelete()
{
```

```c
        if(dq.count <=0)
        {
                printf("deque is empty\n");
                return;
        }

        if(dq.left==0)
        dq.left=MAX;

        dq.elements[--dq.left]=NULL;
        printf("item deleted\n");
        dq.count--;

} /* end leftdelete */

void rightdelete()
{
        if(dq.count <=0)
        {
                printf("deque is empty\n");
                return;
        }

        if(dq.right==MAX)
        dq.right=0;

        dq.elements[dq.right++]=NULL;
        printf("item deleted\n");
        dq.count--;

} /* end rightdelete */

void disp()
{
```

```
        int i;

        for(i=0;i<MAX;i++)
        if(dq.elements[i]==NULL)
        printf("-   ");
        else
        printf("%c   ",dq.elements[i]);

        printf("\n left:%d \n",dq.left);
        printf(" right:%d \n",dq.right+1);
}  /* end disp */

/*
```

After executing:

enter choice
1. Insert an element
2. Delete an element
3. Display
4. Exit
1
1. Insertion at left
2. Insertion at right
1
enter element
A
enter choice
1. Insert an element
2. Delete an element
3. Display
4. Exit
1
1. Insertion at left
2. Insertion at right
1
enter element
B
enter choice
1. Insert an element
2. Delete an element

78

3. Display
4. Exit
3
A B - - -
left:2
right:6
enter choice
1. Insert an element
2. Delete an element
3. Display
4. Exit
1
1. Insertion at left
2. Insertion at right
2
enter element
C
3
A B - - C
left:2
right:5
enter choice
1. Insert an element
2. Delete an element
3. Display
4. Exit
2
1. Deletion at left
2. Deletion at right
1
item deleted
enter choice
1. Insert an element
2. Delete an element
3. Display
4. Exit
3
A - - - C
left:1
right:5
enter choice
1. Insert an element
2. Delete an element
3. Display
4. Exit
4... ... ... (terminated)

*/

****

Steps of the Program:

void leftinsert():

1) If total number of elements in deque are MAX, then print: " deque is full ", and return the control.

2) Because 'elements' is a circular array, so if 'left' pointer reaches MAX, then adjust its position, so that it points to the first room of the deque.

3) Insert the element and increment total number of elements by 1.

void rightinsert():

1) If value of 'count' is MAX, then print: " deque is full ", and do return the control.

2) If 'right' pointer reaches 0, then assign MAX to it, because of circularity of array 'elements'.

3) Insert the element and increment 'count' by 1.

void leftdelete():

1) If 'count<=0', then print: " deque is empty ", and return the control.

2) Adjust the position of 'left' pointer in circular array 'elements', if it has reached 0.

3) Delete the element pointed by 'left' pointer and decrement the total number of elements by 1.

void rightdelete():

1) If there is no element in the deque, then print: " deque is empty ", and do return the control.

2) Adjust the position of 'right' pointer in circular array 'elements', if it has reached MAX.

3) Delete the element pointed by 'right' pointer and decrement 'count' by 1.

void disp():

Display each and every element of deque. And print the location of 'left' and 'right' pointers also.

There are two variations of a Deque :

(1) Input Restricted Deque.

(2) Output Restricted Deque.

3.4   Input Restricted Deque

An input restricted deque is a deque, which allows insertions only at one end of the list but allows deletions at both ends of the list.

EXAMPLE

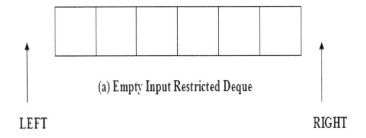

(a) Empty Input Restricted Deque

LEFT   RIGHT

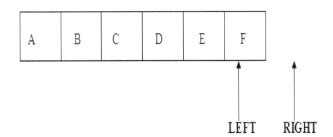

LEFT   RIGHT

(b) Input Restricted Deque after inserting elements A, B, C, D, E and F in turn.

82

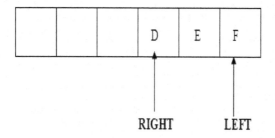

RIGHT   LEFT

(c) Input Restricted Deque after deleting 3 elements at the right in turn.

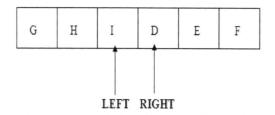

LEFT   RIGHT

(d) Input Restricted Deque after inserting G, H and I in turn.

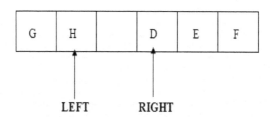

LEFT   RIGHT

(e) Input Restricted Deque after deleting 1 element at the left.

83

Note : In Input Restricted Deque, for insertion, we can choose any one end of the deque. In the above example, we have used left end of the deque .

****

/* *Implementation of Input Restricted Deque* */

```c
#include<stdio.h>
#define MAX 5

struct deque
{
    int count;
    int left;
    char elements[MAX];
    int right;
}dq;

void insert(), del(), disp();
void leftdelete(), rightdelete();

void main()
{
    int x;

    dq.left=0;
    dq.right=MAX;
    dq.count=0;

    while(1)
    {
        printf("enter choice\n");
        printf("1. Insert an element\n");
        printf("2. Delete an element\n");
        printf("3. Display\n");
        printf("4. Exit\n");
```

84

```c
          scanf("%d",&x);

          switch(x)
          {
                  case 1:     insert();        break;
                  case 2:     del();           break;
                  case 3:     disp();          break;
                  case 4:     exit();
          }  /* end switch */
     }  /* end while */
}  /* end main */

void del()
{
     int x;

     printf("1. Deletion at left\n");
     printf("2. Deletion at right\n");
     scanf("%d",&x);

     switch(x)
     {
             case 1:  leftdelete();           break;
             case 2:  rightdelete();          break;
     }
}  /* end del */

void insert()
{
     char item;

     if(dq.count ==MAX)
     {
```

85

```
                    printf("deque is full\n");
                    return;
          }   /* Here 'count' denotes the total number of elements in the
              deque */

          if(dq.left==MAX)
          dq.left=0;

          printf("enter element\n");
          fflush(stdin);
          scanf("%c",&item);

          dq.elements[dq.left++]=item;
          dq.count++;
}   /* end insert */

void leftdelete()
{
          if(dq.count <=0)
          {
                    printf("deque is empty\n");
                    return;
          }

          if(dq.left==0)
          dq.left=MAX;

          dq.elements[--dq.left]=NULL;
          printf("item deleted\n");
          dq.count--;
}   /* end leftdelete */

void rightdelete()
{
```

```
            if(dq.count <=0)
            {

                    printf("deque is empty\n");
                    return;
            }

            if(dq.right==MAX)
            dq.right=0;

            dq.elements[dq.right++]=NULL;
            printf("item deleted\n");
            dq.count--;

}  /* end rightdelete */

void disp()
{
            int i;

            for(i=0;i<MAX;i++)
            if(dq.elements[i]==NULL)
            printf("- ");
            else
            printf("%c ",dq.elements[i]);

            printf("\n left:%d \n",dq.left);
            printf(" right:%d \n",dq.right+1);

}  /* end disp */

/*

After executing:
```

enter choice
1. Insert an element
2. Delete an element
3. Display
4. Exit
1
enter element
A
enter choice
1. Insert an element
2. Delete an element
3. Display
4. Exit
1
enter element
B
enter choice
1. Insert an element
2. Delete an element
3. Display
4. Exit
1
enter element
C
enter choice
1. Insert an element
2. Delete an element
3. Display
4. Exit
3
A   B   C - -
 left:3
 right:6
enter choice
1. Insert an element
2. Delete an element
3. Display
4. Exit
2
1. Deletion at left
2. Deletion at right
2
item deleted
enter choice
1. Insert an element
2. Delete an element

88

****

In program on Deques, we have used four functions: leftinsert, rightinsert, leftdelete, rightdelete. But in the above program, we have used 'insert' function to insert an element, which is same as 'leftinsert' function of deques. Difference between both of these programs is only that, here we are not using 'rightinsert' function, because it is an input restricted deque, and we can have insertion at one end only.

3.5   Output Restricted Deque

An Output Restricted Deque is a deque, which allows deletions only at one end of the list but allows insertions at both ends of the list.

EXAMPLE:

89

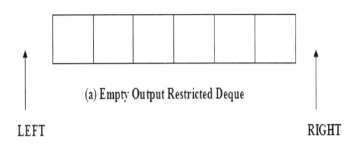

(a) Empty Output Restricted Deque

LEFT   RIGHT

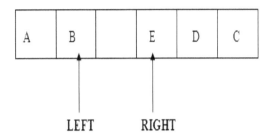

LEFT   RIGHT

(b) Output Restricted Deque after inserting A, B at the left and C, D
    and E at the right.

90

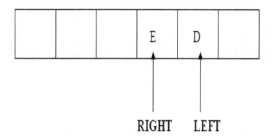

RIGHT   LEFT

(c) Output Restricted Deque after deleting 3 elements in turn.

Note : In Output Restricted Deque, deletion can be done at any one end. In our example, we have used left end of the deque.

****

This program can be implemented as follows :

    (1) To insert an element at the left, use 'leftinsert' function.

    (2) To insert an element at the right, use 'rightinsert' function.

    (3) To delete an element, either use 'leftdelete' function or 'rightdelete' function.

Where functions: leftinsert, rightinsert, leftdelete and rightdelete were used in program on deques.

****

91

Note: Though in various figures, explaining the formation of deques, we have shown various elements of the deque in a straight line, yet it is to be kept in mind that these elements of the deque are in a "Circular Array".

RECURSION

A recursive function is a function that contains either a Call statement to itself or a Call statement to another function, which again results in a Call statement to this. Recursion is a stack making procedure. Each time when a function calls itself, all the auto variables which belong to that function are pushed onto a stack, and a new virtual instance of the function is created, which begins its execution for the new set of auto variables (top cluster of auto variables of the stack). Consider the following recursive function:

```
void process(int n)
{
        if(n<=3)
        {
                printf("Hello\n");       /*   Statement: 1   */
                process(n+1);            /*   Statement: 2   */
                printf("World\n");       /*   Statement: 3   */
        }
}
```

Suppose initially 1 is passed in this function. Then stack created by this function is:

```
4        Instance: 4

3        Instance: 3

2        Instance: 2

1        Instance: 1

n
```

Each time, when 'process' function is called, statement: 1 prints 'Hello', and Statement: 2 again calls 'process' with parameter n+1 i.e. a new instance of 'process' is created and n+1 is pushed onto the stack. This new instance of 'process' executes all of its statements using the top element n+1 of the stack. So when Instance: 3 calls 'process' with parameter 4, Instance: 4 is created. But here condition 'if(n<=3)' is not satisfied, and no statement of 'process' is executed for n=4. Therefore this new Instance: 4 and top element 4 of the stack are popped out from the memory, and control of the program is returned to Instance: 3. Where, after execution of remaining statement: 3, control is again returned to Instance: 2. And so on. So this function gives the following output:

Hello
Hello
Hello
World
World
World

4.1   Backtracking

Consider a problem: Suppose a person wants to go from city A to city B. Further suppose that there are 3 paths, which are going out of city A, and each path is further alienated into 3 paths, as shown in the following figure:

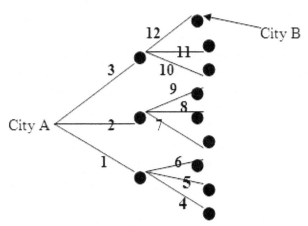

Which way goes to city B is not known. In this problem, we will have to explore all the paths. So, the person starts walking on path: 1 and tries all the paths numbered 4, 5 and 6 one by one. He doesn't find city B. So he comes back to the starting point and now explores path numbered 2 and 3 in the similar fashion. In such type of problems, further moves are affected by previous moves. To come back to the previous move and start performing another move is called backtracking.

4.2   Factorial of a number

Factorial of a number n is the product of positive integers from 1 to n, and is denoted by n!.

n!=n * (n-1) * (n-2)................ * 2 * 1.

So   5!= 5 * 4 * 3 * 2 * 1=120.
         4!= 4 * 3 * 2 * 1=24.
         3!= 3 * 2 * 1=6.
And so on.

Therefore 5!= 5 * 4!.
         4!= 4 * 3!.

Accordingly, a factorial function 'fact' can be defined as follows:

$$Fact(n)= \begin{cases} 1 & \text{if } n=1. \\ n*fact(n-1) & \text{if } n>1. \end{cases}$$

****

/* *Program to find out the factorial of a number using recursion* */

#include<stdio.h>

void main()
{
        int n,p;
        int fact(int);

        printf("enter a number greater than 0\n");
        scanf("%d",&n);

```c
        if(n<=0)
        {
                printf("error");
                exit();
        }

        p=fact(n);

        printf("%d",p);

}  /* end main */


int fact(int n)
{
        if(n==1)
        return 1;
        else
        return n*fact(n-1);

}  /* end fact */
/*

After executing:

enter a number greater than 0
5
120        ................(output)

*/
```

****

97

Logic of the program:

Every time when 'fact' function is called, a new instance of 'fact' is created. And return statement of instance: n returns an integer value to instance: n-1. Here return statement of each instance of 'fact' will be as under:
(Suppose number entered by user is: 5)

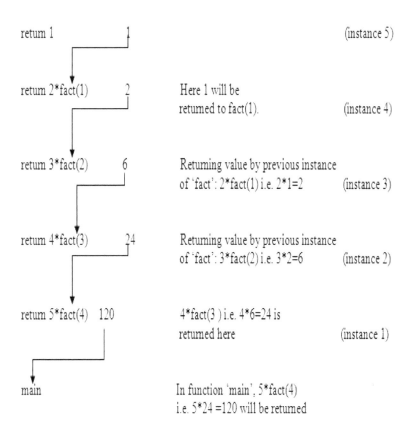

return 1   1   (instance 5)

return 2*fact(1)   2   Here 1 will be
                                     returned to fact(1).   (instance 4)

return 3*fact(2)   6   Returning value by previous instance
                                     of 'fact': 2*fact(1) i.e. 2*1=2   (instance 3)

return 4*fact(3)   24   Returning value by previous instance
                                     of 'fact': 3*fact(2) i.e. 3*2=6   (instance 2)

return 5*fact(4)   120   4*fact(3) i.e. 4*6=24 is
                                     returned here   (instance 1)

main   In function 'main', 5*fact(4)
                                     i.e. 5*24 =120 will be returned

98

4.3 Multiplying Numbers Using Recursion

Multiplication of two numbers x and y can be defined as:

$x + x + x \ldots\ldots\ldots + x$ (y times).

The recursive definition of multiplying two numbers in such a way can be given as follows:

$$\text{Multiply}(m, n) = \begin{cases} m & \text{If } n = 1 \\ m + \text{Multiply}(m, n\text{-}1) & \text{Otherwise} \end{cases}$$

Following is the recursive program of multiplication of two numbers.

```
**************************************************
```

```c
/* Multiplication of two numbers using recursion */

#include<stdio.h>

void main()
{
        int m, n, mult;

        printf("enter two positive numbers \n");
        scanf("%d %d", &m, &n);

        mult=process(m, n);

        printf("result:%d",mult);

} /* end main */
```

99

```
process(int m, int n)
{
          if(n==1)
          return m;
          else
          return (m+process(m,n-1));

}  /* end process  */

/*

After executing:

enter two positive numbers
5 6
result:30      ………….(output)

*/
```

****

Logic of the program:

Function 'process' is called n-1 times by itself. Here 'return' statement of every instance of 'process' is given below, when the two numbers entered are 5 and 4.

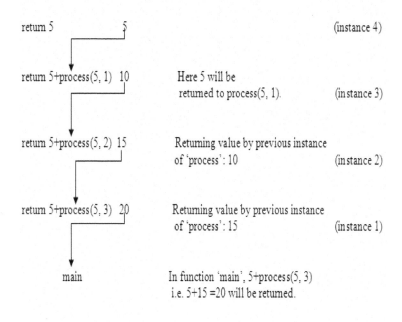

| return 5 | 5 | | (instance 4) |

return 5+process(5, 1) 10   Here 5 will be
                              returned to process(5, 1).   (instance 3)

return 5+process(5, 2) 15   Returning value by previous instance
                              of 'process': 10   (instance 2)

return 5+process(5, 3) 20   Returning value by previous instance
                              of 'process': 15   (instance 1)

main   In function 'main', 5+process(5, 3)
        i.e. 5+15 =20 will be returned.

4.4   Greatest Common Divisor

A greatest common divisor x of two positive numbers y and
z is a positive number, such that:

(1) y%x=0 and z%x=0 i.e. x divides both the numbers y
and z.

(2) For any number k, if y%k=0 and z%k=0, then $k \leq x$.

101

GCD of 5 and 27:

Here 1 is the greatest common divisor of 5 and 27.

The recursive definition of greatest common divisor of two numbers x and y can be given as follows, when $x \geq y$.

$$GCD(x, y) = \begin{cases} y & \text{If x mod y=0} \\ GCD(y, x \bmod y) & \text{Otherwise} \end{cases}$$

****

/* Program to find out the greatest common divisor of two numbers */

```c
#include<stdio.h>

void main()
{
```

102

```c
        int num1, num2, gcd;

        printf("enter two positive numbers \n");
        scanf("%d %d",&num1,&num2);

        if(num1>num2)
        gcd=find_gcd(num1,num2);
        else
        gcd=find_gcd(num2,num1);

        printf("greatest common divisor:%d\n",gcd);
}  /* end main */

find_gcd(int num1,int num2)
{
        if(num1%num2==0)
        return num2;
        else
        return find_gcd(num2, num1%num2);

}  /* end find_gcd */

/*

After executing:

enter two positive numbers
32  40
greatest common divisor:8   (output)

*/


*******************************************
```

Logic to find out the greatest common divisor:

(1) If num2 divides num1 i.e. if num1%num2=0, then num2 is the greatest common divisor of the two numbers.

(2) Otherwise, if value of expression 'num1%num2', say **x** divides num2, then x is the greatest common divisor (Final solution).

(3) Else, step:2 is repeated to find out the greatest common divisor of two numbers num1 and num2, where, num1=num2 and num2=x, now.

4.5   Fibonacci Series

Fibonacci series is a sequence of numbers, in which every number is the sum of previous two numbers in the sequence. First two numbers of this sequence is taken as 0 and 1. So fibonacci series, which is generated as per the definition, is as following:

0,   1,   1,   2,   3,   5,   8,   13,   21,   34,   55,   89
.... and so on.

The recursive definition to generate the Fibonacci sequence is as follows:

$$
Fibonacci(n) = \begin{cases} 0 & \text{If } n = 1 \\ 1 & \text{If } n = 2 \\ Fibonacci(n-1) + Fibonacci(n-2) & \text{If } n > 2 \end{cases}
$$

```
*************************************************

/* Program to generate a Fibonacci series using recursion */

#include<stdio.h>

int fibonacci(int);

void main()
{
        int n, i=1;

printf("how many numbers do you want in Fibonacci series\n");
        scanf("%d",&n);

        if(n<1)
        {
                printf("enter a non-negative integer\n");
                exit();
        }

        while(i<=n)
        {
                printf("%d ", fibonacci(i));
                i++;
        }

} /* end main */

int fibonacci(int n)
{
        if(n==1)
        return 0;
        else
```

```
if(n==2)
return 1;
else
return fibonacci(n-1)+fibonacci(n-2);
```

} /* end fibonacci */

/*

After executing:

how many numbers do you want in fibonacci series
5
0 1 1 2 3 ....(output)

*/

****

Logic of the program:

Each time when 'fibonacci' function is called, the sum of previous two numbers in the series is returned, if value of n is greater than 2. Otherwise, 0 or 1 is returned depending upon whether the value of n is 1 or 2.

4.6   Binary Search Using Recursion

Binary Search means searching an element in a sorted array. In binary search, if array is sorted in ascending order, then we compare the item being searched for, with the item at the middle of the array. If they are equal, then there is no need for further searching. Otherwise, if middle item is greater than the item being searched for, then search procedure is repeated on the first half of the array. Else, if middle item is less than the item, which is to be searched, then search procedure is repeated in the second half of the array.

This procedure for searching can be defined recursively. We can use a function that results in a Call statement to itself with a smaller array as input. This smaller array may be the first half or the second half of the previous subarray, in which we have compared the item, which we are looking for, with the middle item. This process of calling the same function again and again will be continued until we get the item that we are looking for or we reach at the dead state i.e. item, which has to be searched, is not found. In the following program, function 'bsearch' plays a role of such type of function, in which variable 'low' and 'high' are used as the lower and upper bound of the array. And, it returns –1, if we reach at the dead state or the position of the item, which is to be searched in the array if search is completed successfully.

Note: Searching is given in Chapter 9 of this book.

****

```
/* Implementation of Binary Search using recursion */

#include<stdio.h>
#define MAX 100

int bsearch(int *, int, int, int);

void main()
{
        int num[MAX], i, n, item, pos;

        printf("enter total number of elements\n");
```

107

```c
        scanf("%d",&n);
        if(n>MAX)
        {
            printf("Input size is greater than declared size\n");
            exit();
        }

        printf("enter elements in ascending order\n");
        for(i=0;i<n;i++)
        scanf("%d",&num[i]);
        printf("enter element to be searched\n");
        scanf("%d",&item);

        pos=bsearch(num, item, 0, n-1);
            /* Call bsearch function by passing base address of
               array 'num', item to be searched and lower and upper
               bound of array 'num' */

        if(pos==-1)
        printf("element not found \n");
        else
        printf("element found at position :%d",pos+1);
}  /* end main */

int bsearch(int *num, int item, int low, int high)
{
        int mid;

        mid=(low+high)/2;

        if(low>high)               /* element not found */
        return -1;

        if(item==num[mid])    /* element found at position 'mid' */
        return mid;
        else
        if(item<num[mid])
```

108

```
        return bsearch(num,item,low,mid-1);
            /* Recursion is used here. 'bsearch' function is again called
               with lower and upper bound as 'low' and 'mid-1' */
      else
        return bsearch(num,item,mid+1,high);
            /* if item is in between num[mid+1] and num[high] then pass
               lower and upper bound as 'mid+1' and 'high' */
}    /* end bsearch */

/*

After executing:

    enter total number of elements
    5
    enter elements in ascending order
    1  2  3  4  5
    enter element to be searched
    5
    element found at position :5  ............... (output)

*/
```

****

Steps of the program:

Suppose array is:

1   2   3   4   5

And element to be searched is: 5, then

Stack created by function 'bsearch':

low	high	mid		num[mid]
4	4	4	Instance: 3	5
3	4	3	Instance: 2	4
0	4	2	Instance: 1	3

low   high   mid   num[mid]

In instance:3, 'num[mid]=5', which means that 'item' is found at position 'mid' in array 'num'. Value of 'mid' in instance:3 is 4. So 4 is returned to instance:2. Instance:2 will return this value to instance:1, which further returns this value to function 'main'. And there we get the output:

element found at position:5 …………………(output)

4.7   **Towers of Hanoi**

Suppose there are three pegs, labeled A, B and C. Further suppose that on peg A there are n number of disks, which are of decreasing size. Now we want to play a game, which involves the shifting of these disks to peg B in the same pattern, using peg C as an auxiliary peg. The rules of the game are as under:

(a) Only the top disk on any peg may be moved to any other peg, at a time.

(b) The larger disk can never be placed on a smaller disk.

Suppose 3 disks are placed in peg A with decreasing size, then solution of this problem will consists of the following seven moves:

110

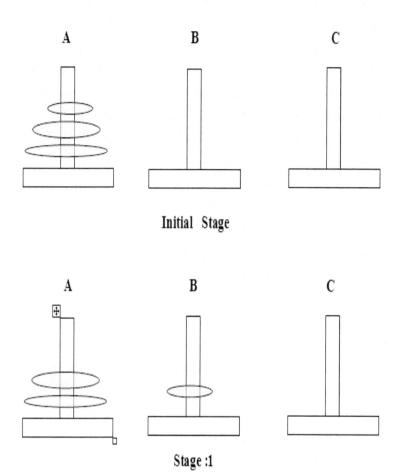

A   B   C

Initial Stage

A   B   C

Stage :1

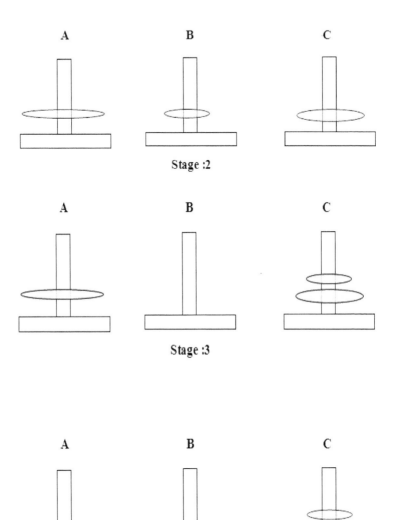

A   B   C

Stage :2

A   B   C

Stage :3

A   B   C

Stage :4

112

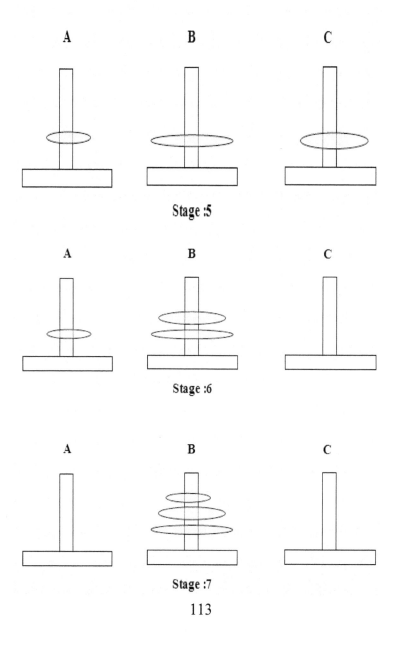

Stage :5

Stage :6

Stage :7

Suppose, there are 'N' numbers of disks, then the solution of this problem can be defined as under:

- ➤ Move N-1 disks from peg A to C using B as an auxiliary peg

- ➤ Move top disk from peg A to B

- ➤ Move N-1 disks from peg C to B using A as an auxiliary peg

Following program prints the solution of this problem when number of disks in peg 'A' are 'N', where, number 'N' is supplied as an input by the user.

****

```c
/* Implementation of Towers of Hanoi using recursion */

#include<stdio.h>

void towers(int, char, char, char);

void main()
{
        int n;

        printf("enter number of  disks\n");
        scanf("%d",&n);

        towers(n,'A','B','C');

}  /* end main */
```

114

```
void towers(int n, char frompeg, char topeg, char auxpeg)
{
        if(n>=1)
        {
                towers(n-1,frompeg,auxpeg,topeg);   /* statement: 1 */
        printf("move disk %d from peg %c to peg %c\n", n, frompeg, topeg);
                                                    /* statement: 2 */
                towers(n-1,auxpeg,topeg,frompeg);   /* statement: 3 */
        }
}       /* end towers */

/*

After executing:

enter number of disks
3

move disk 1 from peg A to peg B
move disk 2 from peg A to peg C
move disk 1 from peg B to peg C
move disk 3 from peg A to peg B
move disk 1 from peg C to peg A
move disk 2 from peg C to peg B
move disk 1 from peg A to peg B .......................(output)
*/
```

****

If number of disks entered by user are 3, then

Stack made by the function 'towers':

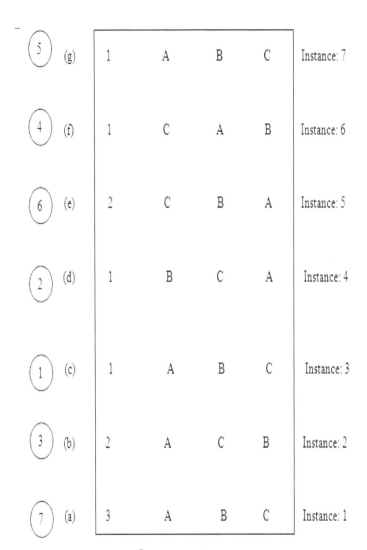

n	frompeg	topeg	auxpeg	
(g) 1	A	B	C	Instance: 7
(f) 1	C	A	B	Instance: 6
(e) 2	C	B	A	Instance: 5
(d) 1	B	C	A	Instance: 4
(c) 1	A	B	C	Instance: 3
(b) 2	A	C	B	Instance: 2
(a) 3	A	B	C	Instance: 1

Above $\left(1\right), \left(2\right), \left(3\right), \left(4\right), \left(5\right), \left(6\right)$ and $\left(7\right)$ denote the precedence of clearing the instance of 'towers' from computer's memory. Instance: 3 and cluster: (c) of auto variables numbered $\left(1\right)$ will be the first cluster, which will be popped out from memory.

Steps of the program:

Note: We will simulate this program with 3 numbers of disks.

(1) First, function 'main' calls 'towers' with parameters n, 'A', 'B' and 'C' respectively, where n, in our case, is 3. Instance: 1 of 'towers' is created and 3, A, B and C are pushed onto the stack.

(2) Statement: 1 of instance: 1 again calls 'towers' with parameters: 2, 'A', 'C' and 'B'. Now instance: 2 is created and cluster: (b) of auto variables: 2, A, C and B are pushed onto the stack.

(3) Similarly instance: 3 is created which works for variables' values: 1, A, B and C. Statement: 1 of instance: 3 again calls 'towers' with parameters: 0, A, C and B, and a new instance of 'towers' would be created. But we have not shown in above figure, because no statement of this instance will be executed because of condition 'if(n>=1)'. So it will be popped out from memory, and control will be returned to instance: 3.

(4) Statement: 2 of instance: 3 will print: " move disk 1 from peg A(frompeg) to peg B(topeg)". And statement: 3 will generate a new instance of 'towers'. This instance will not execute any statement of 'towers', so control will be returned to instance: 3. But, instance: 3 has executed all of its statements already, therefore it will also be erased from the memory and control is returned to instance: 2.

(5) Now, statement: 2 of instance: 2 prints "move disk 2(n) from peg A(frompeg) to peg C(topeg)". And statement: 3 generates instance: 4, which works for variables' values: 1, 'B','C' and 'A'.

(6) In instance: 4, value of n is 1, as it was in case of instance: 3. So instance: 4 prints "move disk 1(n) from peg B(frompeg) to peg C(topeg)". And control is returned to instance: 2(Refer to step: 3 and 4).

(7) Instance: 2 returns control to instance: 1, because it has executed all of its statements.   So, now statement: 2 of instance: 1 prints "move disk 3(n) from peg A(frompeg) to

peg B(topeg)". And statement: 3 creates instance: 5, which starts its execution for   variables' values: 2, 'C', 'B' and 'A'.

(8) Statement: 1 of instance: 5 generates instance: 6, which gives the output "move disk from peg C to peg A". After that, control is returned to instance: 5, that prints "move disk 2 from peg C to peg B" and creates a new instance 7. This instance: 7 produces the final output "move disk 1 from peg A to peg B".

4.8   8 Queens Problem

8 queens problem is to place the eight queens on a 8 X 8 chessboard such that no two of them attack each other i.e. no two cut each other, or we can say that no two of them are on the same row, column, or diagonal. One of the solutions to this problem is given below.

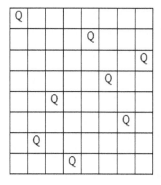

A solution of the 8-queens problem

Following program prints all the solutions of the 8-queens problem by considering that the positions in the chessboard are numbered as follows:

a11	a12	a13	a14	a15	a16	a17	a18
a21	a21	a21	a21	a21	a21	a21	a21
a31	a32	a33	a34	a35	a36	a37	a38
a41	a42	a43	a44	a45	a46	a47	a48
a51	a52	a53	a54	a55	a56	a57	a58
a61	a62	a63	a64	a65	a66	a67	a68
a71	a72	a73	a74	a75	a76	a77	a78
a81	a82	a83	a84	a85	a86	A87	a88

119

```
*************************************************

/* Program to implement 8-queens problem */

#include<stdio.h>
#define true 1
#define false 0

void try(int);
int place_queen(int);
int abs(int);

int column[9];

void main()
{
        int i, j;
printf("there is a chessboard in which positions are numbered from a11 to a88\n");
        for(i=1;i<=8;i++)
        {
            for(j=1;j<=8;j++)
            printf(" a%d%d", i, j);
            printf("\n");
        }
        printf("\n solutions to the 8 queens problem are\n\n");
        try(1);          /* Call the recursive function 'try' */
} /* end main */

void try(int n)
{
                int i, j, check;
                for(i=1;i<=8;i++)
                {
```

120

```
                    column[n]=i;
                              /* nth queen is placed at nth row and
                                 ith column on the chessboard */
                    check=place_queen(n);

                    if(check==true && n!=8)
                    try(n+1);
                              /* if nth queen is not intersecting any
                                 other queen i.e. (check==true) and
                                 total queens(n) which are placed
                                 on the chessboard are less than 8,
                                 then call function 'try' with
                                 argument 'n+1' */

                    if(check==true && n==8)
                    {
                         for(j=1;j<=8;j++)
                         printf("a%d%d ", j, column[j]);

                         printf("\n\n");

                    } /* if all the 8 queens are placed at proper
                         positions, then print the solution */

          } /* end for */

} /* end try */


int place_queen(int n)
{
          int x;

          for(x=1; x<=n-1; x++)
    if((column[x]==column[n]) || (abs(column[x]-column[n])==abs(x-n)))
          return false;
                         /* If two queens (nth queen and any other
                            queen) are in the same column or in the
                            same diagonal, then return false */

          return true;        /* Else, return true */

}      /* end place_queen */
```

```
int abs(int x)
{
            if(x<0)
            return −x;
            else
            return x;
}
```

/*

After executing:

there is a chessboard in which positions are numbered from a11 to a88

a11 a12 a13 a14 a15 a16 a17 a18
a21 a22 a23 a24 a25 a26 a27 a28
a31 a32 a33 a34 a35 a36 a37 a38
a41 a42 a43 a44 a45 a46 a47 a48
a51 a52 a53 a54 a55 a56 a57 a58
a61 a62 a63 a64 a65 a66 a67 a68
a71 a72 a73 a74 a75 a76 a77 a78
a81 a82 a83 a84 a85 a86 a87 a88

solutions to the 8 queens problem are

a11 a25 a38 a46 a53 a67 a72 a84

a11 a26 a38 a43 a57 a64 a72 a85

a11 a27 a34 a46 a58 a62 a75 a83

a11 a27 a35 a48 a52 a64 a76 a83

a12 a24 a36 a48 a53 a61 a77 a85

a12 a25 a37 a41 a53 a68 a76 a84

a12 a25 a37 a44 a51 a68 a76 a83

a12 a26 a31 a47 a54 a68 a73 a85

a12 a26 a38 a43 a51 a64 a77 a85

a12 a27 a33 a46 a58 a65 a71 a84

a12 a27 a35 a48 a51 a64 a76 a83

a12 a28 a36 a41 a53 a65 a77 a84

(total 92 solutions will be printed out of which 12 are given above)

```
*/
```

****

Steps of the program:

No two queens can be placed in the same row, so we place each xth queen ($1 \leq x \leq 8$) at x^{th} row. In our program, we have taken an integer array 'column[9]', where column[n] ($1 \leq n \leq 8$) stores the column number at which n^{th} queen is placed.

void try(int n):

1) For queen 'n', we will try all the 8 positions of the nth row. So set 'column[n]' to 'i', where $1 \leq i \leq 8$.

2) Check whether n^{th} queen is intersecting any other queen out of n-1 queens, which have already been placed on the chessboard.

3) If this queen is not intersecting any other queen and n<8, then call recursive function 'try' with parameter 'n+1' to place $(n+1)^{th}$ queen at $(n+1)^{th}$ row.

4) If all the 8 queens are placed such that no two of them are cutting each other, then print the solution.

In function 'try', backtracking is used. Recursive statement 'try(n+1)' is used in loop 'for(i=1;i<=8;i++)'. So, for each queen 'x' ($1 \leq x \leq 8$), all the 8 positions of xth row are tested to find every solution of this problem.

int place_queen(int n):

This function is used to check whether n^{th} queen, which has been placed on the chessboard at n^{th} row, is rightly placed or not.

4.9 <u>Generating Permutations</u>

Suppose we are given n different objects, then total number of possible permutations for these n objects are n!. Where n! is the product of numbers from 1 to n.

$$n! = 1*2*3*4............*n$$

Again, suppose that there are 2 different objects 1 and 2. We can obtain two permutations (1, 2) and (2, 1) of these two objects {1, 2}, by writing 2 first on the left, then on the right of 1. Similarly, six permutations of {1, 2, 3} can be obtained by taking the permutations (1, 2) and (2, 1) and inserting 3 into all of the three possible positions (left, center, or right), one by one. So, generating n! permutations of n objects can be summarized as follows:

In all the permutations of objects {1, 2, 3, ... n-1}, insert n into each of the n possible positions to obtain n distinct permutations of {1, 2, 3, ... n}. In this way, by each permutation of {1, 2, 3, ... n-1}, n permutations will be generated. Thus a total n! permutations of n objects can be generated.

The following program generates all the permutations of n different objects.

```
**************************************************
/* Program to generate permutations of n different objects */

#include<stdio.h>
#define MAX 20

int permutation[MAX];

void permute(int, int);

void main()
{
        int n, i;

        printf("enter total number of objects\n");
        scanf("%d",&n);

        if(n>MAX)
        {
         printf("Input size is greater than declared size\n");
         exit();
        }
        permute(1,n);
}   /* end main */

void permute(int k, int n)
{
        int i, j;
```

```
        for(i=1; i<=k; i++)
        {
                for(j=1; j<=n; j++)
                if(permutation[j]==k)
                permutation[j]=permutation[k];
                        /* delete 'k' from array 'permutation'
                           and assign a value other than 'k' at
                           that position. Here permutation[k] has
                           been assigned */

                for(j=k; j>i; j--)
                permutation[j]=permutation[j-1];
                        /* shift every element > i at one position
                           right to itself */

                permutation[i]=k; /* assign 'k' to permutation[i] */

                if(k==n)
                {
                        for(j=1; j<=n; j++)
                        printf("%d", permutation[j]);

                        printf("\n");
                }
                else
                permute(k+1,n);

        } /* end for */
} /* end permute */

/*

After executing:

enter total number of objects
3


321
132
123
```

312
231
213   ....*(output)*

*/

****

Steps of the program:

void permute(int k, int n):

Loop 'for(j=1; j<=n; j++)' checks for number 'k' in array 'permutation'. If number is found at location 'j', where $1 \leq j \leq n$, then k is deleted from that location and a different number 'permutation[k]' is assigned to 'permutation[j]'. Suppose, at present, array 'permutation' is: "321" and value of k is 3. Then, in place of 3, 'permutation[3]' which is 1, is assigned to 'permutation[1]'. Now array 'permutation' becomes "121". Now at execution of loop 'for(j=k; j>i; j--)', each element will be shifted one position right to itself, starting from k_{th} element upto $(i-1)_{th}$ element. Consider that, at this moment, value of i is 2, then, after execution of this loop, array 'permutation' becomes "122". And 'k'(3) is assigned to 'permutation[i]'(permutation[2]). So the value in array 'permutation' is converted into "132". Thus, in this way, all the permutations of number 'n' are generated.

4.10   To find out the determinant of a matrix

Let 'A' be a 2 x 2 matrix. For example:

127

$$A = \begin{bmatrix} 1 & 3 \\ 2 & 4 \end{bmatrix}$$

then determinant of matrix A $(|A|) = \begin{vmatrix} 1 & 3 \\ 2 & 4 \end{vmatrix} = 1*4 - 3*2 = -2$

Let 'A' be a 3 x 3 matrix. For example :

$$A = \begin{bmatrix} 1 & 4 & 7 \\ 2 & 5 & 8 \\ 3 & 6 & 9 \end{bmatrix} \quad \text{then}$$

$|A| = 1* \begin{vmatrix} 5 & 8 \\ 6 & 9 \end{vmatrix} - 4* \begin{vmatrix} 2 & 8 \\ 3 & 9 \end{vmatrix} + 7* \begin{vmatrix} 2 & 5 \\ 3 & 6 \end{vmatrix} = 0$

Here, above we have expanded the matrix A according to first row. We can also expand the above matrix according to last row :

$|A| = 9* \begin{vmatrix} 1 & 4 \\ 2 & 5 \end{vmatrix} - 6* \begin{vmatrix} 1 & 7 \\ 2 & 8 \end{vmatrix} + 3* \begin{vmatrix} 4 & 7 \\ 5 & 8 \end{vmatrix} = 0$

Result will be same in both the cases.

Following program prints the determinant of a matrix and logic for expanding the matrix used in this program, is according to the last row.

****

/* Program to find out the determinant of a matrix using recursion */

```
#include<stdio.h>
#define MAX 20

int matrix[MAX][MAX],n;

int process(int, int, int[MAX][MAX]), new_process(int,
int[MAX][MAX]), pow(int, int),
determinant(int[MAX][MAX]);

void main()
{
    int det, i, j, temp[MAX][MAX];

    printf("enter the order of matrix\n");
    scanf("%d",&n);

    if(n>MAX || n<=1)
    {
        printf("Input size is not in the range\n");
        exit();
    }

    printf("enter matrix\n");
    for(i=1;i<=n;i++)
    for(j=1;j<=n;j++)
    {
        scanf("%d", &matrix[i][j]);
        temp[i][j]=matrix[i][j];

    } /* In above loop, first position of the array is taken as matrix[1][1] not
         as matrix[0][0], so don't get confused with it. */

    if(n==2)
    det=determinant(temp);    /* If order of matrix is 2, then use
                                  function 'determinant' */
```

129

```
        else
        det=process(n,n,temp); /* else use recursion to find the determinant */

        printf("determinant:%d",det);

}   /* end main */

int determinant(int matrix_of_order_2[MAX][MAX])
{
        return
(matrix_of_order_2[1][1]*matrix_of_order_2[2][2]-\

matrix_of_order_2[1][2]*matrix_of_order_2[2][1]);
```

}   /* This function is used to find out the determinant of matrix of order 2, which is returned to the function that invokes it. */

```
int process(int expanding_row,int expanding_col,int
new_matrix[MAX][MAX])
{
    int g, h, x, y, prev_matrix[MAX][MAX], order=expanding_row;
```
                                        /* Assign expanding_row to variable 'order'. Here 'order' is the order of new_matrix */

```
        int s=0;

        for(x=1;x<=order;x++)
        for(y=1;y<=order;y++)
        prev_matrix[x][y]=new_matrix[x][y];
```
                        /* assign each element of new_matrix to prev_matrix. */

```
        for(;expanding_col>=1;)   /* loop until expanding_col is greater than or equal to 1 */
        {
            g=0;

            for(x=1;x<=order;x++)
```

```
        {
                h=0;
                if(x!=expanding_row)
                g++;              /* Make a new matrix that doesn't contain
                                   expanding row and expanding column and
                                   is of order, 1 less than the previous matrix
                                   (prev_matrix) */

                for(y=1;y<=order;y++)
                if(y!=expanding_col&&x!=expanding_row)
                {
                        h++;
                        new_matrix[g][h]=prev_matrix[x][y];
                }  /* end for */
        }  /* end for */

s=s+pow(-
1,expanding_row+expanding_col)*prev_matrix[expanding_r
ow][expanding_col]*new_process(order- 1,new_matrix);

        for(x=1;x<=order;x++)
        for(y=1;y<=order;y++)
        new_matrix[x][y]=prev_matrix[x][y];

        expanding_col--;

        }  /* end for */

        return s;

}  /* end process */

int new_process(int order, int new_matrix[MAX][MAX])
{
```

```
        if(order>2)
        return process(order,order,new_matrix);
        else
        return determinant(new_matrix);
}  /* end new_process */

int pow(int l,int m)
{
        int i,mult=1;

        for(i=0;i<m;i++)
        mult=mult*l;

        return mult;
}  /* end pow */

/*

After executing:

Enter the order of matrix
3
enter matrix
1 2 3
4 5 6
7 8 9
determinant:0  ………………….(output)

*/
```

****

Steps of the program:

Input the elements of matrix in array 'matrix'. Suppose matrix entered by user is:

132

$$\begin{bmatrix} 1 & 4 & 7 \\ 2 & 5 & 8 \\ 3 & 6 & 9 \end{bmatrix}.$$

So we will simulate the program according to this matrix.

1) Here order of matrix is 3, so function 'process' is called with parameters 3, 3 and 'temp', where elements of 'temp' matrix are same as elements of 'matrix'.

2) In function 'process', parameters 3, 3 and 'temp' will be received in variables 'expanding_row', 'expanding_col' and 'new_matrix'.

3) In 'process', order of matrix 'new_matrix' is same as 'expanding_row', because we are expanding the matrix according to last row. So assign variable 'expanding_row' to 'order'. And assign each and every element of 'new_matrix' to 'prev_matrix'.

Note: In our case, matrix is:

$$\begin{bmatrix} 1 & 4 & 7 \\ 2 & 5 & 8 \\ 3 & 6 & 9 \end{bmatrix}$$

If we expand this matrix according to last row, then determinant of this matrix is:

133

$$|A| = 9 * \begin{vmatrix} 1 & 4 \\ 2 & 5 \end{vmatrix} - 6 * \begin{vmatrix} 1 & 7 \\ 2 & 8 \end{vmatrix} + 3 * \begin{vmatrix} 4 & 7 \\ 5 & 8 \end{vmatrix}$$

So we have to make these three matrices:

$$\begin{bmatrix} 1 & 4 \\ 2 & 5 \end{bmatrix}, \begin{bmatrix} 1 & 7 \\ 2 & 8 \end{bmatrix} \text{ and } \begin{bmatrix} 4 & 7 \\ 5 & 8 \end{bmatrix}, \text{ one by one and to find out the determinant}$$

of each matrix. In the last, we will have to put all these determinants in abov equation to find out the determinant of actual matrix.

4) As we have to generate above mentioned three matrices one by one, so in our program following steps are used to make a new matrix 'new_matrix' that will not contain 'expanding_row' and 'expanding_col'.

```
for(x=1;x<=order;x++)
{
        h=0;

        if(x!=expanding_row)
        g++;              /* Make a new matrix that doesn't contain
                             expanding row and expanding column  and
                             is of order,  1 less than the previous matrix
                             (prev_matrix)  */

        for(y=1;y<=order;y++)
        if(y!=expanding_col&&x!=expanding_row)
        {
                h++;
```

$$\text{new\_matrix}[g][h]=\text{prev\_matrix}[x][y];$$

}

}

So in our case, at each execution of loop
'for(;expanding_col>=1;)', these matrices

$$\begin{bmatrix} 1 & 4 \\ 2 & 5 \end{bmatrix}, \begin{bmatrix} 1 & 7 \\ 2 & 8 \end{bmatrix} \text{ and } \begin{bmatrix} 4 & 7 \\ 5 & 8 \end{bmatrix} \text{ will be generated in order.}$$

And for each matrix function 'new_process' is called which further calls function 'determinant' that returns the determinant of order 2 matrix.

5) In the last, function 'process' will return the determinant of matrix:

$$\begin{bmatrix} 1 & 4 & 7 \\ 2 & 5 & 8 \\ 3 & 6 & 9 \end{bmatrix} \text{ to function 'main'.}$$

4.11   Inverse of a matrix

Minors(Definition):

Let A= [a_{ij}] be an n rowed square matrix. Then the minor M_{ij} of a_{ij} is the determinant of the submatrix obtained by leaving i^{th} row and j^{th} column of A.

135

For example, if

$$A = \begin{bmatrix} 1 & 4 & 7 \\ 2 & 5 & 8 \\ 3 & 6 & 9 \end{bmatrix}, \text{ then}$$

$$M_{11} = \text{minor of } A_{11} = \begin{vmatrix} 5 & 6 \\ 8 & 9 \end{vmatrix} = -3$$

$$M_{22} = \text{minor of } A_{22} = \begin{vmatrix} 1 & 7 \\ 3 & 9 \end{vmatrix} = -12$$

$$M_{32} = \text{minor of } A_{32} = \begin{vmatrix} 1 & 7 \\ 2 & 8 \end{vmatrix} = -6$$

Cofactor(Definition):

Let A= [a_{ij}] be an n rowed square matrix. Then the cofactor C_{ij} of a_{ij} is equal to $(-1)^{i+j}$ times the minor M_{ij} of a_{ij}, i.e.

$C_{ij} = (-1)^{i+j} * M_{ij}$.

$$\text{Let } A = \begin{bmatrix} 1 & 2 & 3 \\ 4 & 5 & 6 \\ 7 & 8 & 9 \end{bmatrix}, \text{ then}$$

$$C_{11} = (-1)^{1+1} * M_{11} = (-1)^2 * \begin{vmatrix} 5 & 6 \\ 8 & 9 \end{vmatrix} = -3$$

$$C_{22} = (-1)^{2+2} * M_{22} = (-1)^4 * \begin{vmatrix} 1 & 3 \\ 7 & 9 \end{vmatrix} = -12$$

$$C_{32} = (-1)^{3+2} * M_{32} = (-1)^5 * \begin{vmatrix} 1 & 3 \\ 4 & 6 \end{vmatrix} = (-1)*(-6)=6$$

Singular Matrix (Definition):

A square matrix A is called a singular matrix, if $|A|=0$, otherwise A is called a non-singular matrix.

Note: A square matrix A is invertible iff it is non-singular. And the inverse of an invertible matrix is always unique.

Adjoint of a Square Matrix (Definition):

Let $A = [a_{ij}]$ be a square matrix of order n x n, and C_{ij} be the cofactor of a_{ij} in A. Then the transpose of the matrix of cofactors of elements in A is called the adjoint of A and is denoted by adj A.

Thus, adj $A = [C_{ij}]^T$

$\therefore$ (adj A)$_{ij}$ = C_{ji} = Cofactor of A_{ji} in A.

Let $A = \begin{bmatrix} 1 & 2 \\ 3 & 4 \end{bmatrix}$, then

$M_{11} = 4$; $C_{11} = (-1)^2 * 4 = 4$

$M_{12} = 3$; $C_{12} = (-1)^3 * 3 = -3$

$M_{21} = 2$; $C_{21} = (-1)^3 * 2 = -2$

$M_{22} = 1$; $C_{22} = (-1)^4 * 1 = 1$

Adj $A = \begin{bmatrix} 4 & -3 \\ -2 & 1 \end{bmatrix}^T = \begin{bmatrix} 4 & -2 \\ -3 & 1 \end{bmatrix}$

Inverse of a matrix (Definition):

Let A be a non singular matrix of order n. Then a matrix B will be called inverse of A if

$AB = I_n = BA$

The inverse of A is denoted by A^{-1}. And

$A^{-1} = (1/|A|) * (adj\ A).$

****

```c
/*  Program to find out the inverse of a matrix  */
#include<stdio.h>
#define MAX 20

int matrix[MAX][MAX], n;

int determinant(int[MAX][MAX]);
int process(int, int, int[MAX][MAX]);
int new_process(int, int[MAX][MAX]);
int pow(int, int);

void main()
{
    int det, i, j, temp[MAX][MAX], x, y, g, h;
    float inverse[MAX][MAX];

    printf("enter the order of matrix\n");
    scanf("%d",&n);

    if(n>MAX || n<=1)
    {
        printf("Input size is not in the range\n");
        exit();
    }
```

```c
printf("enter matrix\n");
for(i=1;i<=n;i++)
for(j=1;j<=n;j++)
{
    scanf("%d",&matrix[i][j]);
    temp[i][j]=matrix[i][j];

}      /* First element of this matrix is taken as matrix[1][1]  */

if(n==2)
det=determinant(temp);
        /* To find out the determinant of order 2 matrix, use 'determinant'
           function */
else
det=process(n,n,temp); /* else use recursive function 'process' */

if(det==0)
{
    printf("matrix is singular");
    exit();
}

if(n==2)
printf("%f %f\n%f  %f",(float)matrix[2][2]/det,-
(float)matrix[1][2]/det,- (float)matrix[2][1]/det,(float)matrix[1][1]/det);

            /* if order of matrix is 2, then directly print the inverse of
               matrix */
else
{
    for(i=1;i<=n;i++)
    for(j=1;j<=n;j++)
    {
        g=0;
        for(x=1;x<=n;x++)
        {
            h=0;
```

139

```
                    if(x!=i)
                    g++;
                    for(y=1;y<=n;y++)
                    if(y!=j&&x!=i)
                    {
                        h++;
                        temp[g][h]=matrix[x][y];
                    }
```

}   /* Store the submatrix obtained by leaving ith row and
        jth column of 'matrix' in array 'temp'. And if order of
        that 'temp' matrix is 2, then find out the determinant
        of minor Mij, using 'determinant' function, else use
        'process' function */

```
if(n==3)
inverse[i][j]=determinant(temp)*pow(-1,i+j);
```
                                        /* Cofactor Cij */
```
else
inverse[i][j]=process(n-1,n-1,temp)*pow(-1,i+j);
```
/* if n>3 then use 'process' function to find out the cofactor Cij */

}   /* end for */

```
printf("inverse\n");

for(i=1;i<=n;i++)
{
        for(j=1;j<=n;j++)
        printf("%f ",inverse[j][i]/det);
        printf("\n");
```

}   /* Print the result after division of each element of transpose
        of 'inverse' with 'det' */

}   /* end else */

} /* end main */

140

```
int determinant(int order_2_mat[MAX][MAX])
{

    return (order_2_mat[1][1]*order_2_mat[2][2]-
    order_2_mat[1][2]*order_2_mat[2][1]);

}  /* end 'determinant' */
```

/* In the above function find the determinant of the matrix of order 2 and return it to the function that invokes it */

```
int process(int expanding_row, int expanding_col, int new_matrix[MAX][MAX])
{
    int g, h, x, y, prev_matrix[MAX][MAX], order=expanding_row;
                                /* Here order is the order of 'new_matrix' */
    int s=0;

    for(x=1;x<=order;x++)
    for(y=1;y<=order;y++)
    prev_matrix[x][y]=new_matrix[x][y];

    for(;expanding_col>=1;)
    {
        g=0;

        for(x=1;x<=order;x++)
        {
            h=0;
            if(x!=expanding_row)
            g++;
            for(y=1;y<=order;y++)
            if(y!=expanding_col&&x!=expanding_row)
            {
                h++;
                new_matrix[g][h]=prev_matrix[x][y];
            }  /* end if */
```

141

} */* Make a new matrix(new_matrix) that doesn't contain expanding row and expanding column and is of order, 1 less than the previous matrix(prev_matrix) */

```
        s=s+pow(-
1,expanding_row+expanding_col)*prev_matrix[expanding_r
ow][expanding_col]*new_process(order-1,new_matrix);

        for(x=1;x<=order;x++)
        for(y=1;y<=order;y++)
        new_matrix[x][y]=prev_matrix[x][y];
        expanding_col--;

    } /* end for */

    return s;

} /* end 'process' */


int new_process(int order,int new_matrix[MAX][MAX])
{
    if(order>2)
    return process(order,order,new_matrix);
    else
    return determinant(new_matrix);

} /* end new_process */


int pow(int value, int num_of_times)
{
        int i, power=1;
        for(i=0;i<num_of_times;i++)
        power=power*value;

        return power;

} /* end pow */
```

```
/*
```

After executing:

Enter the order of matrix
3
enter matrix
1 2 3
4 9 3
5 1 9
inverse
-0.896552 0.172414 0.241379
0.241379 0.068966 -0.103448
0.471264 -0.103448 -0.011494 ....(output)

```
*/
```

****

Steps of the program:

The logic of this program is same, as it is in the program of finding out the determinant of a matrix. But here we have to find the cofactor of each element of 'matrix'. In function 'main', following steps are used for finding the submatrix 'temp', obtained by leaving i^{th} row and j^{th} column of array 'matrix'.

```
for(i=1;i<=n;i++)
for(j=1;j<=n;j++)
{
    g=0;

    for(x=1;x<=n;x++)
    {
        h=0;
        if(x!=i)
```

143

```
        g++;
        for(y=1;y<=n;y++)
        if(y!=j&&x!=i)
        {
            h++;
            temp[g][h]=matrix[x][y];
        }         /*   end if   */


    }
    .
    .
    .
    .
    .
    .
    .
}      /*   end  for */
```

Now to find out the cofactor of 'matrix[i][j]': find the determinant of 'temp' and multiply it by pow(-1,i+j).

Note: Logic to find the determinant is same, as it is in the previous program.

4.12   A Recursive Problem

A 10 by 10 table of 0's and 1's represents a maze in which a traveller must find a path from maze[0][0] to maze[9][9]. A traveller may move from a square into an adjacent square in the same row or column, but can not skip over any square or move diagonally. In addition, the traveller can not move into any square that contains a 1. Apart from this, maze[0][0] and maze[9][9] must contain 0's.

144

0	0	1	1	1	1	1	1	1	1
1	0	1	1	1	1	1	1	1	1
1	0	0	0	1	1	1	1	1	1
1	1	1	0	1	1	1	1	1	1
1	1	1	0	1	1	1	1	1	1
1	1	1	0	0	1	1	1	1	1
1	1	1	0	0	0	0	0	0	1
1	1	1	0	1	1	1	1	0	1
1	1	1	1	1	1	1	1	0	1
1	1	1	1	1	1	1	1	0	0

Above figure shows a path in such type of a maze. The following program accepts such a maze and either prints a message that no path through the maze exists or prints a list of positions which represent a path from [0][0] to [9][9], where [0][0] is the first location of the maze and [9][9] is the last location of the 'maze'(two dimensional array).

****

/* Program to implement the above problem */

```c
#include<stdio.h>

int maze[10][10], flag[10][10];
void process(int, int);

void main()
{
        int i, j;

printf("enter a 10 by 10 table of 0's and 1's only: first and last element should be 0\n");
```

```
    for(i=0;i<=9;i++)
    for(j=0;j<=9;j++)
    scanf("%d",&maze[i][j]);

    if(maze[0][0]!=0||maze[9][9]!=0)
    {
        printf("wrong maze entered\n");
        exit();
    }

    flag[0][0]=1;
    process(0,0);        /* process is a recursive function, in which initially
                            two arguments '0' and '0' are passed        */

}  /* end main */

void process(int row, int col)
{
    static int end;

    if(row==9&&col==9)
    end=1;

    if(maze[row][col+1]==0 && col!=9 && end==0 && flag[row][col+1]==0)
    {
        flag[row][col+1]=1;
        process(row,col+1);

    }   /* We can move to 'maze[row][col+1]', if : maze[row][col+1]==0
           col!=9 (we shouldn't move out of the boundary of 'maze') end==0
           (if 'end' state is not reached till yet) flag[row][col+1]==0 (if we
           haven't explored element 'maze[row][col+1]' yet). Inside the 'if'
           statement call recursive function 'process' with values 'row' and
           'col+1' but before doing that we have to set the value of
           flag[row][col+1]=1, as by setting this flag value, we will mark
           this position 'maze[row][col+1]' as visited */

if(maze[row+1][col]==0&&row!=9&&end==0&&flag[row+1][col]==0)
    {
```

146

```c
        flag[row+1][col]=1;
        process(row+1,col);

    }  /* move at maze[row+1][col]  */
if(maze[row-1][col]==0&&row!=0&&end==0&&flag[row-1][col]==0)
    {
        flag[row-1][col]=1;
        process(row-1,col);

    }  /* move at maze[row-1][col]  */
if(maze[row][col-1]==0&&col!=0&&end==0&&flag[row][col-1]==0)
    {
        flag[row][col-1]=1;
        process(row,col-1);

    }  /* move at maze[row][col-1]  */

    if(row==0&&col==0&&end==0)
    {
     printf("no path exists");
     exit();

    }       /* after each recursive call if control returns to the first
              instance and this condition is satisfied, then it shows that
              there is no path from maze[0][0] to maze[9][9]  */

    if(end)
    printf("%d%d ",row, col);
}  /* end process */
```

```
/*

After executing:

enter a 10 by 10 table of 0's and 1's only: first and last element should be 0
```

```
0 1 0 0 0 0 0 0 0 0
0 1 0 0 0 0 0 0 0 0
0 0 1 1 1 1 1 1 1 1
1 0 0 0 1 1 1 1 1 1
0 0 1 1 1 1 1 1 1 1
0 0 0 0 0 0 0 0 0 0
1 1 1 1 1 0 0 0 0 0
0 0 0 0 0 0 0 0 1 1
0 0 0 0 0 0 0 0 0 0
1 1 1 1 1 1 0 0 0 0
```

99 89 88 87 77 67 68 69 59 58 57 56 55 54 53 52 51 41 31 21 20 10 00
... ... (output)

It will be the solution printed by the above program. Because it is a recursive program so this solution is in opposite order. Instead of starting from location 00 it is printing the solution from 99th location.

00 ..... 0th row and 0th column
01 ..... 0th row and 1st column
02 ..... 0th row and 2nd column
....
....

*/

****

Steps of the program:

Consider maze is:

```
0 1 0 0 0 0 0 0 0 0
0 1 0 0 0 0 0 0 0 0
0 0 1 0 0 0 0 0 0 0
1 1 0 0 0 0 0 0 0 0
0 0 1 0 0 0 0 0 0 0
0 1 0 0 1 0 0 0 0 1
0 0 0 1 0 0 0 0 0 0
1 0 0 0 0 0 0 1 0 0
```

```
0  0  0  0  0  0  0  0  0  0
0  0  0  1  0  1  1  0  0  0
```

Then, stack created by the function 'process':

Stack

	row	col	end (Static)	maze[row][col] (Globally visible)	flag[row][col] (Globally visible)
Instance:4	2	1	0	0	1
Instance:3	2	0	0	0	1
Instance:2	1	0	0	0	1
Instance:1	0	0	0	0	1

After instance:4, no other instance can be created. Because 'maze[2][2]=1', 'maze[3][1]=1' and also 'maze[1][1]=1'. Thus, the way is blocked. 'maze[2][0]=0', so we can move to this position, but 'flag[2][0]=1', which means that we have already explored this position, so control will be returned to instance:3. In instance:3, row=2 and col=0, and we can move to 'maze[2][1]', but this has, already, been explored, because 'flag[2][1]=1', so control is again returned to instance:2. At the end, control of the program comes at instance:1. Here also, we can't move anywhere else, so now condition: 'if(row==0 && col==0 && end==0)' is satisfied. And we get the following output:

No path exists   ………………..(terminated).

LINKED LISTS

A linked list may be defined as a linear collection of data elements, called nodes. In this list, the pointers represent the linear-order. Each node is divided into two or more parts. A linked list can be of the following types:

- Linear linked list or one-way list.
- Doubly linked list or two-way list
- Circular linked list

5.1   Linear Linked List

In a linear linked list or one-way list, each node is divided in two parts :

- First part contains the information of the element, and
- Second part, stores the address of the next node in the list

Starting address of the linked list may be stored by using, another variable, namely 'start'. Following figure shows the arrangement of the nodes of a linear linked list. In this figure, first part of each node contains the information of the element, denoted as 'Info' and second part contains the address of the next node in the list and has been denoted as 'Next'. The last node (3rd node) of the linked list has 'NULL' value in the 'next' field.

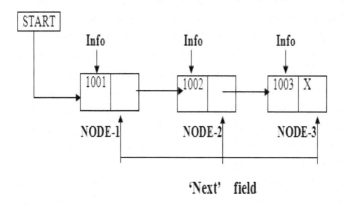

'Next' field

Representation of Linear Linked List :

A Linear Linked List can be stored in memory with the following declarations :

```
typedef struct node_type
{
    int info;
    struct node_type *next;
}node;
```

Here 'info' represents the information part of the node and pointer 'next' is used to store the location of next node of the list.

```
*************************************************
```

```
/* Program to implement the Linear Linked List */

#include<stdio.h>
#include<alloc.h>
```

```c
typedef struct node_type
{
    int info;
    struct node_type *next;
}node;

node *start=NULL;
void add_at_beginning();
void add_at_end();
void add_after_element();
void add_before_element();
void traverse_in_order();
void traverse_in_reverse_order(node *);
void delete_at_beginning();
void delete_at_end();
void delete_after_element();
void delete_before_element();
void sort();

void main()
{
            int x;

            while(1)
            {
                    printf("\nenter choice\n ");
                    printf("1.add at beginning\n ");
                    printf("2.add at end\n ");
                    printf("3.add after element\n ");
                    printf("4.add before element\n ");
                    printf("5.traverse in order\n ");
                    printf("6.traverse in reverse order\n ");
                    printf("7.delete at beginning\n ");
                    printf("8.delete at end\n ");
                    printf("9.delete after element\n ");
```

```c
        printf("10.delete before element\n ");
        printf("11.sort\n ");
        printf("12.exit\n ");
        scanf("%d",&x);

    switch(x)
    {
        case 1: add_at_beginning();    break;
        case 2: add_at_end();          break;
        case 3: add_after_element();   break;
        case 4: add_before_element();  break;
        case 5: traverse_in_order();   break;
        case 6: traverse_in_reverse_order(start);
                                       break;
        case 7: delete_at_beginning(); break;
        case 8: delete_at_end();       break;
        case 9: delete_after_element();   break;
        case 10: delete_before_element(); break;
        case 11: sort();               break;
        case 12: exit();

    }  /* end switch */

}  /* end while */

}  /* end main */

void add_at_beginning()
{
        node *ptr;
        int item;

        printf("enter item\n");
        scanf("%d",&item);
```

153

```
ptr=(node *)malloc(sizeof(node));

if(ptr==NULL)
{
        printf("no space\n");
        return;
}

(*ptr).info=item;
if(start==NULL)  /* If list is empty then create starting node */
{
        (*ptr).next=NULL;
        start=ptr;
}
else
{
        (*ptr).next=start;   /* make  starting node as second
                                    node of the list */
        start=ptr; /* and make this new node as the starting node */
}
}  /* end add_at_beginning */


void add_at_end()
{
        node *ptr, *loc;
        int item;

        printf("enter item\n");
        scanf("%d",&item);

        ptr=(node *)malloc(sizeof(node));
```

```c
        if(ptr==NULL)
        {
                printf("no space\n");
                return;
        }

        (*ptr).info=item;

        if(start==NULL)      /* If list is empty, then create starting node
                                          of the list */
        {
                start=ptr;
                (*start).next=NULL;
        }
        else
        {
                loc=start;

                while((*loc).next != NULL)
                loc=(*loc).next;

                (*loc).next=ptr;
                (*ptr).next=NULL;

        } /* If list is not empty, then add this new node at the end of the last
             node and make it the last node of the list   */
} /* end add_at_end */

void add_after_element()
{
                node *ptr, *loc;
                int item,item1;

    printf("enter item after which a node has to be inserted\n");
                scanf("%d",&item1);
```

```c
if(start==NULL)
{
    printf("no element found\n");
    return;
}

loc=start;

while((*loc).info!=item1 && loc!=NULL)
    loc=(*loc).next;        /* find the location at which 'item1'
                                is found */
if(loc==NULL)    /* if 'item1' is not found then return the
                    control */
{
    printf("element not found\n") ;
    return;
}

if((*loc).next==NULL)  /* If element has to be inserted at
                            the end of the list, then invoke
                            function 'add_at_end'  */
{
    add_at_end() ;
    return;
}
ptr=(node *)malloc(sizeof(node));

if(ptr==NULL)
{
    printf("no space\n");
    return;
}

printf("enter item which has to be inserted\n");
scanf("%d",&item);

(*ptr).info=item;
(*ptr).next=(*loc).next;
```

```c
        (*loc).next=ptr;      /* insert item after 'loc' */
}   /* end add_after_element */

void add_before_element()
{
        node *ptr,*prev, *loc;
        int item,item1;

printf("enter item, before which node has to be inserted\n");
        scanf("%d",&item1);

        if(start==NULL)
        {
                printf("no element found\n");
                return;
        }

        loc=start;

        while((*loc).info!=item1&&loc!=NULL)
        loc=(*loc).next;      /* search for 'item1' and store this
                                 location in 'loc'pointer */
        if(loc==NULL)  /* if 'item1' is not found then return the
                          control */
        {
                printf("element not found\n");
                return;
        }

        if(loc==start)
        {
            add_at_beginning() ;   /* If item has to be inserted
                                      before starting node, then call
                                      this function */
                return;
        }
```

```c
ptr=(node *)malloc(sizeof(node));

if(ptr==NULL)
{
        printf("no space\n");
        return;
}

printf("enter item which has to be inserted\n");
scanf("%d",&item);

(*ptr).info=item;
prev=start;

while((*prev).next!=loc)
prev=(*prev).next;    /* store the previous location of 'loc'
                         in pointer 'prev' */

(*ptr).next=(*prev).next;
(*prev).next=ptr;    /* insert this new node after 'prev' node */

}  /* end add_before_element */

void traverse_in_order()
{
        node *ptr;

        if(start==NULL)
        {
            printf("list is empty\n");
            return;
        }

        for(ptr=start;ptr!=NULL;ptr=(*ptr).next)
        printf("%d",(*ptr).info);  /* print all the elements of the list */

}  /* end traverse_in_reverse_order */
```

```c
void traverse_in_reverse_order(node *ptr)
{
        if(start==NULL)
        {
            printf("list is empty\n");
            return;
        }

        if(ptr!=NULL)
        {
                traverse_in_reverse_order((*ptr).next);
                    /* call this function again and again, until we reach
                       at the last node */
                printf("%d",(*ptr).info);
                        /* now start printing the 'info' part of each node */
        }

} /* end traverse_in_reverse_order */

void delete_at_beginning()
{
        node *ptr;

        if(start==NULL)
        {
            printf("element not found\n");
            return;
        }
        ptr=start;

        start=(*start).next;
        free(ptr);      /* delete the starting node and make second node
                           of the list as the  starting  node */

        printf("item deleted\n");
} /* end delete_at_beginning */
```

```c
void delete_at_end()
{
        node *ptr, *loc;

        if(start==NULL)
        {
            printf("element not found\n");
            return;
        }
        if((*start).next==NULL)  /* if there is only one element in
                                     the list, then empty the list  */
        {
            free(start);
            start=NULL;
            return;
        }
        ptr=start;
        while((*ptr).next!=NULL)
        {
            loc=ptr;
            ptr=(*ptr).next;

        }   /* store location of the second last node in 'loc' pointer  */
        free(ptr);
        (*loc).next=NULL;          /* make 'loc' as the last node  */
        printf("item deleted\n");
}  /* end delete_at_end  */
void delete_after_element()
{
        node *ptr, *loc;
```
160

```c
        int item;

    printf("enter item after which, node is to be deleted\n");
        scanf("%d",&item);

        if(start==NULL)
        {
                printf("element not found\n");
                return;
        }
        ptr=start;

        while((*ptr).info!=item && ptr!=NULL)
        ptr=(*ptr).next;   /* search for the location of 'item' and store this
                                            location in pointer 'ptr' */
        if((*ptr).next==NULL || ptr==NULL)
        {
                printf("element not found\n");
                return;
        }

        loc=(*ptr).next;
        (*ptr).next=(*loc).next;
        free(loc);           /* delete node at location 'loc' */

} /* end delete_after_element */
void delete_before_element()
{
        node *ptr,*prev,*temp, *loc;
        int item;

    printf("enter item before which, node is to be deleted\n");
        scanf("%d",&item);

        if(start==NULL)
        {
                printf("element not found\n");
```

161

```
            return;
        }

        loc=start;

        while((*loc).info!=item && loc!=NULL)
        {
            prev=loc;
            loc=(*loc).next;
        }   /* search for 'item' and store the location of its previous node
                in 'prev' pointer  */

        if(loc==NULL || loc==start)
        {
            printf("element not found\n");
            return;
        }
        if(prev==start)
        {
            delete_at_beginning();
            return;
        }
        temp=start;
        while((*temp).next!=prev)
        temp=(*temp).next;   /* store previous location of 'prev' in
                                pointer 'temp' */
        (*temp).next=loc;   /* delete 'prev' node */
        free(prev);
        printf("item deleted\n");

}  /* end delete_before_element */

void sort()
{
        node *ptr, *loc;
```

```
        int temp;

        for(ptr=start;(*ptr).next!=NULL;ptr=(*ptr).next)
        for(loc=(*ptr).next;loc!=NULL;loc=(*loc).next)
        if((*ptr).info>(*loc).info)
        {
                temp=(*loc).info;
                (*loc).info=(*ptr).info;
                (*ptr).info=temp;
        }                       /* selection sort has been used here */

        printf("list has been sorted now\n");

}   /* end sort */

/*
```

After executing:

enter choice
1.add at beginning
2.add at end
3.add after element
4.add before element
5.traverse in order
6.traverse in reverse order
7.delete at beginning
8.delete at end
9.delete after element
10.delete before element
11.sort
12.exit
1
enter item
1

enter choice
1.add at beginning
2.add at end
3.add after element
4.add before element

163

5.traverse in order
6.traverse in reverse order
7.delete at beginning
8.delete at end
9.delete after element
10.delete before element
11.sort
12.exit
2
enter item
2

enter choice
1.add at beginning
2.add at end
3.add after element
4.add before element
5.traverse in order
6.traverse in reverse order
7.delete at beginning
8.delete at end
9.delete after element
10.delete before element
11.sort
12.exit
3
enter item after which a node is to be inserted
2
enter item
3

enter choice
1.add at beginning
2.add at end
3.add after element
4.add before element
5.traverse in order
6.traverse in reverse order
7.delete at beginning
8.delete at end
9.delete after element
10.delete before element
11.sort
12.exit
4
enter item before which, a node is to be inserted

164

1
enter item
0

enter choice
1.add at beginning
2.add at end
3.add after element
4.add before element
5.traverse in order
6.traverse in reverse order
7.delete at beginning
8.delete at end
9.delete after element
10.delete before element
11.sort
12.exit
5
0123

enter choice
1.add at beginning
2.add at end
3.add after element
4.add before element
5.traverse in order
6.traverse in reverse order
7.delete at beginning
8.delete at end
9.delete after element
10.delete before element
11.sort
12.exit
6
3210

enter choice
1.add at beginning
2.add at end
3.add after element
4.add before element
5.traverse in order
6.traverse in reverse order
7.delete at beginning
8.delete at end
9.delete after element

10.delete before element
11.sort
12.exit
7
item deleted

enter choice
1.add at beginning
2.add at end
3.add after element
4.add before element
5.traverse in order
6.traverse in reverse order
7.delete at beginning
8.delete at end
9.delete after element
10.delete before element
11.sort
12.exit
 8
item deleted

enter choice
1.add at beginning
2.add at end
3.add after element
4.add before element
5.traverse in order
6.traverse in reverse order
7.delete at beginning
8.delete at end
9.delete after element
10.delete before element
11.sort
12.exit
5
12
enter choice
1.add at beginning
2.add at end
3.add after element
4.add before element
5.traverse in order
6.traverse in reverse order
7.delete at beginning
8.delete at end

166

9.delete after element
10.delete before element
11.sort
12.exit
9
enter item after which, a node is to be deleted
1

enter choice
1.add at beginning
2.add at end
3.add after element
4.add before element
5.traverse in order
6.traverse in reverse order
7.delete at beginning
8.delete at end
9.delete after element
10.delete before element
11.sort
12.exit
10
enter item before which, a node is to be deleted
1
element not found

enter choice
1.add at beginning
2.add at end
3.add after element
4.add before element
5.traverse in order
6.traverse in reverse order
7.delete at beginning
8.delete at end
9.delete after element
10.delete before element
11.sort
12.exit
11
list has been sorted now

enter choice
1.add at beginning
2.add at end
3.add after element

*/

****

Steps of the program:

void add_at_beginning() :

1) First we have to allocate the memory to insert a new node. Here 'malloc' is used to allocate the memory and this function returns the base address of allocated memory.

2) Suppose base address of the space allocated in memory is 400. This address will be returned by 'malloc' function to pointer 'ptr'.

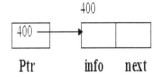

As shown above, pointer 'ptr' will contain the address 400. And at address 400 there is a memory space where an integer 'info' and address of structure 'node_type' can be stored in pointer 'next'.

168

3) If linked list is empty, then make 'ptr' as a starting node. And assign NULL to 'start->next'.

4) If it is not empty, then assign 'start' to 'ptr->next'. And make 'ptr' as the starting node, i.e. assign 'ptr' to 'start'.

void add_at_end() :

1) Use 'malloc' function to allocate the space in the memory. Base address of this memory will be stored in pointer 'ptr'.

2) If list is empty then make 'ptr' as the starting node and assign NULL to 'start->next'.

3)
   (a) If list is not empty, then search for the last node in the list. And store this location in pointer 'loc'.

   (b) Assign 'ptr' to 'loc->next' and assign NULL to 'ptr->next' i.e. make 'ptr' as the last node of the list.

void add_after_element() :

1) Input the element, after which we have to insert a new node. Store this element in variable 'item1'.

2) If list is empty, then print : " no element is found ".

3) If list is not empty, then search for 'item1' and store this location in pointer 'loc'.

4) If 'item1' is not found then print : " no element found ".

5) If 'loc' is the last node of the list, then call function 'add_at_end' i.e. insert the new node at the end of the list.

6) Else, create a new node and store its location in pointer 'ptr'.

7) Store location 'loc->next' in 'ptr->next'. And assign 'ptr' to 'loc->next'. Now 'ptr' is inserted after node 'loc'.

void add_before_element():

1) Input the element, before which we have to insert a new node. Store this element in variable 'item1'.

2) If list is empty, then print : " no element is found ".

3) If list is not empty, then search for 'item1' and store this location in pointer 'loc'.

4) If 'item1' is not found then print : " no element found ".

5) If 'loc' is the starting node of the list, then call function 'add_at_beginning' i.e.   insert the new node at the beginning of the list.

6) Else, create a new node and store its location in pointer 'ptr'.

7) Search for the previous node of node 'loc' and store its location in pointer 'prev'.

8) Store location 'prev->next' in 'ptr->next' and assign 'ptr' to 'prev->next', meaning thereby that, insert 'ptr' after node 'prev'.

void traverse_in_order() :

Print information ('info') part of each and every node, starting from node 'start'.

void traverse_in_reverse_order() :

Call function 'traverse_in_reverse_order' again and again, till we reach at the end of the list. Each time when we call this function, an instance of 'traverse_in_reverse_order' is created and value in 'ptr', which is the address of a node of structure 'node_type', is pushed onto a stack. After we reach at the end of the list, each element of the stack is popped out from memory (Last In First Out order). So 'info' part of each node is printed in reverse order. Suppose currently, linked list in memory is as follows :

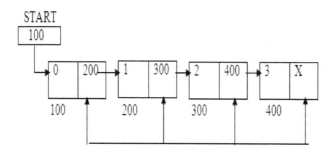

'next' field

Then stack created by function 'traverse_in_reverse_order' is :

Instance:4	400
Instance:3	300
Instance:2	200
Instance:1	100

Ptr

These elements will be popped out from memory in reverse order, so 'info' part of each node will be printed in reverse order.

void delete_at_beginning() :

1) If list is empty, then print : " no element is found ".

2) Else, assign 'start->next' to 'start' and delete the starting node. Now 'start' pointer will point to the second node of the list.

void delete_at_end() :

1) If list is empty then print : "no element found".

2) If there is only one element in the list, then empty the list.

3) Else, search for the last node of the list and store its location in pointer 'ptr', and store the location of previous node of 'ptr' in pointer 'loc'.

4) Delete 'ptr' and assign NULL to 'loc->next' i.e. make second last node of the list as the last node.

void delete_after_element() :

1) Scan 'item' after which, a node has to be deleted.

2) If list is empty, then print : " no element found ".

3) Else, search for 'item' and store its location in pointer 'ptr'.

4) If 'item' is not found or 'ptr' is the last node of the list, then print : " element not found ".

5) Else, assign 'ptr->next->next' to 'ptr->next', and delete node at position 'ptr->next'.

void delete_before_element() :

1) Scan 'item' before which, a node has to be deleted.

2) If list is empty, then print : " no element found ".

3) Else, search for 'item' and store its location in pointer 'loc', and store the location of previous node of 'loc' in pointer 'prev'. .

4) If 'item' is not found or 'loc' is the starting node of the list then print : " element not found " .

5) If 'prev' is the starting node of the list, then we have to delete the starting node, so call function : 'delete_at_beginning'.

6) Else, search for the previous node of 'prev' and store its location in pointer 'temp'.

7) Assign 'loc' to 'temp->next' and delete node 'prev'.

void sort() :

In this function, selection sort is used. (Logic: First find the smallest node in the list i.e. find the node, which has the smallest 'info' part, and interchange the 'info' part of this node with the first node of the list. After that, find the second smallest 'info' part and interchange it with the 'info' part of second node of the list. And so on.)

5.2   Circular Linked List

A linear linked list in which last node points to the starting node is called Circular Linked List. So last node of a circular linked list does not contain the NULL pointer. Following figure illustrates this type of linked list:

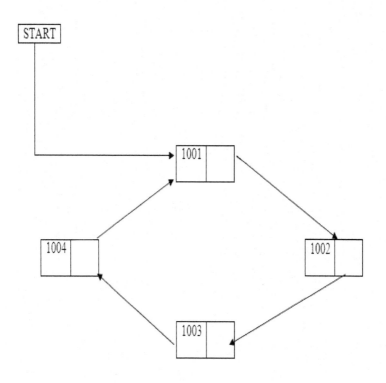

Circular linked list

****

/* *Implementation of Circular Linked List* */

#include<stdio.h>
#include<alloc.h>

```c
typedef struct node_type
{
    int info;
    struct node_type *next;
}node;

node *start=NULL,*end=NULL;

void add_at_beginning();
void add_at_end();
void add_after_element();
void add_before_element();
void traverse_in_order();
void traverse_in_reverse_order(node *);
void delete_at_beginning();
void delete_at_end();
void delete_after_element();
void delete_before_element();
void sort();

void main()
{
        int x;

        while(1)
        {
                printf("\nenter choice\n ");
                printf("1.add at beginning\n ");
                printf("2.add at end\n ");
                printf("3.add after element\n ");
                printf("4.add before element\n ");
                printf("5.traverse in order\n ");
                printf("6.traverse in reverse order\n ");
                printf("7.delete at beginning\n ");
                printf("8.delete at end\n ");
                printf("9.delete after element\n ");
```

176

```c
                printf("10.delete before element\n ");
                printf("11.sort\n ");
                printf("12.exit\n ");
                scanf("%d",&x);

        switch(x)
        {
                case 1: add_at_beginning();      break;
                case 2: add_at_end();            break;
                case 3: add_after_element();     break;
                case 4: add_before_element();    break;
                case 5: traverse_in_order();     break;
                case 6: traverse_in_reverse_order(start); break;
                case 7: delete_at_beginning();   break;
                case 8: delete_at_end();         break;
                case 9: delete_after_element();  break;
                case 10:delete_before_element(); break;
                case 11:sort();                  break;
                case 12:exit();

        }  /*  end switch  */

   }  /*  end while  */

}  /*  end main  */


void add_at_beginning()
{
                node *ptr;
                int item;

                printf("enter item\n");
                scanf("%d",&item);

                ptr=(node *)malloc(sizeof(node));
```

177

```c
        if(ptr==NULL)
        {
                printf("no space\n");
                return;
        }

        (*ptr).info=item;

        if(start==NULL)   /* if list is empty then create
                              starting node   */
        {
                (*ptr).next=ptr;
                   /*  As 'ptr' is the only node of the list as of now,
                       so, 'ptr->next' pointer will point to itself  */
                end=start=ptr;
        }
        else
        {
                (*ptr).next=start;
                     /*  else,  make starting node as second node
                         of the list  */
                start=ptr;   /*  and make this new node as the
                                  starting node   */
                (*end).next=start;   /*  'end->next' will point
                                          to 'start'  */
        }
}  /* end add_at_beginning */

void add_at_end()
{
                node *ptr;
                int item;

                printf("enter item\n");
                scanf("%d",&item);
```

178

```c
        ptr=(node *)malloc(sizeof(node));
        if(ptr==NULL)
        {
            printf("no space\n");
            return;
        }

        (*ptr).info=item;
        if(end==NULL)   /* if list is empty, then create the
                            starting node of the list */
        {
                (*ptr).next=ptr;
                end=start=ptr;
        }
        else
        {
                (*end).next=ptr;
                 end=ptr;
                (*end).next=start;

        }        /* add this new node at the end of the list and make
                    it the last node of the list */

}  /* end add_at_end */

void add_after_element()
{
                node *ptr, *loc;
                int item,item1;

        printf("enter item after which, a node is to be inserted\n");
                scanf("%d",&item1);
```

```c
if(start==NULL)
{
    printf("no element found\n");
    return;
}
loc=start;

while((*loc).info!=item1&&loc!=end)
loc=(*loc).next;
            /* find the location at which 'item1' is found */

if(loc==end && (*loc).info!=item1)
                /* if 'item1' is not found then return the
                    control */
{
    printf("element not found\n") ;
    return;
}

if(loc==end)   /* if element has to be inserted at the end of
                    the list then call 'add_at_end' */
{
    add_at_end() ;
    return;
}

ptr=(node *)malloc(sizeof(node));

if(ptr==NULL)
{
    printf("no space\n");
    return;
}

printf("enter item, which has to be inserted\n");
scanf("%d",&item);
```

```c
        (*ptr).info=item;
        (*ptr).next=(*loc).next;
        (*loc).next=ptr;        /*  insert 'item' after 'loc'  */

}  /* end add_after_element */

void add_before_element()
{
        node *ptr, *prev, *loc;
        int item,item1;

printf("enter item before which, a node is to be inserted\n");
        scanf("%d",&item1);

        if(start==NULL)
        {
                printf("no element found\n");
                return;
        }
        loc=start;

        while((*loc).info!=item1 && loc!=end)
        {
                prev=loc;
                loc=(*loc).next;

        }  /* Search for 'item1'. Store this location in 'loc' pointer and
              store the previous location of 'loc' in 'prev' pointer  */

        if(loc==end && (*loc).info!=item1)
        {
            printf("element not found\n");
            return;
        }  /* if 'item1' is not found then return the control  */

        if(loc==start && (*loc).info==item1)
        {
```

181

```
                add_at_beginning() ;
                        /*    if item has to be inserted at the beginning
                              then call this function */
            return;
    }
    ptr=(node *)malloc(sizeof(node));

    if(ptr==NULL)
    {
            printf("no space\n");
            return;
    }

     printf("enter item, which has to be inserted\n");
     scanf("%d",&item);

    (*ptr).info=item;
    (*ptr).next=(*prev).next;
    (*prev).next=ptr;
                        /*    insert this new node after 'prev' node    */

}  /* end add_before_element */

void traverse_in_order()
{
            node *ptr;

            if(start==NULL)
            {
                printf("list is empty\n");
                return;
            }
             ptr=start;

            do
            {
```

```c
            printf("%d",(*ptr).info);
            ptr=(*ptr).next;

        }while(ptr!=start);
                    /* print all the elements of the list */

}  /* end traverse_in_order */

void traverse_in_reverse_order(node *ptr)
{
        if(start==NULL)
        {
            printf("list is empty\n");
            return;
        }

        if(ptr!=end)
        traverse_in_reverse_order((*ptr).next);
                    /* call this function again and again until we reach
                       at the last node   */
        printf("%d",(*ptr).info);  /* now start printing the 'info'
                                      part of each  node  */
}  /* end traverse_in_reverse_order */

void delete_at_beginning()
{
        node *ptr;

        if(start==NULL)
        {
            printf("element not found\n");
            return;
        }

        if(start==end)
```

183

```c
                    /*  if there is only one element in the list then empty
                        the list  */
        {
                free(start);
                start=end=NULL;
                return;
        }

        ptr=start;
        start=(*start).next;
        (*end).next=start;
        free(ptr);     /*  delete the starting node and make second node of
                           the list as the  starting   node  */

}  /*  end delete_at_beginning  */

void delete_at_end()
{
        node *ptr,*prev;

        if(start==NULL)
        {
                printf("element not found\n");
                return;
        }

        if(start==end)
        {
                free(start);
                start=end=NULL;
                return;                 /*  now list is empty */
        }

        ptr=start;

        while(ptr!=end)
        {
```

```c
                prev=ptr;
                ptr=(*ptr).next;

        }    /* store location of the second last node in 'prev' pointer   */
        (*prev).next=start;
        end=prev;
        free(ptr);        /* make 'prev' as the last node of the list */
}   /* end delete_at_end */

void delete_after_element()
{
        node *ptr, *loc;
        int item;

    printf("enter item after which, a node is to be deleted\n");
        scanf("%d",&item);

        if(start==NULL || start==end)
        {
                printf("element not found\n");
                return;
        }
        loc=start;

        while((*loc).info!=item && loc!=end)
        loc=(*loc).next;

        if(loc==end)
        if((*loc).info!=item)
        {
                printf("element not found\n");
                return;
        }
```

185

```
            else
            {
                delete_at_beginning();
                    /* because it is a circular list and 'item' has been
                          found at the last node, so delete the starting node */
                return;
            }
            ptr=(*loc).next;

            if(ptr==end)
            end=loc;

            (*loc).next=(*ptr).next;
            free(ptr);        /* delete the node, which is at location 'ptr' */
}   /* end delete_after_element */

void delete_before_element()
{
            node *ptr,*ptr1,*prev, *loc;
            int item;

    printf("enter item before which, a node is to be deleted\n");
            scanf("%d",&item);

            if(start==NULL || start==end)
            {
                    printf("element not found\n");
                    return;
            }

            loc=start;
            prev=NULL;

            while((*loc).info!=item&&loc!=end)
            {
                    prev=loc;
```

```c
            loc=(*loc).next;

    }   /* search for 'item' and store its previous location in 'prev'
        pointer   */

    if(loc==start || (loc==end && (*loc).info!=item))
    {
        printf("element not found\n");
        return;
    }

    if(prev==start)
    {
        delete_at_beginning();
        return;
    }

    ptr1=start;

    while(ptr1!=prev)
    {
            ptr=ptr1;
            ptr1=(*ptr1).next;

    }   /* Store the previous location of 'prev' in pointer 'ptr'   */

    (*ptr).next=loc;
    free(prev);          /* delete 'prev' node */

}  /* end delete_before_element */

void sort()
{
        node *ptr, *loc;
        int temp;

        for(ptr=start;ptr!=end;ptr=(*ptr).next)
        for(loc=(*ptr).next;loc!=start;loc=(*loc).next)
```
187

```
        if((*ptr).info>(*loc).info)
        {
                temp=(*loc).info;
                (*loc).info=(*ptr).info;
                (*ptr).info=temp;

        }       /*   Selection Sort has been used here  */

    printf("list has been sorted now\n");

}   /*  end sort  */

/*

After executing:

enter choice
 1.add at beginning
 2.add at end
 3.add after element
 4.add before element
 5.traverse in order
 6.traverse in reverse order
 7.delete at beginning
 8.delete at end
 9.delete after element
 10.delete before element
 11.sort
 12.exit
 1
enter item
 1

enter choice
 1.add at beginning
 2.add at end
 3.add after element
 4.add before element
 5.traverse in order
 6.traverse in reverse order
 7.delete at beginning
 8.delete at end
 9.delete after element
 10.delete before element
```

11.sort
12.exit
2
enter item
2

enter choice
  1.add at beginning
  2.add at end
  3.add after element
  4.add before element
  5.traverse in order
  6.traverse in reverse order
  7.delete at beginning
  8.delete at end
  9.delete after element
  10.delete before element
  11.sort
  12.exit
  3
enter item after which, a node is to be inserted
2
enter item, which has to be inserted
3

enter choice
  1.add at beginning
  2.add at end
  3.add after element
  4.add before element
  5.traverse in order
  6.traverse in reverse order
  7.delete at beginning
  8.delete at end
  9.delete after element
  10.delete before element
  11.sort
  12.exit
  4
enter item before which, a node is to be inserted
1
enter item, which has to be inserted
5

enter choice
  1.add at beginning

189

2.add at end
3.add after element
4.add before element
5.traverse in order
6.traverse in reverse order
7.delete at beginning
8.delete at end
9.delete after element
10.delete before element
11.sort
12.exit
5
5123

enter choice
1.add at beginning
2.add at end
3.add after element
4.add before element
5.traverse in order
6.traverse in reverse order
7.delete at beginning
8.delete at end
9.delete after element
10.delete before element
11.sort
12.exit
6
3215

enter choice
1.add at beginning
2.add at end
3.add after element
4.add before element
5.traverse in order
6.traverse in reverse order
7.delete at beginning
8.delete at end
9.delete after element
10.delete before element
11.sort
12.exit
11
list has been sorted now

190

enter choice
1.add_at_beginning
2.add_at_end
3.add after element
4.add before element
5.traverse in order
6.traverse in reverse order
7.delete at beginning
8.delete at end
9.delete after element
10.delete before element
11.sort
12.exit
5
1235

enter choice
1.add at beginning
2.add at end
3.add after element
4.add before element
5.traverse in order
6.traverse in reverse order
7.delete at beginning
8.delete at end
9.delete after element
10.delete before element
11.sort
12.exit
7

enter choice
1.add at beginning
2.add at end
3.add after element
4.add before element
5.traverse in order
6.traverse in reverse order
7.delete at beginning
8.delete at end
9.delete after element
10.delete before element
11.sort
12.exit
8

enter choice
1.add at beginning
2.add at end
3.add after element
4.add before element
5.traverse in order
6.traverse in reverse order
7.delete at beginning
8.delete at end
9.delete after element
10.delete before element
11.sort
12.exit
9
enter item after which, a node is to be deleted
2

enter choice
1.add at beginning
2.add at end
3.add after element
4.add before element
5.traverse in order
6.traverse in reverse order
7.delete at beginning
8.delete at end
9.delete after element
10.delete before element
11.sort
12.exit
10
enter item before which, a node is to be deleted
2
element not found

enter choice
1.add at beginning
2.add at end
3.add after element
4.add before element
5.traverse in order
6.traverse in reverse order
7.delete at beginning
8.delete at end
9.delete after element

192

10.delete before element
11.sort
12.exit
5
2

enter choice
1.add at beginning
2.add at end
3.add after element
4.add before element
5.traverse in order
6.traverse in reverse order
7.delete at beginning
8.delete at end
9.delete after element
10.delete before element
11.sort
12.exit
12 ....*(terminated)*

*/

****

Steps of the program:

void add_at_beginning() :

1. First we have to allocate the memory to insert a new node. Here 'malloc' is used to allocate the memory and this function returns the base address of allocated memory.

2. Suppose base address of the space allocated in memory is 400. This address will be returned by 'malloc' function to pointer 'ptr'.

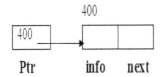

Ptr   info   next

As shown above, pointer 'ptr' will contain the address 400. And at address 400 there is a memory space where an integer 'info' and address of structure 'node_type' can be stored in pointer 'next'.

3. If linked list is empty, then make 'ptr' as the starting node. And because it is a circular list, so assign 'ptr' to 'start->next' i.e. starting node will point to itself.

4. If linked list is not empty, then assign 'start' to 'ptr->next'. And make 'ptr' as the starting node by assigning 'ptr' to 'start'. As it's a circular linked list, so, assign base address of this new starting node to 'end->next'.

void add_at_end() :

1. Use 'malloc' function to allocate the space in the memory. Base address of this memory will be stored in pointer 'ptr'.

2. If list is empty, then make 'ptr' as the starting node and assign 'ptr' to 'start->next'.

3. If list is not empty, then assign 'ptr' to 'end->next' and assign 'ptr' to 'end' i.e. make 'ptr' as the last node of the list. Assign 'start' to 'end->next' as 'ptr' is the last node of the list now, so, 'next' field of 'ptr' should point to the starting node.

194

void add_after_element() :

1. Input the element after which we have to insert a new node. Store this element in variable 'item1'.

2. If list is empty, then print : " no element found ".

3. If list is not empty, then search for 'item1' and store this location in pointer 'loc'.

4. If 'item1' is not found, then print : " no element found ".

5. If 'loc' is the last node of the list, then call function 'add_at_end' i.e. insert the new node at the end of the list.

6. Else, create a new node and store its location in pointer 'ptr'.

7. Store location 'loc->next' in 'ptr->next'. And assign 'ptr' to 'loc->next'. Now 'ptr' is inserted after node 'loc'.

void add_before_element() :

1. Input the element before which we have to insert a new node. Store this element in   variable 'item1'.

2. If list is empty, then print : " no element found ".

3. If list is not empty, then search for 'item1' and store this location in pointer 'loc'. And store the location of previous node of 'loc' in pointer 'prev'.

4. If 'item1' is not found, then print : " no element found ".

5. If 'loc' is the starting node of the list then invoke function 'add_at_beginning' i.e. insert the new node at the beginning of the list.

195

6. Else, create a new node and store its location in pointer 'ptr'.

7. Store location 'prev->next' in 'ptr->next'. And assign 'ptr' to 'prev->next' i.e. insert 'ptr' after node 'prev'.

void traverse_in_order() :

Print information ('info') part of every node, starting from node 'start', by traversing sequentially.

void traverse_in_reverse_order() :

Call function 'traverse_in_reverse_order' again and again till we reach at the end of the list. Each time, when we call this function, a new instance of function 'traverse_in_reverse_order' is created and value in 'ptr', which is the base address of a node of structure 'node_type', is pushed onto a stack. After we reach at the end of the list, each element of the stack is popped out from memory (Last In First Out order). So 'info' part of each node is printed in reverse order.

void delete_at_beginning() :

1. If list is empty, then print : " no element found ".

2. If there is only one element in the list, then make the list empty.

3. Else, assign 'start->next' to 'start', and delete the starting node. Now 'start' pointer will point to the second node of the list. After that, assign 'start' to 'end->next' because starting location of the list has been changed.

void delete_at_end() :

1. If list is empty then print : "no element found".

2. If there is only one element in the list, then empty the list.

3. Else, search for the second last node of the list and store its location in pointer 'prev'.

4. Assign 'start' to 'prev->next' and assign 'prev' to pointer 'end' i.e. make second last element of the list as the last node.

void delete_after_element() :

1. Scan 'item', after which a node has to be deleted.

2. If list is empty, then print : " no element found ".

3. Else, search for the 'item' and store its location in pointer 'loc'.

4. If 'item' is not found, then print : " element not found ".

5. If 'loc' is the last node of the list, then delete the starting node. Because 'end->next' pointer points to the starting node of the list.

6. Else, assign 'loc->next->next' to 'loc->next', and delete the node at position 'loc->next'.

void delete_before_element() :

1. Scan 'item' before which, a node has to be deleted.

2. If list is empty, then print : " no element found ".

3. Else, search for the 'item' and store its location in pointer 'loc'. Store the location of previous node of 'loc' in pointer 'prev'.

4. If 'loc' is the starting node of the list or 'item' is not found, then print : " element not found ".

5. If 'prev' is the starting node, then we have to delete the starting node of the list, so invoke function : 'delete_at_beginning'.

6. Else, search for the previous node of 'prev' and store its location in pointer 'ptr'.

7. Assign 'loc' to 'ptr->next' and delete node 'prev'.

void sort() :

In this function, selection sort is used. So the smallest 'info' part among all the nodes is placed at the first position in the list. Then the second smallest 'info' part is placed at the second position. And so on.

5.3   Doubly Linked List

A Doubly Linked List or Two-Way List is a linear collection of data elements, called nodes, where each node is divided into three parts:

(1) An information field INFO which contains the data of the node.

198

(2) A pointer field NEXT which contains the location of the next node in the list.

(3) A pointer field PREV which contains the location of the preceding node in the list.

This list requires two pointer variables : HEAD, which points to the first node in the
list, and TAIL, which points to the last node in the list. Following figure shows this type
of linked list :

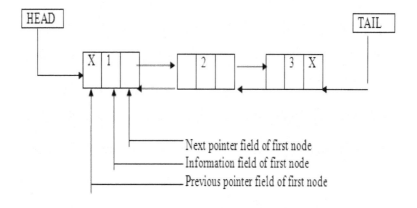

Next pointer field of first node
Information field of first node
Previous pointer field of first node

Doubly linked list

Representation of doubly linked list :

A doubly linked list can be stored in memory with the following declarations :

```c
typedef struct node_type
{
    struct node_type *prev;
    int info;
    struct node_type *next;

}node;
```

Here 'info' represents the information part of the node and pointers 'next' and 'prev' are used to store the locations of next and previous nodes of the list, respectively.

****

/* Implementation of Doubly Linked List */

```c
#include<stdio.h>
#include<alloc.h>

typedef struct node_type
{
    struct node_type *prev;
    int info;
    struct node_type *next;
}node;

node *head=NULL, *tail=NULL;

void add_at_beginning();
void add_at_end();
void add_after_element();
void add_before_element();
void traverse_in_order();
void traverse_in_reverse_order();
void delete_at_beginning();
void delete_at_end();
```

```c
void delete_after_element();
void delete_before_element();
void sort();

void main()
{
        int x;

        while(1)
        {
                printf("\nenter choice\n ");
                printf("1.add at beginning\n ");
                printf("2.add at end\n ");
                printf("3.add after element\n ");
                printf("4.add before element\n ");
                printf("5.traverse in order\n ");
                printf("6.traverse in reverse order\n ");
                printf("7.delete at beginning\n ");
                printf("8.delete at end\n ");
                printf("9.delete after element\n ");
                printf("10.delete before element\n ");
                printf("11.sort\n ");
                printf("12.exit\n ");
                scanf("%d",&x);

                switch(x)
                {
                  case 1:  add_at_beginning();          break;
                  case 2:  add_at_end();                break;
                  case 3:  add_after_element();         break;
                  case 4:  add_before_element();        break;
                  case 5:  traverse_in_order();         break;
                  case 6:  traverse_in_reverse_order(); break;
                  case 7:  delete_at_beginning();       break;
                  case 8:  delete_at_end();             break;
```

```
        case 9:  delete_after_element();  break;
        case 10: delete_before_element();  break;
        case 11: sort();                  break;
        case 12: exit();
```

} */* end switch */

} /* end while */

} /* end main */

```
void add_at_beginning()
{
        node *ptr;
        int item;

        printf("enter item\n");
        scanf("%d",&item);

        ptr=(node *)malloc(sizeof(node));

        if(ptr==NULL)
        {
            printf("no space\n");
            return;
        }

        (*ptr).info=item;

        if(head==NULL)/* if list is empty, then create starting node */
        {
            head=tail=ptr;
            (*ptr).prev=(*ptr).next=NULL;
            return;
        }

        (*ptr).prev=NULL;  /* Else, assign NULL to 'ptr->prev' */
```

202

```c
        (*ptr).next=head;    /* 'ptr->next' will point to 'head' */
        (*head).prev=ptr;    /* assign 'ptr' to 'head->prev' */
        head=ptr;    /* Now 'ptr' will become the starting node of the list */
}    /* end add_at_beginning */
void add_at_end()
{
        node *ptr;
        int item;

        printf("enter item\n");
        scanf("%d",&item);

        ptr=(node *)malloc(sizeof(node));

        if(ptr==NULL)
        {
                printf("no space\n");
                return;
        }

        (*ptr).info=item;

        if(tail==NULL)    /* if list is empty, then create the starting
                                node of the list */
        {
                head=tail=ptr;
                (*ptr).prev=NULL;
                (*ptr).next=NULL;
        }

        else    /* Else, add this new node at the end of the list and
                        make it the last node of the list */
        {
                (*ptr).prev=tail;
                (*ptr).next=NULL;
```

203

```c
            (*tail).next=ptr;
            tail=ptr;
        }

}  /* end add_at_end */

void add_after_element()
{
        node *ptr,*loc;
        int item,item1;

    printf("enter item after which, a node is to be inserted\n");
        scanf("%d",&item1);

        loc=head;

        while(loc!=NULL&&(*loc).info!=item1)
         loc=(*loc).next;          /* search for the location of 'item1' */

         if(loc==NULL)
         {
             printf("element not found\n") ;
             return;
         }

        if(loc==tail)
        {
            add_at_end() ; /* if element has to be inserted at the end of
                               the list, then invoke function 'add_at_end' */
            return;
        }

        ptr=(node *)malloc(sizeof(node));

        if(ptr==NULL)
        {
                printf("no space\n");
                return;
```

```
}
        printf("enter item, which has to be inserted\n");
        scanf("%d",&item);

        (*ptr).info=item;
        (*ptr).prev=loc;
        (*ptr).next=(*loc).next;  /* As we have to insert 'ptr' after
                                      'loc', so, change the 'prev' and 'next'
                                      locations of 'ptr' accordingly */

        (*((*loc).next)).prev=ptr;  /* assign 'ptr' to 'loc->next->prev' */

        (*loc).next=ptr;            /* insert 'ptr' after 'loc'. */

}  /* end add_after_element */

void add_before_element()
{
        node *ptr, *loc;
        int item, item1;

   printf("enter item before which, a node is to be inserted\n");
        scanf("%d",&item1);

        loc=head;

        while(loc!=NULL&&(*loc).info!=item1)
        loc=(*loc).next;        /* search for 'item1' and store this location
                                   in pointer 'loc' */

        if(loc==NULL)
        {
                printf("element not found\n");
                return;
        }

        if(loc==head)
        {
```

205

```c
            add_at_beginning();
                        /*  if item has to be inserted at the beginning,
                            then invoke 'add_at_beginning'  */
        return;
    }

    ptr=(node *)malloc(sizeof(node));

    if(ptr==NULL)
    {
        printf("no space\n");
        return;
    }

    printf("enter item, which has to be inserted\n");
    scanf("%d",&item);

    (*ptr).info=item;
    (*ptr).next=loc;
    (*ptr).prev=(*loc).prev;
                    /*  As 'ptr' has to be inserted before 'loc', so,
                        change the 'prev' and 'next' locations of 'ptr'
                        accordingly   */
    (*((*loc).prev)).next=ptr;  /* assign 'ptr' to 'loc->prev->next' */

    (*loc).prev=ptr;            /* insert 'ptr' before 'loc'. */

}  /* end add_before_element */

void traverse_in_order()
{
    node *ptr;

    if(head==NULL)
    {
        printf("list is empty\n");
        return;
    }
```

```
        for(ptr=head;ptr!=NULL;ptr=(*ptr).next)
        printf("%d",(*ptr).info);  /* print every element of the list */

}  /* end traverse_in_order */

void traverse_in_reverse_order()
{
        node *ptr;

        ptr=tail;

        if(head==NULL)
        {
            printf("list is empty\n");
            return;
        }

        while(ptr!=NULL)
        {
            printf("%d",(*ptr).info);
            ptr=(*ptr).prev;

        }    /* Start traversing from 'tail' pointer in reverse order   */

}  /* end traverse_in_reverse_order */

void delete_at_beginning()
{
        node *ptr;

        ptr=head;

        if(head==NULL)
        {
            printf("list is empty\n");
            return;
        }
```

```
        if(head==tail)
        {
                free(head);
                head=tail=NULL;
                return;
```

} /* if there is only one element in the list, then delete this element
      and make the list empty   */

```
        head=(*head).next;  /* else, make second node of the list as
                                  the starting node */

        (*head).prev=NULL;
        free(ptr);
```

} /* end delete_at_beginning */

```
void delete_at_end()
{
        node *ptr;

        if(head==NULL)
        {
            printf("element not found\n");
            return;
        }

        if(head==tail)
        {
                free(head);
                head=tail=NULL;
                return;
```

} /* if there is only one element in the list, then delete this element */

```
        ptr=tail;
        tail=(*tail).prev;  /* else, make 'tail->prev' as the last node   */
```

208

```
        (*tail).next=NULL;
        free(ptr);

}  /* end delete_at_end */

void delete_after_element()
{
        node *ptr,*loc;
        int item;

    printf("enter item after which, a node is to be deleted\n");
        scanf("%d",&item);

        loc=head;

        while(loc!=NULL && (*loc).info!=item)
        loc=(*loc).next;  /* search for 'item' and store its location in
                                    'loc' */

        if(loc==NULL || loc==tail)
        {
            printf("item not found");
            return;
        }

        if(loc==(*tail).prev)
        {
            delete_at_end();
            return;
        }

        ptr=(*loc).next;
        (*loc).next=(*ptr).next;
        (*((*ptr).next)).prev=loc; /* assign 'loc' to 'ptr->next->prev' */

        free(ptr);          /*  delete node at location 'ptr'  */
}  /* end delete_after_element */
```

```c
void delete_before_element()
{
        node *ptr,*loc;
        int item;

    printf("enter item before which, a node is to be deleted\n");
        scanf("%d",&item);

        loc=head;

        while(loc!=NULL&&(*loc).info!=item)
        loc=(*loc).next;                    /*  search for 'item'    */

        if(loc==NULL || loc==head)
        {
            printf("node not found");
            return;
        }

        if(loc==(*head).next)
        {
            delete_at_beginning();
            return;
        }

         ptr=(*loc).prev;
        (*(*ptr).prev).next=loc;  /* assign 'loc' to 'ptr->prev->next' */

        (*loc).prev=(*ptr).prev; /* assign 'ptr->prev' to 'loc->prev'  */

        free(ptr);                         /*  delete node at location 'ptr'   */

}   /* end delete_before_element  */

void sort()
{
        node *ptr,*loc;
        int temp;
```

```
for(ptr=head;ptr!=tail;ptr=(*ptr).next)
for(loc=(*ptr).next;loc!=NULL;loc=(*loc).next)
if((*ptr).info>(*loc).info)
{
        temp=(*loc).info;
        (*loc).info=(*ptr).info;
        (*ptr).info=temp;

}  /* Selection Sort has been used here   */

printf("list is sorted now\n");

}  /* end sort */
/*
```

After executing :

enter choice
1.add at beginning
2.add at end
3.add after element
4.add before element
5.traverse in order
6.traverse in reverse order
7.delete at beginning
8.delete at end
9.delete after element
10.delete before element
11.sort
12.exit
1
enter item
1
enter choice
1.add at beginning
2.add at end
3.add after element
4.add before element
5.traverse in order
6.traverse in reverse order
7.delete at beginning
8.delete at end
9.delete after element

10.delete before element
11.sort
12.exit
2
enter item
2

enter choice
1.add at beginning
2.add at end
3.add after element
4.add before element
5.traverse in order
6.traverse in reverse order
7.delete at beginning
8.delete at end
9.delete after element
10.delete before element
11.sort
12.exit
3
enter item after which, a node is to be inserted
2
enter item, which has to be inserted
3

enter choice
1.add at beginning
2.add at end
3.add after element
4.add before element
5.traverse in order
6.traverse in reverse order
7.delete at beginning
8.delete at end
9.delete after element
10.delete before element
11.sort
12.exit
4
enter item before which, a node is to be inserted
1
enter item, which has to be inserted
0

enter choice

1.add at beginning
2.add at end
3.add after element
4.add before element
5.traverse in order
6.traverse in reverse order
7.delete at beginning
8.delete at end
9.delete after element
10.delete before element
11.sort
12.exit
5
0123
enter choice
1.add at beginning
2.add at end
3.add after element
4.add before element
5.traverse in order
6.traverse in reverse order
7.delete at beginning
8.delete at end
9.delete after element
10.delete before element
11.sort
12.exit
6
3210
enter choice
1.add at beginning
2.add at end
3.add after element
4.add before element
5.traverse in order
6.traverse in reverse order
7.delete at beginning
8.delete at end
9.delete after element
10.delete before element
11.sort
12.exit
7

enter choice
1.add at beginning

213

2.add at end
3.add after element
4.add before element
5.traverse in order
6.traverse in reverse order
7.delete at beginning
8.delete at end
9.delete after element
10.delete before element
11.sort
12.exit
8

enter choice
1.add at beginning
2.add at end
3.add after element
4.add before element
5.traverse in order
6.traverse in reverse order
7.delete at beginning
8.delete at end
9.delete after element
10.delete before element
11.sort
12.exit
5
12
enter choice
1.add at beginning
2.add at end
3.add after element
4.add before element
5.traverse in order
6.traverse in reverse order
7.delete at beginning
8.delete at end
9.delete after element
10.delete before element
11.sort
12.exit
12   ....(terminated)

*/

****

Steps of the program:

void add_at_beginning() :

1. First we have to allocate the memory to insert a new node. Here 'malloc' is used to allocate the memory and this function returns the base address of allocated memory.

2. Suppose base address of the space allocated in memory is 400. This address will be returned by 'malloc' function to pointer 'ptr'.

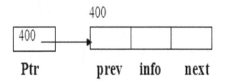

Ptr   **prev**   **info**   **next**

As shown above, pointer 'ptr' will contain the address 400. And at address 400 there is a memory space where an integer 'info' and address of structure 'node_type' can be stored in pointers 'prev' and 'next'.

3. If linked list is empty, then make 'ptr', the starting, as well as the last node of the list. And assign NULL to 'head->next' and 'head-prev'.

4. If list is not empty, then assign 'head' to 'ptr->next' and NULL to 'ptr->prev'. And make 'ptr' as the starting node i.e. assign 'ptr' to 'head'.

void add_at_end() :

1. Use 'malloc' function to allocate the space in the memory. Base address of this memory will be stored in pointer 'ptr'.

2. If list is empty, then make 'ptr' as the starting node and assign NULL to 'prev' and 'next' pointers of this node.

3. If list is not empty, then 'ptr' is to be inserted at the end of the list, so, change the 'prev' and 'next' locations of 'ptr' accordingly i.e. assign 'ptr' to 'tail->next', 'tail' to 'ptr->prev' and NULL to 'ptr->next'. Now, make 'ptr' as the last node of the list by assigning 'ptr' to 'tail'.

void add_after_element() :

1. Input the element after which we have to insert a new node. Store this element in variable 'item1'.

2. If list is not empty, then search for 'item1' and store this location in pointer 'loc'.

3. If list is empty, or 'item1' is not found then print " no element found ".

4. If 'loc' is the last node of the list, then call function 'add_at_end' i.e. insert the new node at the end of the list.

5. Else, create a new node and store its location in pointer 'ptr'.

6. Store location 'loc->next' in 'ptr->next' and 'loc' in 'ptr->prev'. And assign 'loc->next->prev' to 'ptr'.

After that assign 'ptr' to 'loc->next'. Now 'ptr' is inserted after node 'loc'.

void add_before_element() :

1. Input the element before which, we have to insert a new node. Store this element in variable 'item1'.

2. If list is not empty, then search for 'item1' and store this location in pointer 'loc'.

3. If list is empty, or 'item1' is not found then print : " no element found ".

4. If 'loc' is the starting node of the list, then call function 'add_at_beginning' i.e. insert the new node at the beginning of the list.

5. Else create a new node and store its location in pointer 'ptr'.

6. Store location 'loc' in 'ptr->next', and store 'loc->prev' in 'ptr->prev' and change'loc->prev->next' to 'ptr'. And assign 'ptr' to 'loc->prev' i.e. insert 'ptr' after node 'loc->prev'.

void traverse_in_order() :

Print information ('info') part of every node, starting from node 'head', by traversing sequentially.

void traverse_in_reverse_order() :

In this type of list, we don't have any need to use recursion, if we desire to traverse the list in reverse order. Starting from pointer 'tail' we can traverse the whole list, using 'prev' pointer, which is pointing to the previous node in the list. So print every element of the list starting from node 'tail', by traversing the list sequentially in reverse order.

void delete_at_beginning() :

1. If list is empty, then print : " no element found ".

2. If there is only one element in the list, then make the list empty.

3. Else, assign 'head->next' to 'head' and delete the starting node. Now, second node of the list becomes the starting node. Assign NULL to 'head->prev' as 'prev' pointer of this new starting node should contain NULL.

void delete_at_end() :

1. If list is empty then print : "no element found".

2. If there is only one element in the list, then empty the list.

3. Else, make 'tail->prev' as the last node of the list i.e. second last node will become the last node of the list now.

void delete_after_element() :

1. Scan 'item' after which, a node has to be deleted.

2. Search for 'item' and store its location in pointer 'loc'.

3. If 'item' is not found, or list is empty, or there is only one element in the list, or 'loc' is   the last node of the list, then print : " no element found ".

4. If 'loc' is the second last node of the list, then we have to delete the last node, so call function 'delete_at_end'.

5. Else, assign 'loc->next->next' to 'loc->next', and 'loc' to 'loc->next->next->prev'. After that delete node at position 'loc->next'.

void delete_before_element() :

1. Scan 'item' before which, a node has to be deleted.

2. Search for 'item' and store its location in pointer 'loc'.

3. If 'item' is not found, or list is empty, or there is only one element in the list, or 'loc' is the starting node of the list then print : " no element found ".

4. If 'loc' is the second node of the list, then we have to delete the first node, so call function 'delete_at_beginning'.

5. Else, assign 'loc' to 'loc->prev->prev->next' and 'loc->prev->prev' to 'loc->prev'. Then delete node at location 'loc->prev'.

void sort() :

Same sorting technique (Selection Sort) has been used here, as it was done in case of linear linked lists and circular linked lists.

Stacks and Queues Using Linked Lists

6.1   Stacks Using Linked-List

In a linear linked-list, consider that the last node of the list is the top of the stack. And an empty stack can be represented by a NULL list. The following figure illustrates a linked-list, in which 'info' parts of the nodes represent elements of the stack.

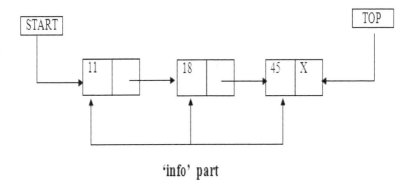

'info' part

In above figure, 11, 18 and 45 are elements of the stack. The following program implements 'push' and 'pop' operations of the stack using linked-list. Here, 'push' operation inserts a node in the linked-list at the end of the list, and 'pop' operation pops the last node of the list.

```
************************************************

/* Implementation of stack using linked-list */

#include<stdio.h>
#include<alloc.h>

void push(), pop();

typedef struct stack
{
    int info;
    struct stack *next;
}stack;

stack *start=NULL, *end=NULL;

void main()
{
            int x;

            while(1)
            {
                    printf("enter choice\n");
                    printf("1.push\n");
                    printf("2.pop\n");
                    printf("3.exit\n");
                    scanf("%d",&x);
                    switch(x)
                    {
                            case 1: push();        break;
                            case 2: pop();         break;
                            case 3:exit();

                    }  /* end switch */

            }  /* end while */

}  /* end main */
```

```c
void push()
{
                int item;
                stack *ptr;

                ptr=(stack *)malloc(sizeof(stack));
                                        /* create a new node */

                if(ptr==NULL)
                {
                    printf("overflow\n");
                    return;
                }

                printf("enter element\n");
                scanf("%d",&item);

            (*ptr).info=item; /* assign 'item' to 'info' part of new node */
            (*ptr).next=NULL;  /* assign NULL to 'next' part of new
                                    node */

                if(start==NULL)
                {
                    start=end=ptr;    /* make this new node as the first
                                        node of the stack   */
                        return;
                }

                (*end).next=ptr;    /* if 'start!=NULL' then make a link
                                        between the last node of the stack
                                        and the new node that has just been
                                        created */

                end=ptr;    /* assign 'ptr' to 'end' i.e make it the last node */

}   /* end push */

void pop()
{
```

```
    stack *ptr,*prev;

    if(start==NULL)              /* no element in stack */
    {
        printf("\nunderflow\n");
        return;

    }  /* end if */

    ptr=start;

    while(ptr!=end)
    {
        prev=ptr;
        ptr=(*ptr).next;

    }  /* search for the second last node and assign the base address
          of this node to pointer 'prev' */

    printf("%d\n",(*end).info);   /* print 'info' part of the
                                     last node */

    if(start==end)
    {
        free(start);
        end=start=NULL;   /* now there is no element in the
                             stack */
    }
    else
    {
        free(end);
        (*prev).next=NULL;
        end=prev;

    }  /* move one position down in the stack and assign base address
          of the second last node to pointer 'end' */

    printf("item deleted\n");

}  /* end pop */
```

/*

After executing:

enter choice
1.push
2.pop
3.exit
1
enter element
1

enter choice
1.push
2.pop
3.exit
1
enter element
2

enter choice
1.push
2.pop
3.exit
1
enter element
3

enter choice
1.push
2.pop
3.exit
2
3
item deleted

enter choice
1.push
2.pop
3.exit
2
2
item deleted

enter choice
1.push

```
2.pop
3.exit
2
1
item deleted

enter choice
1.push
2.pop
3.exit
2
underflow

enter choice
1.push
2.pop
3.exit
3........................(terminated)

*/
```

****

Steps of the program:

void push():

1) Use 'malloc' function to create a new node.

2) If stack is empty, then make this new node as the first node of the stack.

3) Else, add this new node at the top of the stack and make it the last node.

void pop():

1) If stack is not empty, then search for the second last node of the stack. And store the location of this node in pointer 'prev'.

2) If there is only one element in the stack, then empty the stack.

3) Else, delete the last node, and make second last node 'prev' as the last node of the stack.

6.2   Queue Using Linked-List

In a linear linked-list, consider that first node of the list is the front end of the queue and last node of the list is rear end of the queue. And, an empty queue can be represented by a NULL list. The following figure illustrates a linked-list, in which 'info' parts of the nodes represent elements of the queue.

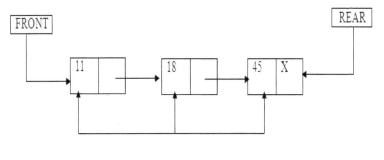

'info' part

I
n above figure, 11, 18 and 45 are elements of the queue. The program mentioned below will implement 'add' and 'del' operations on the queue using linear linked-list. Here, 'add' operation inserts a node in a linked-list at the end of the list and 'del' operation deletes the starting node of the list.

226

```
**************************************************

/* Implementation of queue using linked-list */

#include<stdio.h>
#include<alloc.h>

void add(), del(), disp();

typedef struct queue_type
{
    int info;
    struct queue_type *next;
}queue;

queue *start=NULL,*end=NULL;

void main()
{
            int x;

            while(1)
            {
                        printf("enter choice\n");
                        printf("1.add\n");
                        printf("2.delete\n");
                        printf("3.display\n");
                        printf("4.exit\n");
                        scanf("%d",&x);

                        switch(x)
                        {
                                case 1: add();        break;
                                case 2: del();        break;
                                case 3:disp();        break;
                                case 4:exit();
```

```c
                                   }  /* end switch */
                         }  /* end while */
}  /* end main */
void add()
{
            int item;
            queue *ptr;

            ptr=(queue *)malloc(sizeof(queue));

            if(ptr==NULL)
            {
                        printf("overflow\n");
                        return;
            }

            printf("enter element\n");
            scanf("%d",&item);

            (*ptr).info=item;   /* assign 'item' to 'info' field of the new
                                    node */

            (*ptr).next=NULL;    /* assign NULL to 'next' field of the
                                    new node */

            if(start==NULL)       /* queue is empty */
            {
                        start=end=ptr;  /* create starting node of the queue */
                        return;

            }    /* else insert this new node at the end of queue as shown
                    below */

            (*end).next=ptr;     /* assign 'ptr' to 'end->next' */

            end=ptr;     /* and assign 'ptr' to 'end' i.e. make it(new node)
                             the last node */
}  /* end add */
```

```c
void del()
{
        queue *ptr;

        if(start==NULL)
        {
                printf("\nunderflow\n");    /* no element in queue */
                return;
        }

        if(start==end)    /* if there is only one element in queue,
                             empty the queue */
        {
                free(start);
                start=end=NULL;    /* now queue is empty */
                return;
        }
        /* else do the following: */

        ptr=start;
        start=(*start).next;    /* now 'start' will point to the
                                   second node of queue */
        free(ptr);              /* delete the starting node of the queue */
        printf("item deleted\n");

}  /* end del */

void disp()
{
   queue *ptr;

   for(ptr=start; ptr!=NULL; ptr=(*ptr).next)
   printf("%d ",(*ptr).info);    /* print all the elements of queue */

}  /* end disp */
/*
```

After executing:

229

enter choice
1.add
2.delete
3.display
4.exit
1
enter element
1

enter choice
1.add
2.delete
3.display
4.exit
1
enter element
2

enter choice
1.add
2.delete
3.display
4.exit
1
enter element
3

enter choice
1.add
2.delete
3.display
4.exit
3
1 2 3 enter choice
1.add
2.delete
3.display
4.exit
2
item deleted

enter choice
1.add
2.delete
3.display

230

```
4.exit
3
2 3 enter choice
1.add
2.delete
3.display
4.exit
4            ...........(terminated)

*/
```

****

Steps of the program:

void add():

1) Create a new node 'ptr'.

2) If queue is empty, then make it the starting node.

3) Else, insert this node at the end of the queue and make it the last node of the queue.

void del():

5) If there is only one element in the queue, then empty the queue by assigning NULL to 'start' & 'end'.

6) Else, delete the starting node and make second node of the queue as the starting node.

6.3   Priority Queue Using Linked-List

We have implemented the linear queue using linked-list. Now, if we divide each node of the queue in three parts, where

- First part contains the information part
- Second part contains the priority of the element of the queue and
- Third part contains the location of the next node in the queue

then we can maintain a queue in memory, so that each node is placed in the queue at its proper position according to its priority part. In such a way, we can implement Priority Queue using linear linked list.

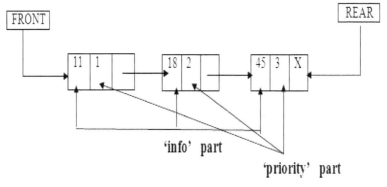

'info' part

'priority' part

In above figure, 11, 18 and 45 are elements of the queue with priorities 1, 2 and 3. The program mentioned below will implement 'add' and 'del' operations on the priority-queue using linear linked-list. Here, 'add' operation inserts a node in the linked-list at its proper position in the list depending upon the priority of the element and 'del' operation deletes the first node of the list.

****

/* Implementation of priority queue using linked-list */

```c
#include<stdio.h>
#include<alloc.h>

void add(), del(), disp();

typedef struct queue_type
{
    int info;
    int priority;
    struct queue_type *next;
}queue;

queue *start=NULL,*end=NULL;

void main()
{
        int x;
        while(1)
        {
                printf("enter choice\n");
                printf("1.add\n");
                printf("2.delete\n");
                printf("3.display\n");
                printf("4.exit\n");
                scanf("%d",&x);

                switch(x)
                {
                        case 1: add();      break;
                        case 2: del();      break;
                        case 3:disp();      break;
                        case 4:exit();
                } /* end switch */
        } /* end while */
} /* end main */
```

233

```
void add()
{
        int item, prn;
        queue *ptr, *temp, *prev;

        ptr=(queue *)malloc(sizeof(queue));

        if(ptr==NULL)
        {
                printf("overflow\n");
                return;
        }
        printf("enter element\n");
        scanf("%d",&item);

        printf("enter priority of the element\n");
        scanf("%d",&prn);

        (*ptr).info=item;       /* assign 'item' to 'info' field of the new
                                   node */

        (*ptr).priority=prn;    /* assign 'prn' to 'priority' part of the
                                   new node */

        (*ptr).next=NULL;       /* assign NULL to 'next' field of the
                                   new node */

        if(start==NULL)         /* If queue is empty, then create
                                   starting node of the queue */
        {
                start=end=ptr;
                return;
        }
        for(temp=start; temp!=NULL &&
                (*temp).priority<prn; temp=(*temp).next)
        prev=temp;      /* Search for node 'prev', after which 'ptr' is to
                           be inserted */
```

234

```c
            if(temp==start)
            {
                        (*ptr).next=start;
                        start=ptr;
                        return;

            } /* If 'ptr' is to be inserted in the beginning, then make it the
                 starting node of the list   */

            (*ptr).next=(*prev).next;
            (*prev).next=ptr;   /* Else, insert node 'ptr' after 'prev' */

            if(prev==end)
            end=(*end).next;

}  /* end add */

void del()
{
            queue *ptr;
            if(start==NULL)
            {
                printf("\nunderflow\n");  /* no element in queue */
                return;
            }

            if(start==end)   /* It means that there is only one element in
                                the queue, empty the queue */
            {
                free(start);
                start=end=NULL;   /* now queue is empty */
                return;
            }
            /* else do the following:  */

            ptr=start;
            start=(*start).next;  /* now 'start' will point to the second
                                     node */
```
235

```
            free(ptr);
            printf("item deleted\n");
}   /* end del */

void disp()
{
    queue *ptr;

    for(ptr=start; ptr!=NULL; ptr=(*ptr).next)
    printf("%d ",(*ptr).info);   /* print all the elements of queue */

}   /* end disp */
/*

After executing:

enter choice
1.add
2.delete
3.display
4.exit
1
enter element
45
enter priority of the element
3
enter choice
1.add
2.delete
3.display
4.exit
1
enter element
18
enter priority of the element
2
enter choice
1.add
2.delete
3.display
4.exit
1
```

```
enter element
11
enter priority of the element
1
enter choice
1.add
2.delete
3.display
4.exit
3
11 18 45 enter choice
1.add
2.delete
3.display
4.exit
4............................................(terminated)

*/
```

****

Steps of the program:

void add():

1) Create a new node 'ptr'.

2) If queue is empty, then make it the starting node and return the control to the previous function (calling function).

3) Traverse the list until we get a node 'temp', 'priority' part of which is greater than 'priority' of 'ptr'. Store the location of previous node of 'temp' in pointer 'prev'.

4) Insert 'ptr' after 'prev'. And if 'prev' is the last node of the list, then change the location of the last node in 'end' pointer accordingly.

void del():

1) If there is only one element in the queue, then make the queue empty and assign NULL to 'start'.

2) Else, delete the starting node and make second node of the queue as the starting node.

TREES

A tree may be defined as a set of certain elements called as nodes. One of the node is named as the root node, while the remaining nodes may be grouped into sub-sets, each of which is a tree in itself. This hierarchical relationship of the various nodes may be described by referring to each such subtree as a **child** of the root, while the root is referred to as the **parent** of each subtree. If a tree consists of a single node, then that node is called a **leaf** node.

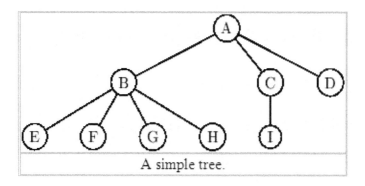

A simple tree.

The above figure represents a simple tree. In this figure, the root node is *A*, and there are three subtrees rooted at *B*, *C* and *D*. Subtree *D* is a leaf node, as are the remaining nodes, *E*, *F*, *G*, *H* and *I*. The node *C* has a single child *I*, where as B has four children E, F, G and H.

7.1   BINARY TREES

A **Binary Tree** is a tree, which is either empty, or the one in which every node:

- has no children; or

- has just a left child; or

- has just a right child; or

- has both a left and a right child.

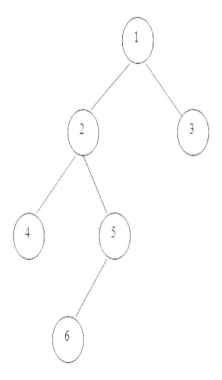

Binary Tree T

Level of a Node: The level of a node refers to its distance from the root node. If we assign level number 0 to the root node, then in above tree T, the nodes 2 and 3 are level 1 nodes, the nodes 4 and 5 are level 2 nodes. And node 6 is a level 3 node.

7.2 Complete Binary Trees

Consider a binary tree T, in which, root of the tree is assigned the level 0 and every other node in the tree is assigned a level number, which is 1 more than the level number of its parent. Then it can be verified that level x of T can have at most 2^x nodes. The tree T is said to be complete if all its levels, except, possibly the last, have the maximum number of possible nodes. In other words, a complete binary tree may be defined as a tree in which, except the last level, at each level x, there should be 2^x nodes. For example, following binary tree is a complete binary tree with 32 nodes.

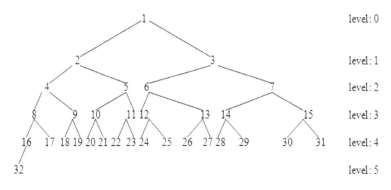

Complete Binary Tree

241

7.3   Depth (or Height) of a tree

If every branch(edge) of a tree is assigned a weight 1(or length 1), then length of the path from a node x to node y can be defined as the sum of the weights of branches(edges) along that path or we can say that length of path from x to y is the total number of branches(edges) lying along that path. The depth of a tree may be defined as the length of the longest path from the root to any leaf. In short, we can say that the maximum level number of a binary tree is known as its height (or depth). Consider the following tree:

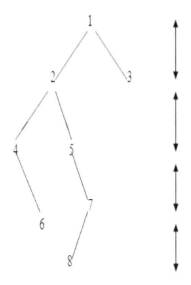

Binary Tree

Depth of above tree is 4. Depth of a complete binary tree with n nodes is given by:

$D_n = \log_2 n$ (Only integer part)

Consider the following complete binary tree:

242

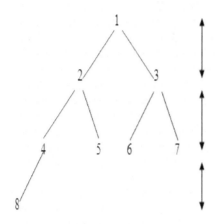

Complete Binary Tree

Depth of above tree is: $\log_2 8 = \log_2 2^3 = 3$.

7.4 Binary Search Trees

Suppose T is a binary tree. Then T will be called a Binary Search Tree, if value at each node N of T is greater than every value in left subtree of N and is less than every value in the right subtree of N.

Inserting into a binary search tree:

Suppose we have to insert a node Y in tree T, then:

1) Compare Y with root node N of the tree. If Y<N, then proceed to left child of N. Else, proceed to the right child of N.

2) Repeat above step until we meet an empty subtree. Insert node Y in place of empty subtree.

Example:

Suppose binary search tree T in memory is:

Below mentioned figures represent the tree T in memory, after inserting elements 8, 11 and 25 respectively:

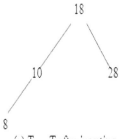

(a) Tree T after inserting 8

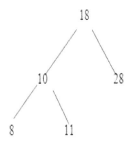

(b) Tree T after inserting 11

244

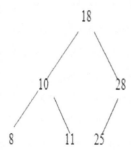

(c) Tree T after inserting 25

Traversing in a Binary Search Tree:

Let R be the root of a binary search tree. Then the three traversal techniques are as under:

Inorder traversing:

   (1) Traverse the left subtree of root R in inorder.

   (2) Visit the root R.

   (3) Traverse the right subtree of R in inorder.

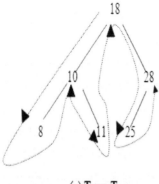

(a) Tree T

inorder traversal of tree T:

8   10   11   18   25   28

Note that the inorder traversal of a binary search tree yields a sorted listing of the elements of T.

Preorder traversing:

(1) Visit the root R.

(2) Traverse the left subtree of root R in preorder.

(3) Traverse the right subtree of root R in preorder.

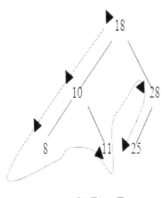

(b) Tree T

preorder traversal of tree T:

18   10   8   11   28   25

Postorder traversing:

(1) Traverse the left subtree of root R in postorder.

246

(2) Traverse the right subtree of root R in postorder.

(3) Visit the root R.

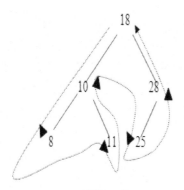

(c) Tree T

postorder traversal of tree T:

8 11 10 25 28 18

Deletion in a binary search tree:

Suppose we want to delete node N of the tree, which contains information ITEM. Then find the location of N and, also, the location of the parent node P(N). The procedure of deletion of node N depends on the number of children of node N. There may be three situations :

Situation 1: If N has no children, then N will be deleted from the tree T by simply replacing the location of N in the parent node P(N) by the NULL pointer.

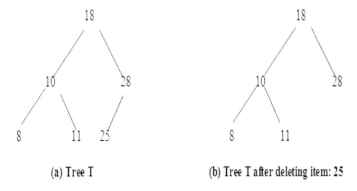

(a) Tree T   (b) Tree T after deleting item: 25

Situation 2: If N has exactly one child, then N will be deleted from the tree T by simply replacing the location of N in P(N) by the location of the only child of N.

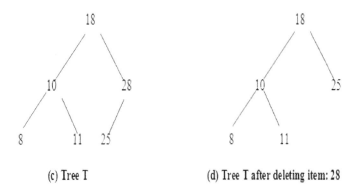

(c) Tree T   (d) Tree T after deleting item: 28

Situation 3: If N has two children, then N will be deleted from the tree T by first deleting S(N) from tree T (by using situation 1 or situation 2), where S(N) is the inorder successor of N and then replacing value in node N by the value of node S(N).

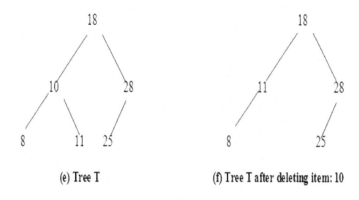

(e) Tree T   (f) Tree T after deleting item: 10

Note that S(N) can not have a left child. In above figure (e), inorder successor S(N) of 10 is 11.

Leaf Nodes: The nodes which don't have any child are called leaf nodes or terminal nodes.

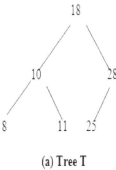

(a) Tree T

Leaf nodes in tree T are: 8,   11,   25.

Non Leaf Nodes: The nodes which are not leaf nodes are called non leaf nodes.

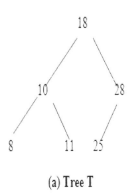

(a) Tree T

Non leaf nodes in above tree T are: 18,   10,   28.

Searching in a Binary Search Tree:

First, we compare the element to be searched with the root node. If it matches with the root node, then the search terminates here; otherwise search is continued in the left subtree of the node if the element is less than the root node or in the right subtree if the element is greater than the root node.

****

/* Implementation of binary search tree */

```
#include<stdio.h>
#include<alloc.h>

typedef struct tree_type
{
    struct tree_type *left;
    int info;
    struct tree_type *right;
}tree;

tree *root=NULL;
void insert();
void del();
void delete_with_no_child(tree*, tree*);
void delete_with_left_child(tree*, tree*);
void delete_with_right_child(tree*, tree*);
void delete_with_two_children(tree*);
void in_ord(tree*);
void pre_ord(tree*);
void post_ord(tree*);
int count_nodes(tree*);
int count_leaf_nodes(tree*);
int count_non_leaf_nodes();
```

251

```c
int count_height(tree*);
int max(int, int);
int smallest_node(tree*);
int largest_node(tree*);

void main()
{
            int x;

            while(1)
            {
                    printf("\nenter choice\n ");
                    printf("1.add an element\n ");
                    printf("2.delete an element\n ");
                    printf("3.traverse in order\n ");
                    printf("4.traverse in pre order\n ");
                    printf("5.traverse in post order\n ");
                    printf("6.count nodes\n ");
                    printf("7.count leaf nodes\n ");
                    printf("8.count non leaf nodes\n ");
                    printf("9.count height\n ");
                    printf("10.smallest node\n ");
                    printf("11.largest node\n ");
                    printf("12.exit\n ");
                    scanf("%d",&x);

                    switch(x)
                    {
                            case 1:  insert();                                          break;
                            case 2:  del();                                             break;
                            case 3:  in_ord(root);                                      break;
                            case 4:  pre_ord(root);                                     break;
                            case 5:  post_ord(root);                                    break;
case 6:  printf("total nodes are %d",count_nodes(root));                              break;
case 7:  printf("total leaf nodes are %d",count_leaf_nodes(root));   break;
```

```
case 8:  printf("non leaf nodes:%d ",count_non_leaf_nodes()); break;
case 9:  printf("height of tree is %d",count_height(root));        break;
case 10: printf("smallest node:%d ",smallest_node(root));          break;
case 11: printf("largest node:%d ",largest_node(root));            break;
                      case 12:  exit();

                   }  /* end switch */

              }  /* end while */

}  /* end main */

void insert()
{
        tree *ptr, *loc, *daddy;
        int item;

        printf("enter item\n");
        scanf("%d",&item);

        ptr=(tree *)malloc(sizeof(tree));

        if(ptr==NULL)
        {
                printf("no space\n");
                return;
        }

        (*ptr).info=item;
        (*ptr).left=(*ptr).right=NULL;
        if(root==NULL)    /* if tree is empty, then create 'root' of the
                                tree */
        {
                root=ptr;
                return;
        }

        loc=root;
```

```c
    while(loc!=NULL)        /* search for the empty subtree where
                               'item' can be inserted */
    {
            daddy=loc;

            if(item<(*loc).info)
            loc=(*loc).left;
            else
            loc=(*loc).right;

    }        /* store the location of parent node of empty subtree in
               pointer 'daddy' */

    if(item<(*daddy).info)
    (*daddy).left=ptr;      /* if 'item' is less than 'info' part of parent
                               node, then insert 'ptr' at 'daddy->left' */
    else
    (*daddy).right=ptr;      /*  else insert it at 'daddy->right'  */

}    /*  end insert  */

void del()
{
        tree *loc, *daddy;
        int item;

        if(root==NULL)
        {
            printf("tree is empty\n");
            return;
        }

        printf("enter item which is to be deleted\n");
        scanf("%d",&item);

        loc=root;

        daddy=NULL;
```

```
while((*loc).info!=item&&loc!=NULL)
        /* search for the node, which contains 'item' and store
           the base address of this node in pointer 'loc' */
{
    daddy=loc;

    if(item<(*loc).info)
    loc=(*loc).left;
    else
    loc=(*loc).right;

}   /* store the location of parent node of 'loc' in pointer 'daddy' */

if(loc==NULL)
{
        printf("element not found\n");
        return;
}

if((*loc).left==(*loc).right&&(*loc).right==NULL)
delete_with_no_child(loc,daddy);
        /* if 'loc' has no child, then call function 'delete_with_no_child'
           with parameters 'loc' and its parent node 'daddy' */
else
if((*loc).left==NULL&&(*loc).right!=NULL)
delete_with_right_child(loc,daddy);
        /* if 'loc' has only right child, then call this function */
else
if((*loc).left!=NULL&&(*loc).right==NULL)
delete_with_left_child(loc,daddy);
        /* if 'loc' has only left child, then call 'delete_with_left_child' */
else
delete_with_two_children(loc);
        /* if 'loc' has two children, then call 'delete_with_two_children' */
}   /* end del */
```

```c
void delete_with_no_child(tree *loc, tree *daddy)
{
        if(loc==root)
        {
                free(root);
                root=NULL;
                return;
        }        /* if there is only one node in the tree, then delete this node and
                    assign NULL to 'root' */

        if((*loc).info<(*daddy).info)
        (*daddy).left=NULL;        /* if 'loc' is left child of 'daddy', then
                                      assign NULL to 'daddy->left' */
        else
        (*daddy).right=NULL; /* else assign NULL to 'daddy->right' */

        free(loc);        /* free the memory space that was allocated to
                             node 'loc'*
/
}  /* end delete_with_no_child  */

void delete_with_right_child(tree *loc, tree *daddy)
{
                if(loc==root)
                {
                    root=(*root).right;
                    free(loc);
                    return;
                }        /* make right child of 'root' as new 'root' of the tree   */

                if((*loc).info<(*daddy).info)
                {
                    (*daddy).left=(*loc).right;
                    free(loc);
                }        /* if 'loc' is left child of 'daddy', then make right child of 'loc'
                            as left child of 'daddy' and delete 'loc' */
```

```c
        else
        {
                (*daddy).right=(*loc).right;
                free(loc);
        }        /* else if 'loc' is right child of 'daddy', then make right child
                    of 'loc' as right child of 'daddy' */

}  /* end delete_with_right_child */

void delete_with_left_child(tree *loc, tree *daddy)
{
        if(loc==root)
        {
                root=(*root).left;
                free(loc);
                return;
        }

        if((*loc).info<(*daddy).info)
        {
                (*daddy).left=(*loc).left;
                free(loc);

        }        /* if 'loc' is left child of 'daddy', then make left child of 'loc'
                    as left child of 'daddy' */
        else
        {
                (*daddy).right=(*loc).left;
                free(loc);

        }        /* else assign 'loc->left' to 'daddy->right' */

}  /* end delete_with_left_child */

/* In the following function, we will replace the 'info' part of 'loc' with inorder
   successor of 'loc' and thereafter we will delete the inorder successor of 'loc' */
```

```
void delete_with_two_children(tree *loc)
{
        tree *ptr, *dadu, *inord_daddy;

        ptr=(*loc).right;

        while(ptr!=NULL)
        {
            inord_daddy=ptr;
            ptr=(*ptr).left;

        }    /* store location of inorder successor of 'loc' in pointer
                 'inord_daddy' */

        (*loc).info=(*inord_daddy).info; /* change 'loc->info' with
                                              'inord_daddy->info' */
        dadu=loc;              /* initialize 'dadu' */

        ptr=(*loc).right;

        while(ptr!=inord_daddy)
        {
           dadu=ptr;
           ptr=(*ptr).left;

        }   /* now store parent node of 'inord_daddy' in 'dadu'  */

        if(dadu==loc)
        (*loc).right=(*inord_daddy).right;
                        /* if 'loc->right' has no left child then assign
                           'loc->right->right' to 'loc->right' */
        else
        (*dadu).left=(*inord_daddy).right;
                        /* beacause 'inord_daddy' has no left child, so
                           delete 'inord_daddy' and assign its  right node to
                           'dadu->left' as it was  in case  of
                           'delete_with_right_child' */

        free(inord_daddy);    /* free the memory that was allocated to
                                  'inord_daddy'  */
}  /* end delete_with_two_children */
```

```
void in_ord(tree *ptr)
{
        if(ptr!=NULL)
        {
            in_ord((*ptr).left);  /* call recursively with left child of 'ptr' */
            printf("%d ",(*ptr).info);
            in_ord((*ptr).right);  /* call this function again with right
                                        child of 'ptr' */
        }

}   /* print 'info' part of left child of 'ptr', 'info' part of 'ptr' itself and then print
        'info' of right child of 'ptr' recursively */

void pre_ord(tree *ptr)
{
        if(ptr!=NULL)
        {
                    printf("%d ",(*ptr).info);
                    pre_ord((*ptr).left);
                    pre_ord((*ptr).right);
        }

}   /* print 'info' part of 'ptr', 'info' part of left child of 'ptr' and then print
        'info' of right child of 'ptr' recursively */

void post_ord(tree *ptr)
{
        if(ptr!=NULL)
        {
                    post_ord((*ptr).left);
                    post_ord((*ptr).right);
                    printf("%d ",(*ptr).info);
        }

}   /* print 'info' part of left child of 'ptr', 'info' part of right child of
        'ptr' and then print 'info' of 'ptr' recursively */
```

```
int count_nodes(tree *ptr)
{
        if(ptr==NULL)
        return 0;
        else
  return(count_nodes((*ptr).left)+count_nodes((*ptr).right)+1);

}    /* traverse each node and add 1 to the  previous counted nodes after
        traversing a node  */

int count_leaf_nodes(tree *ptr)
{
        if(ptr==NULL)
        return 0;
        else
        if((*ptr).left==(*ptr).right&&(*ptr).left==NULL)
        return 1;
        else
return(count_leaf_nodes((*ptr).left)+count_leaf_nodes((*ptr).right));

}        /*  return 1 if 'ptr' is a leaf node and  add this value to the total of
            previous counted leaf nodes */

int count_non_leaf_nodes()
{
        int total, leaf;

        total=count_nodes(root);
        leaf=count_leaf_nodes(root);
        return(total-leaf);

}  /* end count_non_leaf_nodes  */

int count_height(tree *ptr)
{
        if(ptr==NULL)
        return -1;
```

```
        else
        return max(count_height(ptr->left), count_height(ptr->right))+1;
```

} /* *count height of left subtree and right subtree of each node N and return the bigger of these plus 1 to the previous instance, which further returns the height of parent node P(N), where P(N) is the parent of current node N* */

```
int max(int item1, int item2)
{
        if(item1>item2)
        return item1;
        else
        return item2;
```

} /* *end max* */

```
int smallest_node(tree *ptr)
{
        if(root==NULL)
        {
            printf("tree is empty");
            return 0;
        }

        while((*ptr).left!=NULL)
        ptr=(*ptr).left;

        return((*ptr).info);
```

} /* *it is a binary search tree, so leftmost child of 'root' will be the smallest node* */

```
int largest_node(tree *ptr)
{
        if(root==NULL)
        {
            printf("tree is empty");
            return 0;
        }
```

261

```
        while((*ptr).right!=NULL)
        ptr=(*ptr).right;

        return((*ptr).info);    /* rightmost child of 'root' will be the largest
                                   node */

}  /* end largest_node */

/*

After executing:

enter choice
  1.add an element
  2.delete an element
  3.traverse in order
  4.traverse in pre order
  5.traverse in post order
  6.count nodes
  7.count leaf nodes
  8.count non leaf nodes
  9.count height
  10.smallest node
  11.largest node
  12.exit
  1
enter item
6
enter choice
  1.add an element
  2.delete an element
  3.traverse in order
  4.traverse in pre order
  5.traverse in post order
  6.count nodes
  7.count leaf nodes
  8.count non leaf nodes
  9.count height
  10.smallest node
  11.largest node
  12.exit
  1
enter item
9
enter choice
  1.add an element
```

2.delete an element
3.traverse in order
4.traverse in pre order
5.traverse in post order
6.count nodes
7.count leaf nodes
8.count non leaf nodes
9.count height
10.smallest node
11.largest node
12.exit
1
enter item
7

enter choice
1.add an element
2.delete an element
3.traverse in order
4.traverse in pre order
5.traverse in post order
6.count nodes
7.count leaf nodes
8.count non leaf nodes
9.count height
10.smallest node
11.largest node
12.exit
2
enter item which is to be deleted
9

enter choice
1.add an element
2.delete an element
3.traverse in order
4.traverse in pre order
5.traverse in post order
6.count nodes
7.count leaf nodes
8.count non leaf nodes
9.count height
10.smallest node
11.largest node
12.exit
3

263

6 7
enter choice
  1.add an element
  2.delete an element
  3.traverse in order
  4.traverse in pre order
  5.traverse in post order
  6.count nodes
  7.count leaf nodes
  8.count non leaf nodes
  9.count height
  10.smallest node
  11.largest node
  12.exit
  4
6 7
enter choice
  1.add an element
  2.delete an element
  3.traverse in order
  4.traverse in pre order
  5.traverse in post order
  6.count nodes
  7.count leaf nodes
  8.count non leaf nodes
  9.count height
  10.smallest node
  11.largest node
  12.exit
  5
7 6
enter choice
  1.add an element
  2.delete an element
  3.traverse in order
  4.traverse in pre order
  5.traverse in post order
  6.count nodes
  7.count leaf nodes
  8.count non leaf nodes
  9.count height
  10.smallest node
  11.largest node
  12.exit
  6
total nodes are 2

264

enter choice
1.add an element
2.delete an element
3.traverse in order
4.traverse in pre order
5.traverse in post order
6.count nodes
7.count leaf nodes
8.count non leaf nodes
9.count height
10.smallest node
11.largest node
12.exit
7
total leaf nodes are 1
enter choice
1.add an element
2.delete an element
3.traverse in order
4.traverse in pre order
5.traverse in post order
6.count nodes
7.count leaf nodes
8.count non leaf nodes
9.count height
10.smallest node
11.largest node
12.exit
8
non leaf nodes: 1

enter choice
1.add an element
2.delete an element
3.traverse in order
4.traverse in pre order
5.traverse in post order
6.count nodes
7.count leaf nodes
8.count non leaf nodes
9.count height
10.smallest node
11.largest node
12.exit
9
height of tree is 1

265

```
enter choice
 1.add an element
 2.delete an element
 3.traverse in order
 4.traverse in pre order
 5.traverse in post order
 6.count nodes
 7.count leaf nodes
 8.count non leaf nodes
 9.count height
 10.smallest node
 11.largest node
 12.exit
 10
smallest node:6
enter choice
 1.add an element
 2.delete an element
 3.traverse in order
 4.traverse in pre order
 5.traverse in post order
 6.count nodes
 7.count leaf nodes
 8.count non leaf nodes
 9.count height
 10.smallest node
 11.largest node
 12.exit
 11
largest node:7
enter choice
 1.add an element
 2.delete an element
 3.traverse in order
 4.traverse in pre order
 5.traverse in post order
 6.count nodes
 7.count leaf nodes
 8.count non leaf nodes
 9.count height
 10.smallest node
 11.largest node
 12.exit
 12            ...............(terminated)          */
```

****

266

Steps of the Program:

void insert():

1) Create a new node 'ptr'. If tree is empty then make 'ptr' as the root node of the tree.

2) If tree is not empty then search for the empty location, where 'ptr' can be inserted. Let this empty location is 'loc' and parent node of 'loc' is 'daddy'.

3) If 'item', which has to be inserted, is less than 'daddy->info', then insert 'ptr' at location 'daddy->left', else insert 'item' at 'daddy->right'.

void del():

1) If tree is not empty then search for the location 'loc' of 'item', which is to be deleted.

2) If 'loc' is a leaf node, then call 'delete_with_no_chid(loc, daddy)', where 'daddy' is the parent node of 'loc'.

3) If 'loc' has only left child, then call 'delete_with_left_child(loc, daddy)'.

4) If 'loc' has only right child, then call 'delete_with_right_child(loc, daddy)'.

5) If 'loc' has two children, then call 'delete_with_two_children(loc, daddy)'.

*void delete_with_no_child(tree *loc, tree *daddy):*

1) If there is only one node in the tree, then empty the tree.

2) Else, if 'loc' is left child of 'daddy' then assign NULL to 'daddy->left'. If 'loc' is right child of 'daddy' then assign NULL to 'daddy->right'.

*void delete_with_right_child(tree *loc, tree *daddy):*

1) If 'loc' is the root node, then delete this node and make 'root->right' as the new root.

2) Else, if 'loc' is left child of 'daddy' then assign 'loc->right' to 'daddy->left'. If 'loc' is right child of 'daddy' then assign 'loc->right' to 'daddy->right'. Thereafter delete node 'loc'.

*void delete_with_left_child(tree *loc, tree *daddy):*

1) If 'loc' is the root node, then delete this node and make 'root->left' as the new root.

2) Else, if 'loc' is left child of 'daddy' then assign 'loc->left' to 'daddy->left'. If 'loc' is right child of 'daddy' then assign 'loc->left' to 'daddy->right'. Thereafter delete node 'loc'.

*void delete_with_two_children(tree *loc, tree *daddy):*

1) Inorder successor of 'loc' will be the leftmost child of 'loc->right'. In case if 'loc->right' has no left child then 'loc->right' will be the inorder successor of 'loc' Store the location of inorder successor of 'loc' in pointer 'inord_daddy'.

2) Replace the 'info' part of 'loc' with 'info' part of 'inord_daddy'.

3) Store the location of parent node of 'inord_daddy' in pointer 'dadu'.

4) If 'loc->right' has no left child, then make 'loc->right->right' as the right child of 'loc'.

5) Else, make right child of 'inord_daddy' as left child of 'dadu', and free the memory space that was allocated to 'inord_daddy'.

void in_ord(tree *ptr):

For each node print: 'info' part of left child, 'info' part of the node itself and in the last print 'info' part of right child. This can be accomplished by using recursion:

Suppose tree in memory is:

Then, values in 'info' field of the nodes, which are pushed onto the stack created by function 'in_ord', are:

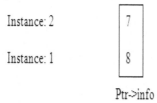

Ptr->info

1) 'info' part: 7, of 'ptr' of last created instance will be printed. Since 'ptr' in instance: 2 is a leaf node, so this instance will be cleared from memory.

269

2) Now 'info' part: 8, of root node is printed, and 'in_ord' is called with right child of 'ptr'.

Now stack in memory becomes:

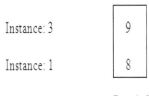

Ptr->info

3) At this time, 'info' part of 'ptr' of instance: 3 is printed. Thereafter, this instance will also be erased from memory. Now control of the program comes at instance: 1. But there is no other statement, which has to be executed so output for this tree is:
7   8   9...................(inorder traversal).

void pre_ord(tree *ptr):

For each node print: 'info' part of the node, 'info' part of the left child and 'info' part of the right child.

void post_ord(tree *ptr):

For each node print: 'info' part of the left child, 'info' part of the right child and 'info' part of the node itself.

int count_height(tree *ptr):

For each node N, find the height of its left and right subtree recursively. Thereafter return the bigger of these plus 1 as the height of node N to the previous instance.

7.5 Traversing in trees without using Recursion

The modules to traverse a binary tree could be written non-recursively by using stacking and un-stacking explicitly. We can maintain our own stack in memory and can perform the desired operations on the stack.

In-order Traversal:

Initially set ptr=root. And do following:

    1)

        a) Proceed down the left-most path of ptr, processing each node N on the path and pushing it onto the stack i.e.

```
while(ptr!=NULL)
{
    push ptr onto the stack
    ptr=ptr->left
}
```

        b) Pop and print the topmost element say ptr of the stack, and set ptr=ptr->right.

    2) Repeat step: 1, till the stack becomes empty and ptr becomes NULL.

271

Pre-order Traversal:

Initially set ptr=root. And do following:

1)

    a) If ptr is not NULL, then proceed down the left-most path of ptr, printing each node N on the path and pushing it onto the stack i.e.

```
while(ptr!=NULL)
{
        print: ptr
        push ptr onto the stack
        ptr=ptr->left
}
```

    b) Pop the topmost node say ptr from the stack, and set ptr=ptr->right.

2) Repeat step: 1, till the stack becomes empty and ptr becomes NULL.

Post-order Traversal:

Initially set ptr=root. And do following:

1)

    a) If ptr is not NULL, then proceed down the left-most path of ptr, processing each node N on the path and pushing it onto the stack i.e.

```
while(ptr!=NULL)
{
        push ptr onto the stack
        ptr=ptr->left
}
```

b) For top node say 'ptr' of the stack, set ptr=ptr->right. If ptr has already been processed or ptr is NULL, then pop and print the topmost node of the stack. And set ptr=NULL(if it has already been processed).

2) Repeat step: 1, till the stack becomes empty.

****

```c
/* Pre-order, post-order & in-order traversing without using recursion */
#include<stdio.h>
#include<alloc.h>
#define MAX 100

typedef struct node_type
{
    struct node_type *left;
    int info;
    struct node_type *right;
}tree;

tree *root=NULL;
void insert(), in_ord(tree *), pre_ord(tree *), post_ord(tree *);

void main()
{
        int x;

        while(1)
        {
                printf("\nenter choice\n ");
                printf("1.Insert an element\n ");
                printf("2.Traverse in order\n ");
                printf("3.Traverse in pre order\n ");
                printf("4.Traverse in post order\n ");
```

273

```c
            printf("5.Exit\n ");
            scanf("%d",&x);
            switch(x)
            {
                    case 1:  insert();                break;
                    case 2:  in_ord(root);            break;
                    case 3:  pre_ord(root);           break;
                    case 4:  post_ord(root);          break;
                    case 5:  exit();

            }  /* end switch */

      }  /* end while */

}  /* end main */

void insert()
{
        tree *ptr, *loc, *prev;
        int item;

        printf("enter item\n");
        scanf("%d",&item);

        ptr=(tree *)malloc(sizeof(tree));

        if(ptr==NULL)
        {
                printf("no space\n");
                return;
        }

        (*ptr).info=item;
        (*ptr).left=(*ptr).right=NULL;

        if(root==NULL)
        {
            root=ptr;
```

```
            return;
      }
      loc=root;

      while(loc!=NULL)
      {
            prev=loc;

            if(item<(*loc).info)
            loc=(*loc).left;
            else
            loc=(*loc).right;

      } /* end while */

      if(item<(*prev).info)
      (*prev).left=ptr;
      else
      (*prev).right=ptr;

} /* end insert */

void in_ord(tree *ptr)
{
      tree *stack[MAX];
      int i=0;

      do
      {
            /* In the following loop, push the nodes along the left branch of
               'ptr' in array 'stack' */

            while(ptr!=NULL)
            {
                  stack[i++]=ptr;
                  ptr=(*ptr).left;
            }
```

```
            if(i!=0)
            {
                    ptr=stack[--i];
                    printf("%d ",(*ptr).info);   /* print 'info' part of last
                                                    node of array 'stack' */
                    ptr=(*ptr).right;   /* and then explore right subtree of
                                           this node */
            }
       }while(ptr!=NULL || i!=0);
}  /* end in_ord */

void pre_ord(tree *ptr)
{
       tree *stack[MAX];
       int i=0;
       do
       {
            while(ptr!=NULL)
            {
                    printf("%d ",(*ptr).info);   /* print 'info' part of
                                                    node 'ptr' */
                    stack[i++]=ptr;   /* and push this node on to array
                                         'stack' */
                    ptr=(*ptr).left;   /* traverse left branch of node 'ptr' */
            }
            if(i!=0)
            {
                    ptr=stack[--i];   /* Assign last element of array
                                         'stack' to pointer 'ptr' */
                    ptr=(*ptr).right;   /* now we have to explore right
                                           subtree of node 'ptr', so assign
                                           'ptr->right' to 'ptr' */
            }
```

```
        }while(ptr!=NULL || i!=0);

}   /* end pre_ord */

void post_ord(tree *ptr)
{
        tree *stack[MAX],*prev;
        int i=0,j,max,flag;

        do
        {
                /* In the following loop, explore left branch of node 'ptr' */

                while(ptr!=NULL)
                {
                        stack[i++]=ptr;   /* Push each node of this branch
                                              on to array 'stack' */
                        ptr=(*ptr).left;
                        max=i;
                }

                if(i!=0)      /* If all the nodes of array 'stack' have not been
                                 printed till yet, then do following: */
                {
                        ptr=stack[i-1];   /* Assign last node of array 'stack'
                                              to pointer 'ptr' */

                        ptr=(*ptr).right;   /* assign 'ptr->right' to 'ptr' */

                        flag=0;
                        for(j=0;j<max;j++)
                        if(stack[j]==ptr)
                        flag=1;
                                /* Now in the above loop, set the value of
                                   'flag' as 1, if node 'ptr' has already been
                                   added to array 'stack' */

                        if(ptr==NULL || flag==1)
                        {
```

```
                    ptr=NULL;
                    printf("%d ",(*stack[--i]).info);

         }   /*  If 'ptr' is NULL or if value in 'ptr' has already been
                 explored then print stack[i-1] */

      }   /*  end if  */

   }while(i!=0);

}   /*  end post_ord  */

/*

After executing:

enter choice
 1.Insert an element
 2.Traverse in order
 3.Traverse in pre order
 4.Traverse in post order
 5.Exit
 1
enter item
 8

enter choice
 1.Insert an element
 2.Traverse in order
 3.Traverse in pre order
 4.Traverse in post order
 5.Exit
 1
enter item
 9
enter choice
 1.Insert an element
 2.Traverse in order
 3.Traverse in pre order
 4.Traverse in post order
 5.Exit
 1
enter item
 7
```

```
enter choice
1.Insert an element
2.Traverse in order
3.Traverse in pre order
4.Traverse in post order
5.Exit
1
enter item
6

enter choice
1.Insert an element
2.Traverse in order
3.Traverse in pre order
4.Traverse in post order
5.Exit
2
6 7 8 9
enter choice
1.Insert an element
2.Traverse in order
3.Traverse in pre order
4.Traverse in post order
5.Exit
3
8 7 6 9
enter choice
1.Insert an element
2.Traverse in order
3.Traverse in pre order
4.Traverse in post order
5.Exit
4
6 7 9 8
enter choice
1.Insert an element
2.Traverse in order
3.Traverse in pre order
4.Traverse in post order
5.Exit
5 ... ... ... ... ... ... ... ... ... ... ...(terminated)

*/
```

****

Steps of the Program:

Suppose tree in memory is:

Further suppose that these three nodes 8, 7 and 9 are at addresses: 100, 200 and 300.

void in_ord(tree *ptr):

1) In first iteration of 'do-while' loop, following steps are executed:

   a) All the locations 'ptr', 'ptr->left', 'ptr->left->left'............are stored in array 'stack' until a NULL pointer is encountered. At the first iteration of the above loop, there are only two such nodes found at locations 100 and 200. So after execution of this step array 'stack' will contain: 100 and 200.

   b) The top node 'ptr' of array 'stack' is popped out and 'info' part of 'ptr' is printed. This means 7 is printed, and 'i' is decremented by 1, meaning thereby that node is deleted from array 'stack'. Now 'stack' contains: 100.

2) At second iteration of 'do-while' loop, top element from array 'stack', which is 100, is popped out and 'info' part of this node, which is 8, is printed.

3) At third iteration of 'do-while' loop:

300 is pushed onto array 'stack'. Now 'stack' contains element: 300.

Thereafter this is popped out from array 'stack' and 'info' part of this node, which is 9, is printed.

void pre_ord(tree *ptr):

1) In first iteration of 'do-while' loop, following steps are executed:

   a) The 'info' parts of 'ptr', 'ptr->left', 'ptr->left->left'..............are printed one by one and locations 'ptr', 'ptr->left', 'ptr->left->left'............ are pushed onto array 'stack' until a NULL pointer is encountered. In our case there are only two such nodes at locations 100 and 200. So after execution of this step, output will be: 8, 7 and array 'stack' will contain(locations): 100 and 200.

   b) Top node 'ptr' of array 'stack' is popped out and 'i' is decremented by 1 meaning thereby that this node is deleted from array 'stack'. Now 'stack' contains: 100.

2) At second iteration of 'do-while' loop, 100 is also popped out from 'stack'.

3) At third iteration, 'info' part of 300, which is 9, is printed onto the screen and the 'do-while' loop terminates here.

void post_ord(tree *ptr):

1) At each iteration of 'do-while' loop, following steps are executed:

    a) All the locations 'ptr', 'ptr->left', 'ptr->left->left'............ (Until a NULL pointer is encountered) are stored in array 'stack', one by one.

    b)

    (i)   For top node say 'ptr' of array 'stack', 'ptr' is set to 'ptr->right'.

    (ii)   If 'ptr' is NULL or 'ptr' is found in array 'stack', then top node of 'stack' is popped out and 'info' part of this node is printed onto the screen. Thereafter 'ptr' is set to NULL.

7.6   Height Balanced Trees; AVL Trees

In a balanced binary tree, the difference between the heights of two subtrees of every node is never more than 1. The balance of a node in a binary tree may be defined as the height of its left subtree minus height of its right subtree. Each node, in a balanced binary tree, has a balance of 1, -1 or 0, depending on whether the height of its left subtree is greater than, less than, or equal to the height of its right subtree.

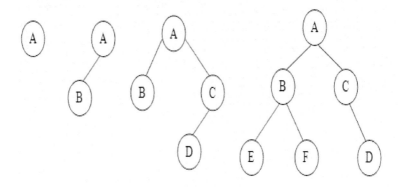

AVL Trees: Balanced Binary Trees

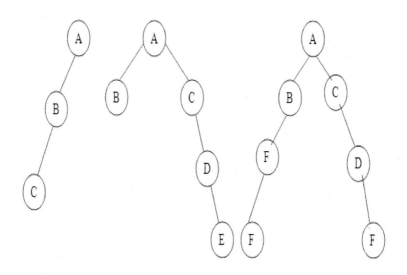

Non-AVL Trees

Insertion of a node in AVL Tree:

We can insert a new node into an AVL tree by first using the simple insertion algorithm (used in binary search trees), that is by comparing the key of the new node with that of the root, and inserting the new node into the left or right subtree as appropriate. The resulting tree may or may not remain balanced. If resulting tree is unbalanced, then that is transformed into a balanced tree.

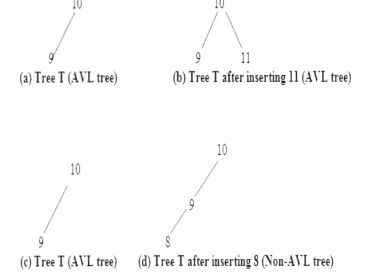

(a) Tree T (AVL tree)   (b) Tree T after inserting 11 (AVL tree)

(c) Tree T (AVL tree)   (d) Tree T after inserting 8 (Non-AVL tree)

In above figure (d), balance of node 10 is 2, so it is a non-AVL Tree.

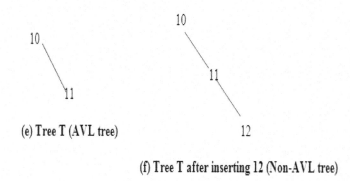

(e) Tree T (AVL tree)

(f) Tree T after inserting 12 (Non-AVL tree)

In above figure (f), balance of node 10 is -2.

It will be seen from above, that a tree becomes unbalanced, if the newly inserted node is a left descendant of a node that previously had a balance of 1, as shown in above figure (d) or if it is a right descendant of a node that previously had a balance of −1, as shown in above figure (f). Thus a tree becomes unbalanced when there exists a node N such that

(i)   It's balance is 1 and the newly created node is inserted into the left subtree of N, changing the balance of node N from 1 to 2.

(ii)   It's balance is -1 and the newly created node is inserted into the right subtree of N, changing the balance of node N from −1 to −2.

To maintain a balanced tree, it is necessary to perform a transformation on the tree so that the inorder traversal of the

285

transformed tree remains the same, as that of the original tree (that is, the transformed tree remains a binary search tree).

An unbalanced tree T is transformed into a balanced tree either by left rotating or by right rotating the subtree rooted at node N, depending upon whether the node N has a balance of –2 or a balance of 2, where node N belongs to the unbalanced tree T.

Left Rotation:

Left rotation of a subtree rooted at node N with left child L and right child R may be defined as follows:
(Consider left child of node R is L_1)

1) Rotate node N and all of its left descendents, to one position down in the tree in anticlockwise direction.

2) Make node L1 as the right child of N.

3) Make node R as the new root of the subtree.

Right Rotation:

Right rotation of a subtree rooted at node N with left child L and right child R may be defined as follows:
(Consider right child of node L is R_1)

1) Rotate node N and all of its right descendents, to one position down in the tree in clockwise direction.

2) Make node R1 as left child of node N.

3) Make node L as the new root of the subtree.

EXAMPLE:

Left Rotation:

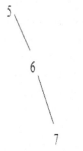

(a) Tree T

[Node: 5 has balance of –2]

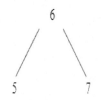

(b) Tree T

⎡After performing left rotation on⎤
⎣tree rooted at node 5.   ⎦

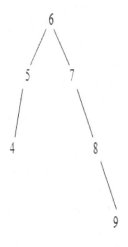

(c) Tree T

[Node: 7 has balance of –2]

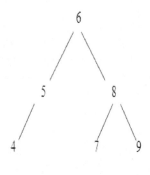

(d) Tree T

⎡After performing left rotation on⎤
⎣subtree rooted at node:7   ⎦

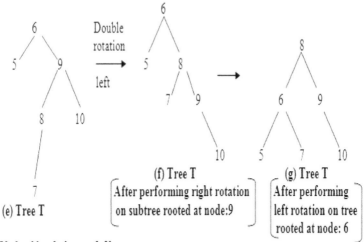

(f) Tree T
[After performing right rotation on subtree rooted at node:9]

(g) Tree T
[After performing left rotation on tree rooted at node: 6]

(e) Tree T

[Node: 6 has balance of -2]

Note that in above figure: (e), if left rotation is applied on tree rooted at node: 6, then resulting tree will have a balance of 2, which will also be an unbalanced tree. So, in this case, we will have to perform the double rotation. First perform right rotation on subtree rooted at node: 9 and then left rotation on tree rooted at node: 6. The question arises, when should we perform double rotation. Suppose a tree T becomes unbalanced after inserting 'item', changing the balance of node N from –1 to –2. Then we will have to perform the double rotation (First right rotation on right child of N and then left rotation on N), if 'item' has been inserted into the left subtree of right child of N (i.e. item < N->right->item). Else, we perform the single left rotation on node N.

Right Rotation:

288

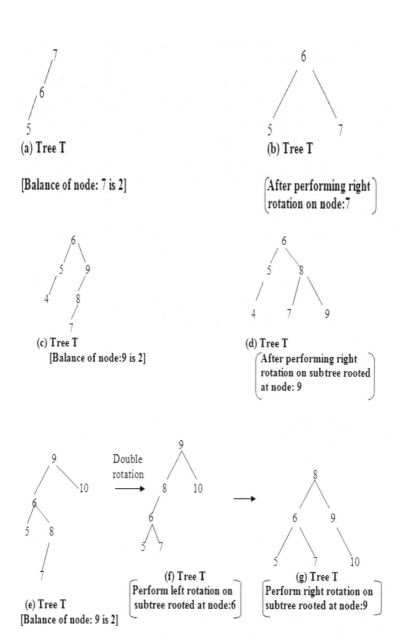

(a) Tree T

[Balance of node: 7 is 2]

(b) Tree T

$\left(\begin{array}{l}\text{After performing right}\\ \text{rotation on node:7}\end{array}\right)$

(c) Tree T
[Balance of node:9 is 2]

(d) Tree T
$\left(\begin{array}{l}\text{After performing right}\\ \text{rotation on subtree rooted}\\ \text{at node: 9}\end{array}\right)$

Double
rotation

(e) Tree T
[Balance of node: 9 is 2]

(f) Tree T
$\left[\begin{array}{l}\text{Perform left rotation on}\\ \text{subtree rooted at node:6}\end{array}\right]$

(g) Tree T
$\left[\begin{array}{l}\text{Perform right rotation on}\\ \text{subtree rooted at node:9}\end{array}\right]$

Note that, in above figure: (e), if right rotation is applied on tree rooted at node: 9, then resulting tree will have a balance of -2, which will also be an unbalanced tree. So in this case we perform the left rotation on subtree rooted at node: 6, thereafter we perform the right rotation on node: 9. Now, similar question arises here: When to perform the double rotation. Suppose a tree T becomes unbalanced after inserting 'item', changing the balance of node N from 1 to 2. *Answer is:* We perform the double rotation (First left rotation on left child of N, then right rotation on node N), if 'item' is inserted into the right subtree of left child of node N. Else, we perform the single right rotation on node N.

Note: Searching of a node in a balanced tree requires less time than that in an unbalanced tree. Because, in a balanced tree, only few comparisons are required to search a node.

****

/* *Implementation of Height Balanced Tree* */

```
#include<stdio.h>
#include<alloc.h>

typedef struct tree_type
{
        struct tree_type *daddy;
        int height;
        struct tree_type *left;
        int info;
        struct tree_type *right;
 }tree;

tree *root = NULL;

void insert();
```

```c
void checkbal(tree *, int);
void in_order(tree *);
void leftrotate(tree *, tree *);
void rightrotate(tree *, tree *);
void adjust_height(tree *);
int find_height(tree *);
int max(int, int);

void main()
{
        int x, h;

        while(1)
        {
                printf("enter choice\n");
                printf("1.Insert an element\n");
                printf("2.Inorder Traversal\n");
                printf("3.Height of the tree\n");
                printf("4.Exit\n");
                scanf("%d",&x);

                switch(x)
                {
                        case 1:  insert();           break;
                        case 2:  in_order(root);   break;
                        case 3:  h = find_height(root);

                        printf("Height of tree is %d\n"); break;

                        case 4:  exit();

                } /* end switch */

        } /* end while */

} /* end main */

void insert()
{
```

```c
tree *ptr, *loc, *prev;
int item;

printf("enter item\n");
scanf("%d",&item);

ptr=(tree *)malloc(sizeof(tree));

if(ptr==NULL)
{
    printf("no space\n");
    return;
}

(*ptr).info=item;
(*ptr).daddy = (*ptr).left = (*ptr).right = NULL;
(*ptr).height=0;   /* 'ptr->height' variable stores the height
                         of subtree rooted at node 'ptr' */

    if(root==NULL)
    {
            root=ptr;
            return;
    }

    loc=root;

    while(loc!=NULL)
    {
            prev=loc;

            if(item<(*loc).info)
            loc=(*loc).left;
            else
            loc=(*loc).right;

    }   /*  Search for the empty subtree where 'item' can be
            inserted. Here 'prev' denotes the location of parent
            node of empty subtree */
```

```
            (*ptr).daddy = prev;   /* 'ptr->daddy' stores the
                                       parent node of 'ptr' */

            if(item<(*prev).info)
            (*prev).left = ptr;
            else
            (*prev).right = ptr;
                                  /* In place of empty subtree,
                                     insert 'ptr' */
            adjust_height(ptr);   /* After insertion of node 'ptr',
                                     modify the heights of
                                     parental nodes */

            checkbal(ptr, item);

}  /* end insert */


void adjust_height(tree *loc)
{
            while(loc!=root)
            {
            loc=(*loc).daddy;
(*loc).height = max(find_height((*loc).left), find_height((*loc).right))+1;

            }   /* Modify the heights of parental nodes of node 'loc'  */

}  /* end adjust_height */

void checkbal(tree *ptr, int item)
{
            int hleft, hright, bal;

            while( ptr->daddy != NULL )
            {

                    ptr = (*ptr).daddy;
                    hleft = find_height((*ptr).left);
                    hright = find_height((*ptr).right);
                    bal = hleft-hright;
```

293

```
                                if(bal>1)
                                {
                                            if(item>ptr->left->info)
                                            {
                                                leftrotate((*ptr).left, ptr);
                                                rightrotate(ptr, (*ptr).daddy);

                                            }    /*  Double rotation   */
                                            else
                                                rightrotate(ptr, (*ptr).daddy);
                                                        /*  Single rotation  */
                                }  /* end if */

                                else
                                if(bal<-1)
                                {
                                            if(item<ptr->right->info)
                                            {
                                                rightrotate((*ptr).right, ptr);
                                                leftrotate(ptr, (*ptr).daddy);

                                            }    /*  Double rotation   */
                                            else
                                                leftrotate(ptr, (*ptr).daddy);
                                                        /*  Single rotation  */
                                }  /* end if */

                        }  /* end while */

}  /* end checkbal  */

void rightrotate(tree *ptr, tree *prev)
{
                        tree *hold, *temp;

                        temp = (*ptr).left;
                        hold = (*temp).right;
                        (*temp).right = ptr;
```

294

```c
            (*ptr).left = hold;

            if(ptr==root)
            root = temp;
            else
            if(ptr == (*prev).left)
            (*prev).left = temp;
            else
            (*prev).right = temp;
```

(*ptr).height = max(find_height((*ptr).left), find_height((*ptr).right))+1;
(*temp).height = max(find_height((*temp).left), find_height((*temp).right))+1;

```c
            adjust_height(temp);
                            /* Adjust the heights of 'ptr', 'temp' and
                               parental nodes of 'temp' accordingly */

            (*temp).daddy = prev;
            if(hold!=NULL)
            (*hold).daddy = ptr;

            (*ptr).daddy = temp;
} /* end rightrotate */

void leftrotate(tree *ptr, tree *prev)
{
            tree *hold, *temp;

            temp = (*ptr).right;
            hold = (*temp).left;
            (*temp).left = ptr;
            (*ptr).right = hold;

            if(ptr==root)
            root = temp;
            else
            if(ptr == (*prev).right)
            (*prev).right = temp;
```

```
                                    else
                                    (*prev).left = temp;
(*ptr).height = max(find_height((*ptr).left), find_height((*ptr).right))+1;
(*temp).height = max(find_height((*temp).left), find_height((*temp).right))+1;
                                    adjust_height(temp);
                                              /*  Adjust the heights of 'ptr', 'temp' and
                                                  parental nodes of 'temp' accordingly  */

                                    (*temp).daddy = prev;
                                    if(hold!=NULL)
                                    (*hold).daddy = ptr;

                                     (*ptr).daddy = temp;
}  /* end leftrotate */

int find_height(tree *ptr)
{
        if(ptr==NULL)
        return -1;
        else
        return (*ptr).height;

}  /* end find_height */

int max(int item1, int item2)
{
        if(item1>item2)
        return item1;
        else
         return item2;

}  /* end max */

void in_order(tree *ptr)
{
        if(ptr!=NULL)
        {
            in_order((*ptr).left);
                                    296
```

```
                    printf("%d ",(*ptr).info);
                    in_order((*ptr).right);
            }

    }  /* end in_order */
```

/*

After executing:

enter choice
1.Insert an element
2.Inorder Traversal
3.Height of the tree
4.Exit
1
enter item
7
enter choice
1.Insert an element
2.Inorder Traversal
3.Height of the tree
4.Exit
1
enter item
6
enter choice
1.Insert an element
2.Inorder Traversal
3.Height of the tree
4.Exit
1
enter item
5
enter choice
1.Insert an element
2.Inorder Traversal
3.Height of the tree
4.Exit
2
5 6 7 enter choice
1.Insert an element
2.Inorder Traversal
3.Height of the tree

4.Exit
3
Height of tree is 1
enter choice
1.Insert an element
2.Inorder Traversal
3.Height of the tree
4.Exit
4 ... ...(terminated)

*/

****

Steps of the Program:

void insert():

1) Create a new node 'ptr'. If tree is empty then make 'ptr' as the root node of the tree and return the control. Else do the following:

2) Insert this new node 'ptr' at its proper location in the binary search tree. And adjust the 'daddy' pointer, which stores the location of parent node, accordingly.

3) Modify the heights and check the balance of the parental nodes of 'ptr'. If resulting tree is not balanced, then transform the tree into a balanced tree.

*void adjust_height(tree *loc):*

We have to change the 'height' variable of parental nodes of 'loc'. So do the following until 'loc' reaches at the 'root' node:

        (a) Assign 'loc->daddy' to loc.

298

(b) Find the heights of left subtree and right subtree of 'loc' and assign the larger of these plus 1 to 'loc->height'.

*void checkbal(tree *ptr, int item):*

Do the following until 'ptr' reaches at the 'root' node:

(a) assign 'ptr->daddy' to 'ptr'.

(b) Find the heights of left subtree and right subtree of 'ptr' and store these in variables 'hleft' and 'hright'.

(c) bal=hleft - hright, so if (bal>1) i.e. if left subtree is heavy then :

    (i)   If 'item' was inserted into the right subtree of 'ptr->left' then perform the double rotation.

    (ii)   Else, perform single right rotation on 'ptr'.

(d) If (bal<-1) i.e. if right subtree is heavy then:

    (i)   If 'item' was inserted into the left subtree of 'ptr->right' then perform the double rotation.

    (ii)   Else, perform single left rotation on 'ptr'.

*void rightrotate(tree *ptr, tree *prev):*

1) For right rotation of subtree rooted at node 'ptr', do the following :

```
temp = ptr->left;
hold = temp->right;
temp->right = ptr;
ptr->left = hold;
```

2) If 'ptr' was the root node of the tree, then make 'temp' as the new root.

3) Else, check whether 'ptr' was the left child of 'prev' or the right child of 'prev'. In place of 'ptr' make 'temp' as its new child.

4) Adjust the heights of 'ptr', 'temp' and parental nodes of 'temp' accordingly.

5) Also adjust the 'daddy' pointer of 'temp', 'hold' and 'ptr' accordingly.

void leftrotate(tree *ptr, tree *prev):

1) For left rotation of subtree rooted at node 'ptr', do the following :

```
temp = ptr->right;
hold = temp->left;
temp->left = ptr;
ptr->right = hold;
```

2) If 'ptr' was the root node of the tree, then make 'temp' as the new root.

3) Else, check whether 'ptr' was the left child of 'prev' or the right child of 'prev'. In place of 'ptr' make 'temp' as its new child.

4) Adjust the heights of 'ptr', 'temp' and parental nodes of 'temp' accordingly.

5) Also adjust the 'daddy' pointer of 'temp', 'hold' and 'ptr' accordingly.

7.7 Threaded Binary Trees; Inorder Threading

In a linked representation of a binary tree T, approximately half of the entries in the pointer fields LEFT and RIGHT will contain NULL elements. These null entries may be replaced by some special links, called threads, which may more efficiently utilize this space. Changing the null links by threads will make it possible to perform inorder traversal without using either a stack or recursion. There are two types of inorder threading.

- One way inorder threading
- Two way inorder threading

In a one-way inorder threading of T, a thread will appear in the right field of a node and will point to the next node in the inorder traversal of T. Using this, we can traverse the whole tree in inorder without using recursion. Now the question arises, how will we come to know that which node contains a thread and which doesn't. For that, we can use a 1 bit flag for each node N, which is set to 1, when node N contains a thread to its inorder successor.

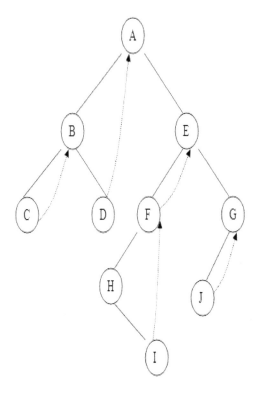

One Way Inorder Threading

In a two way inorder threading of T, a thread will also appear in the LEFT field of a node and will point to the preceding node in the inorder traversal of T.

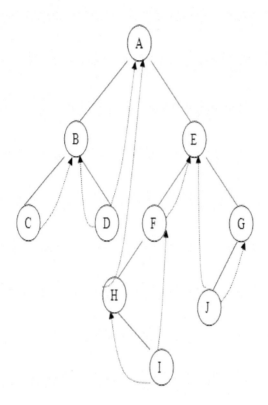

Two Way Inorder Threading

****

/* *Implementation of one-way inorder threading* */

```
#include<stdio.h>
#include<alloc.h>

enum boolean { false, true };
```

```c
typedef struct node_type
{
        unsigned int flag:1;   /*   1 bit flag   */
        struct tree_type *left;
        int info;
        struct tree_type *right;
}tree;

tree *root=NULL;

void setleft(tree *, tree *), setright(tree *, tree *);
void insert(), in_order(tree *);

void main()
{
            int x;

            while(1)
            {
                        printf("enter choice\n");
                        printf("1.Insert a node\n");
                        printf("2.Inorder Traversal\n");
                        printf("3.Exit\n");
                        scanf("%d",&x);

                        switch(x)
                        {
                                    case 1:   insert();             break;
                                    case 2:   in_order(root);   break;
                                    case 3:   exit();

                        }  /* end switch */

            }  /* end while */

}  /* end main */
```

304

```
void insert()
{
        tree *ptr, *loc, *prev;
        int item;

        printf("enter item\n");
        scanf("%d",&item);

        ptr=(tree *)malloc(sizeof(tree));

        if(ptr==NULL)
        {
                printf("no space\n");
                return;
        }

        (*ptr).info=item;
        (*ptr).flag=false;
        (*ptr).left=(*ptr).right=NULL;

        if(root==NULL)
        {
                root=ptr;
                return;

        } /* end if */

        loc=prev=root;

while(loc!=NULL && ((*prev).right!=loc || (*prev).flag==false))
        {
                /* loop until, either we get the empty left
                subtree(loc!=NULL) or we get the empty right
                subtree(prev->right!=loc || prev->flag==false) */

                prev=loc;
```

305

```
                    if(item<(*loc).info)
                    loc=(*loc).left;
                    else
                    loc=(*loc).right;

    }   /* end while */

                    if(item<(*prev).info)
                    setleft(prev, ptr);
                    else
                    setright(prev, ptr);

}   /* end insert */

void setleft(tree *prev, tree *ptr)
{
                    (*ptr).left=NULL;
                    (*ptr).right=prev;      /*  Inorder thread  */
                    (*ptr).flag=true;
                    (*prev).left=ptr;

}   /* end setleft */

void setright(tree *prev, tree *ptr)
{
                    tree *loc;

                    loc=(*prev).right;

                    (*ptr).left=NULL;
                    (*ptr).right=loc;       /*  Inorder thread. 'loc' is the
                                               inorder successor of 'ptr'  */
                    (*prev).right=ptr;
                    (*ptr).flag=(*prev).flag;
                    (*prev).flag=false;

}   /* end setright */
```

```c
void in_order(tree *ptr)
{
                tree *loc;

                do
                {
                        loc=NULL;

                        while(ptr!=NULL)
                        {
                                loc=ptr;
                                ptr=(*ptr).left;
                        }
                        if(loc!=NULL)
                        {

                                printf("%d ",(*loc).info);
                                ptr=(*loc).right;
                        while(ptr!=NULL && (*loc).flag==true)
                                {
                                printf("%d ",(*ptr).info);
                                loc=ptr;
                                ptr=(*ptr).right;
                                }

                        } /* end if */
                }while(loc!=NULL);
} /* end in_order */
/*
```

After executing:

enter choice
1.Insert a node
2.Inorder Traversal
3.Exit

```
1
enter item
10
enter choice
1.Insert a node
2.Inorder Traversal
3.Exit
1
enter item
8
enter choice
1.Insert a node
2.Inorder Traversal
3.Exit
1
enter item
9
enter choice
1.Insert a node
2.Inorder Traversal
3.Exit
1
enter item
7
enter choice
1.Insert a node
2.Inorder Traversal
3.Exit
1
enter item
11
enter choice
1.Insert a node
2.Inorder Traversal
3.Exit
2
7 8 9 10 11 enter choice
1.Insert a node
2.Inorder Traversal
3.Exit
3... ... ... ... ... ... ... ... ... ......(terminated)

*/
```

****

Steps of the Program:

Suppose elements to be inserted in the tree are: 9, 8, 10.

void insert():

1) First time when this function is called, root is NULL. So a new node 'ptr' is created, where ptr->info is set as 9 and the location of this node is stored in 'root'.

2) Second time, 8 is inserted to the left of 9. So 'setleft' is called with parameters: node containing 9, and the new node containing 8 which is to be inserted.

   void setleft(tree *prev, tree *ptr):

   Assign 'prev' to 'ptr->right'. Set 'ptr->flag' to true and insert 'ptr' to the left of 'prev' (by executing statement: prev->left=ptr). Now tree in memory is:

3) Third time, 10 will be inserted to the right of 9. So 'setright' is called with parameters: node containing 9, and the node containing 10, which is to be inserted.

   void setright(tree *prev, tree *ptr):

   Assign 'prev->right' to 'ptr->right' i.e. insert a thread between inorder successor of 'prev' (which is NULL at present) and 'ptr'. Then make 'ptr' as the right child of 'prev' (by executing statement: prev->right=ptr), and set 'prev->flag' to false.

Now tree in memory becomes:

Inorder Traversal:

void in_order(tree *ptr):

Algorithm, which is used in function 'in_order' is as follows:

Repeat the following steps until 'loc' becomes NULL. Initially, loc ≠ NULL.

1) Search for the leftmost node of 'ptr', and assign base address of that node to pointer 'loc'.

2) Print the 'info' part of node 'loc'. Then assign 'loc->right' to 'ptr' i.e. move towards the right child of 'loc'.

3) If 'loc' is not a leaf node then repeat steps: (1) and (2) again. Else

    (i)   Move towards the inorder successor(loc->right) of 'loc' and print the 'info' part of that node. After that assign 'loc->right' to 'loc'. Repeat this step: (i) until we get a node that doesn't contain a thread.

310

GRAPHS

A Graph G is an ordered set (V, E) where

- V is a set of vertices (or nodes).
- E is a set of edges connecting the vertices.

A Graph can be either directed or undirected. In an undirected graph, there is no specific direction associated with the edges. For example an edge e, in an undirected graph can be represented by an unordered pair [u, v] of vertices that can be traversed from u to v or vice versa, (i.e. e=[u, v] or e=[v, u]). Vertices u and v associated with edge e are called the end vertices of e.

EXAMPLE:

V= {V1, V2, V3, V4, V5, V6}
E= {   (V1, V2), (V1, V3), (V2, V4), (V4, V5), (V5, V3),
       (V5, V6), (V1, V5), (V2, V5), (V3, V4), (V1, V1),
       (V1, V2)   }

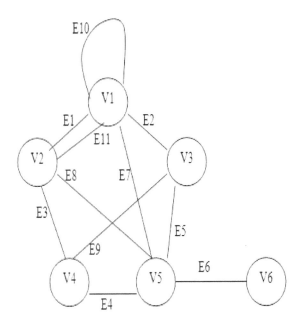

(a) Undirected graph with 6 vertices and 11 edges

The figure (a) shows a graph with 6 nodes and 11 edges. The edges E1 and E11 are said to be parallel, since both the edges are associated with the same pair of vertices V1 and V2. The edge E10 is a self-loop(or simply a loop), because E10 is having the same vertex V1 as its both end vertices.

8.1   Simple Graph

A graph, which has neither self-loops nor parallel edges is called a simple graph.

EXAMPLE:

312

V={V1, V2, V3, V4, V5, V6}
E={ (V1, V2), (V1, V3), (V2, V4), (V4, V5), (V5, V3),
(V5, V6), (V1, V5), (V2, V5), (V3, V4) }

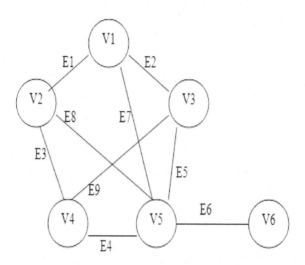

(b) Undirected graph with 6 vertices and 9 edges

8.2 Digraph (Directed graph)

A digraph is a graph, in which edges have a direction i.e. an
edge e=(u,v) can be traversed only from u to v, not from v to
u, where u is called the initial vertex of e and v is called the
terminal vertex of e.

EXAMPLE:

V={V1, V2, V3, V4, V5, V6}

313

E={ (V1, V2), (V1, V3), (V2, V4), (V4, V5), (V5, V3),
(V5, V6), (V1, V5), (V2, V5), (V3, V4), (V1, V1),
(V1, V2) }

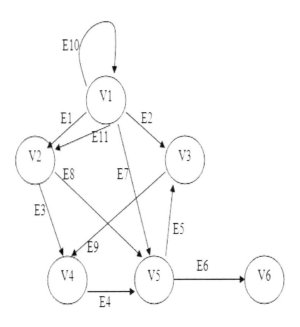

(c) Directed graph with 6 vertices and 11 edges

In a directed graph if an edge e =(Vi, Vj), then e ≠ (Vj, Vi).

Above figure (c) shows a directed graph with 6 nodes and
11(directed) edges. The edges E1 and E11 are said to be
parallel, since each begins from V1 and ends at V2. The edge
E10 is a loop, since it begins from and ends at the same
vertex, V1.

314

8.3   Simple Directed Graph

Simple directed graph is a simple graph in which edges have a direction.

EXAMPLE:

V={V1, V2, V3, V4, V5, V6}
E={   (V1, V2), (V1, V3), (V2, V4), (V4, V5), (V5, V3),
     (V5, V6), (V1, V5), (V2, V5), (V3, V4)   }

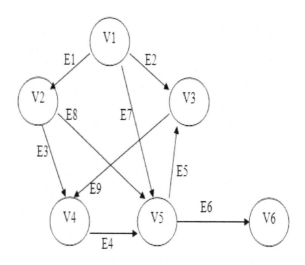

(d) Directed graph with 6 vertices and 9 edges

8.4   Weighted Graph

In a weighted graph, each edge is assigned some weight i.e. a real positive number is associated with each edge. For example, suppose in a road map of a state, there are two

315

cities A and B, which are at a distance of 10 Km. from each other. Then an edge(road), which connects these two vertices A and B, can be assigned a number 10, which is called the weight of that edge. In a non-weighted graph, each edge is assumed to be of equal length, which is normally taken as a positive number 1.

8.5   Path

In a non-weighted graph, a path P of length n from u to v can be defined as follows:
$P=\{v_0, v_1, v_2, \ldots\ldots v_n\}$ Where $u=v_0$ and $v= v_n$ and there is an edge from v_{i-1} to v_i ($0 < i \leq n$). In a directed graph, v_{i-1} is taken as the initial vertex and v_i is taken as the terminal vertex. For example, in figure (c), {V1, V1, V2, V5, V3} is a path of length 4 from V1 to V3. A simple path from u to v is a path, where no vertex appears more than once. For example, in above figure (d), {V3, V4, V5} is a simple path of length 2 from V3 to V5. In a weighted graph, length of a path can be defined as the sum of the weights of the edges lying along that path.

8.6   Cycle

A path $P=\{v_0, v_1, v_2, \ldots\ldots v_n\}$ is said to be a cycle, when all the vertices are distinct except v_0 and v_n, meaning thereby if $v_0 = v_n$, then a simple path P is called a cycle. For example, in figure (d), {V3, V4, V5, V3} is a cycle.

8.7   Connected Graph

A graph G is called a connected graph, if there is at least one path between every pair of vertices. For example, following graph is a connected graph.

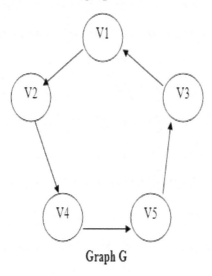

Graph G

8.8   Complete Graph

A graph with an edge between each pair of vertices is said to be a complete graph.

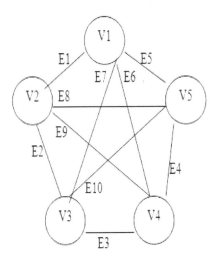

(e) Complete graph with 5 nodes

Note that, for any graph G = (V, E), if n is the total number of vertices and |E| is the total number of edges, then we have $0 \le |E| \le n*(n-1)/2$.

For a complete graph, $|E| = n * (n-1)/2$.

8.9   **Incidence and Degree**

When a vertex v is an end vertex of an edge e, then v and e are said to be incident on each other. For example, in above figure (e), edges E1, E5, E6 and E7 are incident on vertex V1. Two non-parallel edges are said to be adjacent, if they are incident on the same vertex. For example, in above figure (e), E4 and E5 are adjacent edges. The number of edges, incident on a vertex v is called the degree of v and is denoted by d(v). For example, in figure (e), degree of each vertex is

318

4, i.e. d(V1) = d(V2) = d(V3) = d(V4) = d(V5) = 4. In a directed graph, degree of a vertex is divided into two parts known as in-degree and out-degree of the vertex. In-degree of a vertex v, is said to be the total number of edges, for which, v is the terminal vertex. And out-degree of vertex v is called the total number of edges, for which, v is the initial vertex. For example, in figure (d), in-degree of vertex V3 is 2 and out-degree of V3 is 1.

8.10   Null Graph

Two vertices are said to be adjacent, if there is an edge between them. A vertex, which is not adjacent to any other vertex in the graph is called an isolated vertex. A graph containing only isolated vertices is called null graph.

8.11   Adjacency Matrix

A standard way to represent a graph in memory is by using an adjacency matrix. A simple directed graph with n nodes v_1, v_2, ... v_n can be represented in memory by following n x n matrix $A=(a_{ij})$.

For a non-weighted graph G:

$$a_{ij} = \begin{cases} 1 & \text{if there is an edge } (v_i, v_j) \text{ from } v_i \text{ to } v_j. \\ 0 & \text{if no edge exists from } v_i \text{ to } v_j. \end{cases}$$

For a weighted graph G:

319

$$a_{ij} = \left\{ \begin{array}{ll} w(e) \text{ if there is an edge } (v_i, v_j) \text{ from } v_i \text{ to } v_j. \\ 0 \quad \text{if no edge exists from } v_i \text{ to } v_j. \end{array} \right\}$$

Where w(e) is the weight of edge (v_i, v_j).

Consider the following non-weighted graph G:

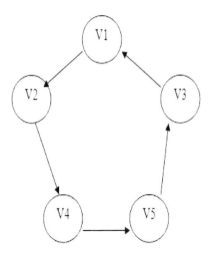

Adjacency matrix A for this graph is:

$$A = \begin{pmatrix} 0 & 1 & 0 & 0 & 0 \\ 0 & 0 & 0 & 1 & 0 \\ 1 & 0 & 0 & 0 & 0 \\ 0 & 0 & 0 & 0 & 1 \\ 0 & 0 & 1 & 0 & 0 \end{pmatrix}$$

An undirected simple graph G can be represented in memory by setting $a_{ij} = a_{ji}$. That is, if there exists an edge e between i and j, then e can be traversed from i to j and also from j to i. Therefore, adjacency matrix for an undirected simple graph is a symmetric matrix.

****

```
/* Implementing simple directed graph using adjacency matrix. */

#include<stdio.h>
#define MAX 100

int adj[MAX][MAX];          /* Adjacency matrix */
int n;                      /* Total number of nodes */

void insert_edge(), delete_edge(), disp();

void main()
{
        int x, i, j;

        printf("Enter number of nodes in the graph\n");
        scanf("%d",&n);

        if(n>MAX)
        {
                printf("Input size is greater than declared size\n");
```

```c
        exit();
}               /* In this program, we will take first node as adj[1][1]
                   and not as adj[0][0]. So don't get confused with it  */

for(i=1;i<=n;i++)
for(j=1;j<=n;j++)
adj[i][j]=0;            /* Create a NULL graph */

while(1)
{
        printf("Enter choice\n");
        printf("1.Insert an edge\n");
        printf("2.Delete an edge\n");
        printf("3.Display the graph\n");
        printf("4.exit\n");
        scanf("%d",&x);

        switch(x)
        {
                case 1:  insert_edge();      break;
                case 2:  delete_edge();      break;
                case 3:  disp();             break;
                case 4:  exit();

        }       /* end switch */

}       /* end while */
}       /* end main */

void insert_edge()
{
        int x, y, wt;

        printf("Enter first node\n");
        scanf("%d",&x);
```

```c
        printf("Enter second node\n");
        scanf("%d",&y);

        if(x>n || x<1 || y>n || y<1)
        {
                printf("Node doesn't exist\n");
                return;
        }

        if(x==y || adj[x][y]!=0)    /* Loops and parallel edges
                                        are not allowed */
        {
          printf("Edge can not be inserted; there is already an edge\n");
                return;
        }

        printf("Enter weight of the edge\n");
        scanf("%d",&wt);

        if(wt==0)
        {
          printf("Weight of an edge should be a non-zero value \n");
                return;
        }

        adj[x][y]=wt;

}   /* end insert_edge */

void delete_edge()
{
        int x, y;

        printf("Enter first node\n");
        scanf("%d",&x);

        printf("Enter second node\n");
        scanf("%d",&y);
```

```
            if(x>n || x<1 || y>n || y<1 || adj[x][y]==0)
            {
                        printf("Edge doesn't exist\n");
                        return;
            }

            adj[x][y]=0;
            printf("Edge is deleted\n");

}  /* end delete_edge */

void disp()
{
            int row, col;

            for(row=1; row<=n; row++)
            for(col=1; col<=n; col++)
            if(adj[row][col]!=0)
    printf("%d->%d (weight: %d)\n", row, col, adj[row][col]);

}   /* end disp */

/*

After executing:

Enter number of nodes in the graph
5
Enter choice
1.Insert an edge
2.Delete an edge
3.Display the graph
4.exit
1
Enter first node
1
Enter second node
2
Enter weight of the edge
1
Enter choice
```

1.Insert an edge
2.Delete an edge
3.Display the graph
4.exit
1
Enter first node
2
Enter second node
3
Enter weight of the edge
1
Enter choice
1.Insert an edge
2.Delete an edge
3.Display the graph
4.exit
1
Enter first node
3
Enter second node
4
Enter weight of the edge
1
Enter choice
1.Insert an edge
2.Delete an edge
3.Display the graph
4.exit
1
Enter first node
4
Enter second node
5
Enter weight of the edge
1
Enter choice
1.Insert an edge
2.Delete an edge
3.Display the graph
4.exit
3
1->2 (weight: 1)
2->3 (weight: 1)
3->4 (weight: 1)
4->5 (weight: 1)
Enter choice

325

```
1.Insert an edge
2.Delete an edge
3.Display the graph
4.exit
2
Enter first node
4
Enter second node
5
Edge is deleted
Enter choice
1.Insert an edge
2.Delete an edge
3.Display the graph
4.exit
4......................................................(terminated)

*/
```

****

Steps of the program:

void insert_edge():

1) We have to insert an edge from node x to node y. If either of the node doesn't belong to the graph then print: "node doesn't exists".

2) If user wants to insert a loop or a parallel edge, then also print a message.

3) Else, assign weight of the edge to element adj[x][y] subject to the condition that weight is of non-zero value.

void delete_edge():

1) We have to delete an edge from node x to node y. If either of the node doesn't belong to the graph or edge doesn't appear in the graph then print: "edge doesn't exist".

2) Else, assign 0 to element adj[x][y] and print: "Edge is deleted".

8.12   Path Matrix

Let G be a simple directed graph with n nodes v_1, v_2, v_3, ... v_n. Then path matrix P of G is a square matrix of order n, which can be defined as follows:

$$P_{ij} = \begin{cases} 1 & \text{if there is a path from } v_i \text{ to } v_j \\ 0 & \text{if no path exists from } v_i \text{ to } v_j \end{cases}$$

EXAMPLE:

Consider the following graph G:

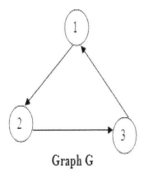

Graph G

Path matrix P for above graph G is:

$$P = \begin{pmatrix} 1 & 1 & 1 \\ 1 & 1 & 1 \\ 1 & 1 & 1 \end{pmatrix}$$

Above matrix P shows that in above graph G, there is a path from every vertex to every other vertex.

8.13   Warshall's Algorithm

For a directed graph G, warshall's algorithm finds the path matrix of G. Consider the following graph:

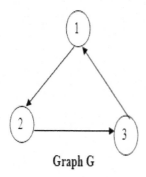

Graph G

Adjacency matrix for this graph is:

$$Adj = \begin{pmatrix} 0 & 1 & 0 \\ 0 & 0 & 1 \\ 0 & 0 & 0 \end{pmatrix}$$

Initially consider that the elements of path matrix P are the same as that of adjacency matrix:

$$P_0 = \begin{pmatrix} 0 & 1 & 0 \\ 0 & 0 & 1 \\ 1 & 0 & 0 \end{pmatrix}$$

Procedure to obtain the final path matrix P_3 from P_0 is as follows:

   a. Consider a graph G_1, adjacency matrix of which is P_0. Now, between any two vertices of G_1, if there is a path from vertex 1, then convert matrix P_0 into P_1 as follows:

329

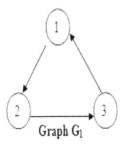

Graph G₁

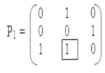

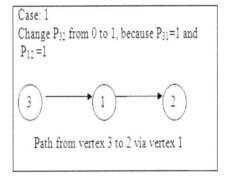

b. Consider a graph G2, adjacency matrix of which is P1. Now, between any two vertices of G2, if there is a path from vertex 2, then convert matrix P1 into P2 as follows:

330

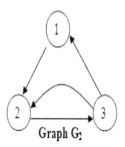

Graph G₂

$$P_2 = \begin{pmatrix} 0 & 1 & \boxed{1} \\ 0 & 0 & 1 \\ 1 & 1 & \boxed{1} \end{pmatrix}$$

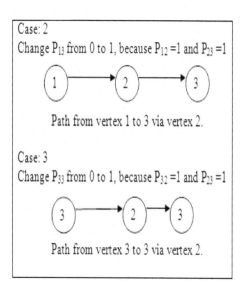

Case: 2
Change P_{13} from 0 to 1, because $P_{12}=1$ and $P_{23}=1$

Path from vertex 1 to 3 via vertex 2.

Case: 3
Change P_{33} from 0 to 1, because $P_{32}=1$ and $P_{23}=1$

Path from vertex 3 to 3 via vertex 2.

   c. Similarly, consider a graph G3, adjacency matrix of which is P2. Now, between any two vertices of G3, if there is a path from vertex 3, then convert matrix P2 into P3 by the same procedure.

331

$$P_3 = \begin{pmatrix} 1 & 1 & 1 \\ 1 & 1 & 1 \\ 1 & 1 & 1 \end{pmatrix}$$

This matrix P_3 is the final path matrix of graph G.

****

/* *Implementation of Warshall's Algorithm* */

```c
#include<stdio.h>
#define MAX 100

int adj[MAX][MAX];
int n;

void insert_edge(), delete_edge(), disp(), warshall();

void main()
{
        int x, i, j;

        printf("Enter number of nodes in the graph\n");
        scanf("%d",&n);

        if(n>MAX)
        {
          printf("Input size is greater than declared size\n");
            exit();
        }

        for(i=1;i<=n;i++)
        for(j=1;j<=n;j++)
        adj[i][j]=0;            /* Create a NULL graph */
```

```c
        while(1)
        {
                printf("Enter choice\n");
                printf("1.Insert an edge\n");
                printf("2.Delete an edge\n");
                printf("3.Display the graph\n");
                printf("4.Path Matrix\n");
                printf("5.exit\n");
                scanf("%d",&x);

                switch(x)
                {
                        case 1:  insert_edge();        break;
                        case 2:  delete_edge();        break;
                        case 3:  disp();               break;
                        case 4:  warshall();           break;
                        case 5:   exit();

                }       /* end switch */
        }       /* end while */
}       /* end main */

void insert_edge()
{
        int x, y;

        printf("Enter first node\n");
        scanf("%d",&x);
        printf("Enter second node\n");
        scanf("%d",&y);

        if(x>n || x<1 || y>n || y<1)
        {
                printf("Node doesn't exist\n");
                return;
        }
```

```c
        if(x==y || adj[x][y]!=0)        /* Loops and parallel edges
                                            are not allowed   */
        {
printf("Edge can not be inserted because there is already an edge\n");
                return;
        }
        adj[x][y]=1;

}  /* end insert_edge */

void delete_edge()
{
        int x, y;

        printf("Enter first node\n");
        scanf("%d",&x);

        printf("Enter second node\n");
        scanf("%d",&y);

        if(x>n || x<1 || y>n || y<1 || adj[x][y]==0)
        {
                printf("Edge doesn't exist\n");
                return;
        }
        adj[x][y]=0;
        printf("Edge is deleted\n");

}  /* end delete_edge */

void disp()
{
        int row, col;
```

334

```
        for(row=1; row<=n; row++)
        for(col=1; col<=n; col++)
        if(adj[row][col]!=0)
            printf("%d->%d\n", row, col);
}  /* end disp */

void warshall()
{
        int i, j, k, P[MAX][MAX];

        for(i=1;i<=n;i++)
        for(j=1;j<=n;j++)
        P[i][j]=adj[i][j];

        for(k=1;k<=n;k++)
        for(i=1;i<=n;i++)
        for(j=1;j<=n;j++)
        P[i][j]=(P[i][j]) || (P[i][k] && P[k][j]);
                /* For each vertex i and j, if there exists a path from i to j
                   via vertex k then change P[i][j] to P[i][k]&&P[k][j] */

        printf("path exists from:\n");

        for(i=1;i<=n;i++)
        for(j=1;j<=n;j++)
        if(P[i][j]!=0)
            printf("%d to %d\n", i, j);
}  /* end warshall */

/*
```

After executing:
Enter number of nodes in the graph
3
Enter choice
1.Insert an edge
2.Delete an edge
3.Display the graph

4.Path Matrix
5.exit
1
Enter first node
1
Enter second node
2
Enter choice
1.Insert an edge
2.Delete an edge
3.Display the graph
4.Path Matrix
5.exit
1
Enter first node
2
Enter second node
3
Enter choice
1.Insert an edge
2.Delete an edge
3.Display the graph
4.Path Matrix
5.exit
1
Enter first node
3
Enter second node
1
Enter choice
1.Insert an edge
2.Delete an edge
3.Display the graph
4.Path Matrix
5.exit
4
path exists from:
1 to 1
1 to 2
1 to 3
2 to 1
2 to 2
2 to 3
3 to 1
3 to 2
3 to 3

****

Steps of the program:

void warshall():

Consider the following graph:

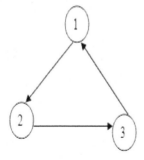

Where path matrix for this graph is:

$$P = \begin{pmatrix} 1 & 1 & 1 \\ 1 & 1 & 1 \\ 1 & 1 & 1 \end{pmatrix}$$

At the start of warshall's algorithm, while obtaining the final path matrix, we had generated three matrices: P_1, P_2 and P_3 in order, where P_3 was the final matrix, which showed the paths between the nodes. In our program, at each iteration of loop

337

'for(k=1;k<=n;k++)', matrix P_k is generated from matrix P_{k-1}. And, at the last iteration of this loop, matrix P_n is generated, which is the final matrix, and shows the paths between the nodes.

Note that, initial path matrix P_0 is the same as that of adjacency matrix.

8.14   Shortest Path Algorithm

A path from source vertex v to destination vertex w may be defined as the shortest path if, it is of minimum length of all the paths from v to w. The shortest paths are not necessarily unique.

Consider the following example:

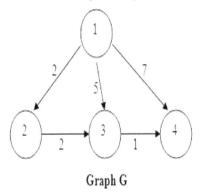

Graph G

In above graph G, the shortest path from vertex 1 to vertex 3 is of length 4, and from vertex 1 to 4 is of length 5. As is evident from the above figure, the shortest path from vertex 1 to 3 is via vertex 2, and from vertex 1 to 4 is via vertex 2 and 3.

338

Shortest path from vertex 1 to 3: 1→ 2 → 3 (weight:4)
Shortest path from vertex 1 to 4: 1→ 2 → 3 → 4 (weight:5)

The **distance** from a vertex x to a vertex y is known as the weight (length) of the shortest path from x to y.

A weighted graph may be maintained in memory by an adjacency matrix. Let G be a directed graph with n nodes, v_1, v_2, v_3, ..., v_n and G is weighted; that is, each edge e in G is assigned a non-negative number w(e), called the weight or length of each edge e. Then G may be maintained in memory by a matrix $A(A=a_{ij})$, defined as follows:

$$a_{ij} = \begin{cases} W(e) & \text{if there is an edge from } v_i \text{ to } v_j \\ 0 & \text{if there is no edge from } v_i \text{ to } v_j \end{cases}$$

Now we can find a matrix say B, which will tell us the lengths of shortest paths between the nodes. More precisely, matrix $B(B=b_{ij})$ can be defined as:
b_{ij} = length of the shortest path from v_i to v_j .

EXAMPLE:

Consider the weighted graph G, in the following figure.

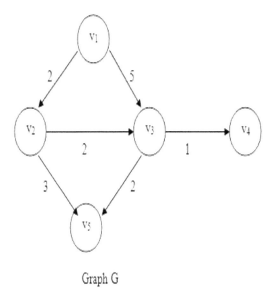

Graph G

This graph can be represented in memory by the following weight matrix:

$$A = \begin{pmatrix} 0 & 2 & 5 & 0 & 0 \\ 0 & 0 & 2 & 0 & 3 \\ 0 & 0 & 0 & 1 & 2 \\ 0 & 0 & 0 & 0 & 0 \\ 0 & 0 & 0 & 0 & 0 \end{pmatrix}$$

Matrix B, which contains the lengths of shortest paths between the nodes, can be obtained by the following steps:

Initially consider matrix $B(B=b_{ij})$ is

$$b_{ij} = \begin{cases} W(e) & \text{if there is an edge } e \text{ from vertex } v_i \text{ to } v_j \\ \infty & \text{if there is no edge from vertex } v_i \text{ to } v_j \end{cases}$$

We consider a matrix B_0, where

$$B_0 = \begin{pmatrix} \infty & 2 & 5 & \infty & \infty \\ \infty & \infty & 2 & \infty & 3 \\ \infty & \infty & \infty & 1 & 2 \\ \infty & \infty & \infty & \infty & \infty \\ \infty & \infty & \infty & \infty & \infty \end{pmatrix}, \quad \begin{pmatrix} v_{11} & v_{12} & v_{13} & v_{14} & v_{15} \\ v_{21} & v_{22} & v_{23} & v_{24} & v_{25} \\ v_{31} & v_{32} & v_{33} & v_{34} & v_{35} \\ v_{41} & v_{42} & v_{43} & v_{44} & v_{45} \\ v_{51} & v_{52} & v_{53} & v_{54} & v_{55} \end{pmatrix}$$

Consider a graph G, adjacency matrix of which is B_0. For every vertex v_i and v_j ($1 \le i, j \le n$) of G, if there is any shorter path from v_i to v_j via vertex v_1, then convert matrix B_0 into B_1. Here, for each i and j, matrix B_1 can be generated by changing the weight of v_{ij} to $v_{i1}+v_{1j}$, if $v_{i1}+v_{1j}$ is less than v_{ij} $\forall\ 1 \le i, j \le n$. (Note that, here B_0 and B_1 are same, but it is not necessarily true in all the cases.

$$B_1 = \begin{pmatrix} \infty & 2 & 5 & \infty & \infty \\ \infty & \infty & 2 & \infty & 3 \\ \infty & \infty & \infty & 1 & 2 \\ \infty & \infty & \infty & \infty & \infty \\ \infty & \infty & \infty & \infty & \infty \end{pmatrix}, \quad \begin{pmatrix} v_{11} & v_{12} & v_{13} & v_{14} & v_{15} \\ v_{21} & v_{22} & v_{23} & v_{24} & v_{25} \\ v_{31} & v_{32} & v_{33} & v_{34} & v_{35} \\ v_{41} & v_{42} & v_{43} & v_{44} & v_{45} \\ v_{51} & v_{52} & v_{53} & v_{54} & v_{55} \end{pmatrix}$$

Now consider another graph say G_1, adjacency matrix of which is B_1. For every vertex v_i and v_j ($1\le i, j \le n$) of G_1, if there is a shorter path from v_i to v_j via v_2, then convert matrix B_1 into B_2 by the same procedure.

Note: Each matrix B_x can be generated by changing the weight of v_{ij} to $v_{ix}+v_{xj}$, if $v_{ix}+v_{xj}$ is less than v_{ij}.

$$B_2 = \begin{pmatrix} \infty & 2 & \boxed{4} & \infty & \boxed{5} \\ \infty & \infty & 2 & \infty & 3 \\ \infty & \infty & \infty & 1 & 2 \\ \infty & \infty & \infty & \infty & \infty \\ \infty & \infty & \infty & \infty & \infty \end{pmatrix} , \quad \begin{pmatrix} v_{11} & v_{12} & v_{13} & v_{14} & v_{15} \\ v_{21} & v_{22} & v_{23} & v_{24} & v_{25} \\ v_{31} & v_{32} & v_{33} & v_{34} & v_{35} \\ v_{41} & v_{42} & v_{43} & v_{44} & v_{45} \\ v_{51} & v_{52} & v_{53} & v_{54} & v_{55} \end{pmatrix}$$

In this way, following matrices: B_3, B_4 and B_5 can be generated in order.

$$B_3 = \begin{pmatrix} \infty & 2 & 4 & 5 & 5 \\ \infty & \infty & 2 & 3 & 3 \\ \infty & \infty & \infty & 1 & 2 \\ \infty & \infty & \infty & \infty & \infty \\ \infty & \infty & \infty & \infty & \infty \end{pmatrix} , \quad \begin{pmatrix} v_{11} & v_{12} & v_{13} & v_{14} & v_{15} \\ v_{21} & v_{22} & v_{23} & v_{24} & v_{25} \\ v_{31} & v_{32} & v_{33} & v_{34} & v_{35} \\ v_{41} & v_{42} & v_{43} & v_{44} & v_{45} \\ v_{51} & v_{52} & v_{53} & v_{54} & v_{55} \end{pmatrix}$$

$$B_4 = \begin{pmatrix} \infty & 2 & 4 & 5 & 5 \\ \infty & \infty & 2 & 3 & 3 \\ \infty & \infty & \infty & 1 & 2 \\ \infty & \infty & \infty & \infty & \infty \\ \infty & \infty & \infty & \infty & \infty \end{pmatrix}, \quad \begin{pmatrix} v_{11} & v_{12} & v_{13} & v_{14} & v_{15} \\ v_{21} & v_{22} & v_{23} & v_{24} & v_{25} \\ v_{31} & v_{32} & v_{33} & v_{34} & v_{35} \\ v_{41} & v_{42} & v_{43} & v_{44} & v_{45} \\ v_{51} & v_{52} & v_{53} & v_{54} & v_{55} \end{pmatrix}$$

$$B_5 = \begin{pmatrix} \infty & 2 & 4 & 5 & 5 \\ \infty & \infty & 2 & 3 & 3 \\ \infty & \infty & \infty & 1 & 2 \\ \infty & \infty & \infty & \infty & \infty \\ \infty & \infty & \infty & \infty & \infty \end{pmatrix}, \quad \begin{pmatrix} v_{11} & v_{12} & v_{13} & v_{14} & v_{15} \\ v_{21} & v_{22} & v_{23} & v_{24} & v_{25} \\ v_{31} & v_{32} & v_{33} & v_{34} & v_{35} \\ v_{41} & v_{42} & v_{43} & v_{44} & v_{45} \\ v_{51} & v_{52} & v_{53} & v_{54} & v_{55} \end{pmatrix}$$

Here B_5 is the final matrix, which shows the shortest paths between the nodes. For aforesaid graph G, shortest path:

From vertex 1 to 2 is of length: 2
From vertex 1 to 3 is of length: 4
From vertex 1 to 4 is of length: 5
From vertex 1 to 5 is of length: 5
From vertex 2 to 3 is of length: 2
From vertex 2 to 4 is of length: 3
From vertex 2 to 5 is of length: 3
From vertex 3 to 4 is of length: 1
From vertex 3 to 5 is of length: 2

```
************************************************
/* Implementation of shortest path algorithm  */

#include<stdio.h>
#define INF 9999
#define MAX 100

int adj[MAX][MAX], n;
void insert_edge(), delete_edge(), disp(), shortest_path(int, int);
int min(int, int);

void main()
{
            int x, i, j;

        printf("Enter the number of nodes in the graph\n");
            scanf("%d",&n);

            if(n>MAX)
            {
        printf("Input size is greater than declared size\n");
                    exit();
            }
            for(i=1;i<=n;i++)
            for(j=1;j<=n;j++)
            adj[i][j]=0;            /* Create a NULL graph  */

            while(1)
            {
                    printf("Enter choice\n");
                    printf("1.Insert an edge\n");
                    printf("2.Delete an edge\n");
                    printf("3.Display the graph\n");
                    printf("4.Shortest path\n");
                    printf("5.Exit\n");
                    scanf("%d",&x);
```

```c
                switch(x)
                {
                        case 1: insert_edge();    break;
                        case 2: delete_edge();    break;
                        case 3: disp();                break;
                        case 4:
                        printf("Enter source vertex\n");
                                scanf("%d",&i);
                        printf("Enter destination vertex\n");
                                scanf("%d",&j);
                                shortest_path(i, j);    break;

                        case 5:  exit();

                }    /* end switch */

        }    /* end while */

}   /* end main */

void insert_edge()
{
        int x, y, wt;

        printf("Enter first node\n");
        scanf("%d",&x);

        printf("Enter second node\n");
        scanf("%d",&y);

        if(x>n || x<1 || y>n || y<1)
        {
                printf("Node doesn't exist\n");
                return;
        }
```

```c
        if(x==y || adj[x][y]!=0)        /* Loops and parallel edges
                                            are not allowed   */
        {
printf("Edge can not be inserted since there is already an edge\n");
                        return;
        }
        printf("Enter weight of the edge\n");
        scanf("%d",&wt);

        if(wt==0)
        {
printf("Weight of an edge should be a non-zero value \n");
                        return;
        }
        adj[x][y]=wt;
}    /* end insert_edge */
void delete_edge()
{
        int x, y;

        printf("Enter first node\n");
        scanf("%d",&x);

        printf("Enter second node\n");
        scanf("%d",&y);

        if(x>n || x<1 || y>n || y<1 || adj[x][y]==0)
        {
                printf("Edge doesn't exist\n");
                return;
        }
        adj[x][y]=0;
        printf("Edge is deleted\n");
}  /* end delete_edge */
```

```
void disp()
{
        int row, col;

        for(row=1; row<=n; row++)
        for(col=1; col<=n; col++)
        if(adj[row][col]!=0)
    printf("%d->%d (weight: %d)\n", row, col, adj[row][col]);

} /* end disp */

void shortest_path(int x, int y)
{
        int i, j, k, B[MAX][MAX];

        for(i=1;i<=n;i++)
        for(j=1;j<=n;j++)
        if(adj[i][j]==0)
        B[i][j]=INF;
        else
        B[i][j]=adj[i][j];        /* Initial matrix 'B'(B0) is same as that of
                                     adjacency matrix, except that, in place of
                                     zeros in adjacency matrix, matrix 'B'
                                     contains INF(infinity) */

        for(k=1;k<=n;k++)
        for(i=1;i<=n;i++)
        for(j=1;j<=n;j++)
        B[i][j]=min(B[i][j], B[i][k]+B[k][j]);
                                  /* For each vertex i and j, if there exists a shorter path
                                     from i to j via vertex k then change the length of
                                     shortest path B[i][j] to B[i][k]+B[k][j] */

        if(B[x][y]>=INF)
printf("path does not exist between vertices: %d and %d\n", x, y);
        else
printf("Shortest path between vertices: %d and %d is of length: %d\n", x, y, B[x][y]);

} /* end shortest_path */
```

```
int min(int x, int y)
{
    if(x<y)
    return x;
    else
    return y;

}   /* end min */

/*

After executing:

Enter the number of nodes in the graph
3
Enter choice
1.Insert an edge
2.Delete an edge
3.Display the graph
4.Shortest path
5.Exit
1
Enter first node
1
Enter second node
3
Enter weight of the edge
5
Enter choice
1.Insert an edge
2.Delete an edge
3.Display the graph
4.Shortest path
5.Exit
1
Enter first node
1
Enter second node
2
Enter weight of the edge
2
Enter choice
1.Insert an edge
2.Delete an edge
```

****

Steps of the program:

Consider the following example, where graph G is as shown below:

349

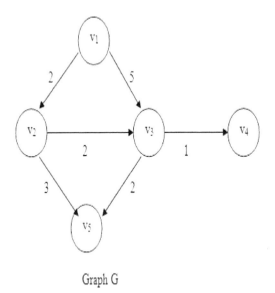

Graph G

In the beginning of shortest path algorithm, while obtaining the shortest paths between the nodes, we had generated five matrices: B_1, B_2, B_3, B_4 and B_5 in order. Among these matrices, B_5 was the final matrix, which showed the shortest paths between the nodes. In our program, at each iteration of loop 'for(k=1;k<=n;k++)', matrix B_k is generated from matrix B_{k-1}. And, at the last iteration of this loop, matrix B_n is generated, which is the final matrix, and contains the lengths of shortest paths between the nodes.

8.15   GRAPH COLORING

Suppose we are given an undirected graph G, and a positive integer m. Then coloring of graph G with m given colors is the process of coloring the nodes of G in such a way, that no

350

two adjacent nodes have the same color. Note that, if d is the degree of the given graph, then it can be colored with d+1 colors. However, it depends upon the graph as to how much minimum number of colors are needed to color it. But, for a complete graph, minimum d+1 colors are required. The minimum number of colors, with which a graph G can be colored, is called the chromatic number of the graph. For example, the graph in the following figure can be colored with three colors 1, 2, and 3. It can be seen that minimum 3 colors are needed to color this graph and hence this graph's chromatic number is 3.

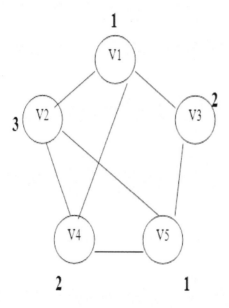

An example of graph coloring

The following program prints all the solutions of coloring the graph with m given colors.

```
************************************************

/*  Implementation of graph coloring  */

#include<stdio.h>
#define MAX 100

int adj[MAX][MAX];        /*    Adjacency matrix    */
int n;                    /*    Total number of nodes      */
int m;                    /*    Total number of colors    */
int color[MAX];           /*    'color' array will contain the solutions i.e.
                               color[x] will contain the color which have
                               been assigned to node 'x'  */

void insert_edge(), delete_edge(), disp(), start_coloring(int), nextcolor(int);

void main()
{
          int x, i, j;
          printf("Enter number of nodes in the graph\n");
          scanf("%d",&n);

          if(n>MAX)
          {
          printf("Input size is greater than declared size\n");
               exit();
          }

          for(i=1;i<=n;i++)
          for(j=1;j<=n;j++)
          adj[i][j]=0;              /*    Create a NULL graph  */

          while(1)
          {
                    printf("Enter choice\n");
                    printf("1.Insert an edge\n");
                    printf("2.Delete an edge\n");
                    printf("3.Display the graph\n");
```

352

```c
                printf("4.To color the graph\n");
                printf("5.exit\n");
                scanf("%d",&x);

                switch(x)
                {
                        case 1:  insert_edge();      break;
                        case 2:  delete_edge();      break;
                        case 3:  disp();             break;
                        case 4:
                        printf("Enter number of colors\n");
                                scanf("%d",&m);

                                for(i=1;i<=n;i++)
                                color[i]=0;

                                start_coloring(1);   break;
                        case 5:  exit();
                }   /* end switch */
        }   /* end while */
}   /* end main */

void insert_edge()
{
        int x, y;

        printf("Enter first node\n");
        scanf("%d",&x);

        printf("Enter second node\n");
        scanf("%d",&y);

        if(x>n || x<1 || y>n || y<1)
        {
                printf("Node doesn't exist\n");
```
353

```c
                        return;
            }
            if(x==y || adj[x][y]!=0)        /* Loops and parallel edges
                                                are not allowed */
            {
printf("Edge can not be inserted since there is already an edge\n");
                        return;
            }
            adj[x][y]=adj[y][x]=1;
                        /* Note that it is an undirected graph, so in adjacency
                        matrix, adj[x][y] and adj[y][x] will contain equal
                        values, which means that there will be an edge
                        from x to y and also from y to x */
}  /* end insert_edge */

void delete_edge()
{
            int x, y;

            printf("Enter first node\n");
            scanf("%d",&x);

            printf("Enter second node\n");
            scanf("%d",&y);

            if(x>n || x<1 || y>n || y<1 || adj[x][y]==0)
            {
                        printf("Edge doesn't exist\n");
                        return;
            }
            adj[x][y]=adj[y][x]=0;

            printf("Edge is deleted\n");
}  /* end delete_edge */
```

```c
void disp()
{
        int row, col;

        for(row=1; row<=n; row++)
        for(col=row+1; col<=n; col++)
        if(adj[row][col]!=0)
        printf("%d<->%d \n", row, col);

} /* end disp */

void start_coloring(int k)
{
        int i;

        while(1)
        {
                nextcolor(k);    /* Generate all possible colors for
                                    node 'k' */

                if(color[k]==0)
                return;          /* If no new color can be assigned to
                                    node 'k', then return */
                if(k==n)
                {
                        printf("\n");
                        for(i=1;i<=n;i++)
                        printf("node: %d color: %d \n", i, color[i]);
                }
                else
                start_coloring(k+1);    /* Choose a color for
                                           node 'k+1' */

        } /* end while */

} /* end start_coloring */
```

355

```
void nextcolor(int k)
{
          int j;

          while(1)
          {
                    color[k]=(color[k]+1)%(m+1);
                              /* If previously color[k] was assigned to node 'k',
                                 then this time assign color[k]+1 to node 'k' */
                    if(color[k]==0)
                    return;        /* If all the possible colors have been
                                      used for node 'k', then return */

                    for(j=1;j<=k-1;j++)
                    if(adj[k][j]!=0 && color[k]==color[j])
                    break;         /* For each adjacent node 'j' of 'k' if
                                      color[k] and color[j] are same, then try
                                      to assign another color to node 'k' */
                    if(j==k)
                    return;

          } /* end while */

} /* end nextcolor */
```

/*

After executing:

Enter number of nodes in the graph
4
Enter choice
1.Insert an edge
2.Delete an edge
3.Display the graph
4.To color the graph
5.exit
1
Enter first node
1
Enter second node
2

356

Enter choice
1.Insert an edge
2.Delete an edge
3.Display the graph
4.To color the graph
5.exit
1
Enter first node
2
Enter second node
3
Enter choice
1.Insert an edge
2.Delete an edge
3.Display the graph
4.To color the graph
5.exit
1
Enter first node
3
Enter second node
4
Enter choice
1.Insert an edge
2.Delete an edge
3.Display the graph
4.To color the graph
5.exit
1
Enter first node
4
Enter second node
1
Enter choice
1.Insert an edge
2.Delete an edge
3.Display the graph
4.To color the graph
5.exit
4
Enter number of colors
2

node: 1 color: 1
node: 2 color: 2
node: 3 color: 1

357

node: 4 color: 2

node: 1 color: 2
node: 2 color: 1
node: 3 color: 2
node: 4 color: 1
Enter choice
1.Insert an edge
2.Delete an edge
3.Display the graph
4.To color the graph
5.exit
5 ... ... (Terminated)

*/

****

Steps of the program:

void start_coloring(int k):

1) Call 'nextcolor(k)', which assigns a color to node 'k' and assign 0 if there is no new color that can be assigned to 'k'.

2) If there is no new color that can be assigned to node 'k' that is if 0 has been assigned to k, then return.

3) If all the nodes of the graph have been colored, then print the solution. Else repeat the same procedure for node 'k+1'.

In this function 'while' loop is an infinite loop, which is used for backtracking. Suppose, first solution is printed for n number of nodes, then to find the next solution, a different color is assigned to node n. In case, if no new color is possible for node n, then a distinct color is assigned to node n-1. After assigning a distinct color to node n-1, all the

358

possible legal colors for node n are generated. Again, if no distinct color is possible for node n-1, then this method is repeated for node n-2, and so on i.e. this procedure is repeated for all the nodes 1 to n.

void nextcolor(int k):

1) Statement 'color[k]=(color[k]+1)%(m+1)' assigns the next higher color to node k i.e. if previously k was colored with color x, then this time it will be assigned color x+1. And if all the colors have been used for k (considering the previous color to be m) then 0 will be assigned to it.

2) Return, if 0 has been assigned to k.

3) For each node j, which has been assigned a color, check that if j is adjacent to k or not. If j is adjacent to node k, then verify that node j contains a color other than color[k]. If not, then again repeat the above procedure for assigning a different color to k.

8.16   HAMILTONIAN CYCLES

Let G be a connected graph with n vertices. It may be a directed graph or an undirected graph. Then a Hamiltonian cycle can be defined as a circular path (of length n) along n edges of G, that explores every vertex once and returns to its starting vertex. Suppose G is a graph with n vertices: V_1, V_2, V_3.......V_n , then a Hamiltonian cycle is defined as a path: P_1, P_2, P_3,........., P_n, P_1.
where $P_i = V_j$. ($1 \le i, j \le n$). And
$P_i \ne P_j \, \forall \, i \ne j$ ($1 \le i, j \le n$).

359

EXAMPLE:

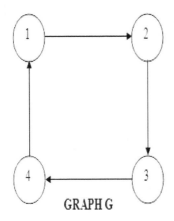

GRAPH G

Hamiltonian cycles in this graph are:

1 2 3 4 1

2 3 4 1 2

3 4 1 2 3

4 1 2 3 4

Now consider the following graph:

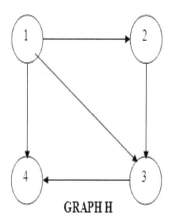

GRAPH H

This graph doesn't contain any Hamiltonian cycle.

The following program prints all the Hamiltonian cycles of a simple directed graph.

****

```
/* Program to print all the Hamiltonian cycles of a simple directed graph */

#include<stdio.h>
#define MAX 100

int adj[MAX][MAX];        /* Adjacency matrix */
int n;                    /* Total number of nodes */
int solution[MAX];

void insert_edge(), delete_edge(), disp();
void hamiltonian(int), nextvertex(int);

void main()
{
        int x, i, j;
```

```c
printf("Enter number of nodes in the graph\n");
scanf("%d",&n);

if(n>MAX)
{
printf("Input size is greater than declared size\n");
    exit();
}

for(i=1;i<=n;i++)
for(j=1;j<=n;j++)
adj[i][j]=0;          /* Create a NULL graph  */

while(1)
{
        printf("Enter choice\n");
        printf("1.Insert an edge\n");
        printf("2.Delete an edge\n");
printf("3.To print all the Hamiltonian cycles of the graph\n");
        printf("4.Display the graph\n");
        printf("5.exit\n");
        scanf("%d",&x);

        switch(x)
        {

                case 1:  insert_edge();    break;
                case 2:  delete_edge();    break;
                case 3:  hamiltonian(1);   break;
                case 4:  disp();           break;
                case 5:  exit();

        }    /* end switch  */

    }    /* end while  */

}  /* end main  */
```

362

```
void insert_edge()
{
        int x, y;

        printf("Enter first node\n");
        scanf("%d",&x);

        printf("Enter second node\n");
        scanf("%d",&y);

        if(x>n || x<1 || y>n || y<1)
        {
                printf("Node doesn't exist\n");
                return;
        }

        if(x==y || adj[x][y]!=0)    /* Loops and parallel edges
                                       are not allowed */
        {
printf("Edge can not be inserted since there is already an edge\n");
                return;
        }

        adj[x][y]=1;
}  /* end insert_edge */

void delete_edge()
{
        int x, y;

        printf("Enter first node\n");
        scanf("%d",&x);

        printf("Enter second node\n");
        scanf("%d",&y);

        if(x>n || x<1 || y>n || y<1 || adj[x][y]==0)
        {
```

363

```c
                printf("Edge doesn't exist\n");
                return;
        }
        adj[x][y]=0;
        printf("Edge is deleted\n");
}   /* end delete_edge */

void disp()
{
        int row, col;

        for(row=1; row<=n; row++)
        for(col=1; col<=n; col++)
        if(adj[row][col]!=0)
        printf("%d->%d \n", row, col);
}  /* end disp */

void hamiltonian(int k)
{
        int i;

        while(1)
        {
                nextvertex(k);
                /* This function assigns a vertex to solution[k], if there
                   is an edge from solution[k-1] to that vertex */
                if(solution[k]==0)
                return;

                if(k==n)
                {
                        for(i=1; i<=n; i++)
                        printf("%d ",solution[i]);
```

```
                    printf("\n");
                }
                else
                    hamiltonian(k+1);

        }    /* end while */

}    /* end hamiltonian */


void nextvertex(int k)
{
        int j;
        while(1)
        {
                solution[k]=(solution[k]+1)%(n+1);
                            /* Assign the next highest vertex
                               possible to solution[k]  */
                if(solution[k]==0 || k==1)
                return;

                if(adj[solution[k-1]][solution[k]]!=0)
                {
                        for(j=1;j<=k-1;j++)
                        if(solution[j]==solution[k])
                        break;
                                /* If vertex has already been added
                                   in array 'solution', then break  */

                        if(j==k)    /* It means that, vertex(recently
                                       added) is distinct */
        if( (k<n) || ((k==n) && adj[solution[n]][solution[1]]!=0) )
                        return;

                }    /* end if */

        }    /* end while */

}    /* end nextvertex */
```

365

/*

After executing:

Enter number of nodes in the graph
4
Enter choice
1.Insert an edge
2.Delete an edge
3.To print all the Hamiltonian cycles of the graph
4.Display the graph
5.exit
1
Enter first node
1
Enter second node
2
Enter choice
1.Insert an edge
2.Delete an edge
3.To print all the Hamiltonian cycles of the graph
4.Display the graph
1
Enter first node
2
Enter second node
3
Enter choice
1.Insert an edge
2.Delete an edge
3.To print all the Hamiltonian cycles of the graph
4.Display the graph
5.exit
1
Enter first node
3
Enter second node
4
Enter choice
1.Insert an edge
2.Delete an edge
3.To print all the Hamiltonian cycles of the graph
4.Display the graph
5.exit
1
Enter first node

366

```
4
Enter second node
1
Enter choice
1.Insert an edge
2.Delete an edge
3.To print all the Hamiltonian cycles of the graph
4.Display the graph
5.exit
4
1->2
2->3
3->4
4->1
Enter choice
1.Insert an edge
2.Delete an edge
3.To print all the Hamiltonian cycles of the graph
4.Display the graph
5.exit
3
1 2 3 4
2 3 4 1
3 4 1 2
4 1 2 3
Enter choice
1.Insert an edge
2.Delete an edge
3.To print all the Hamiltonian cycles of the graph
4.Display the graph
5.exit
5.......................................(terminated)

*/
```

****

Steps of the program:

void hamiltonian(int k):

1) Call 'nextvertex(k)', which assigns a vertex say x to solution[k], only when there is an edge from vertex

'solution[k-1]' to x. If no vertex can be assigned to solution[k], then 0 is assigned to solution[k].

2) If no new vertex is possible, then return.

3) If a solution is found then print it. Else, repeat above procedure (call recursive function 'hamiltonian') for k+1.

In this function, 'while' loop is an infinite loop, which is used for backtracking. Suppose first Hamiltonian cycle is printed, then to find the next cycle, a different vertex is assigned to solution[k]. In case, if no new vertex is possible, then a distinct vertex is assigned to solution[k-1]. After assigning a distinct vertex to solution[k-1], all the possible legal vertices for solution[k] are generated. Again, if no distinct vertex is possible for 'solution[k-1]', then this method is repeated for solution[k-2] and so on.

void nextvertex(int k):

1) Statement 'solution[k]=(solution[k]+1)%(n+1)' assigns the next higher vertex to solution[k] which means that if previously suppose x was assigned to solution[k] then this time x+1 will be assigned to solution[k]. And if all the vertices have been used for solution[k] (considering previous vertex to be n), then 0 will be assigned to it.

2) Return if all the vertices have been used for solution[k].

3) If there is no edge from 'solution[k-1]' to 'solution[k]' or vertex 'solution[k]', which has been recently added in array 'solution', already exists in

the array then reiterate   the above procedure (i.e. assign next higher vertex to 'solution[k]').

4) Else, if k=n then verify that there is an edge from solution[k] to solution[1]. Thus   make sure that vertex 'solution[k]' forms a cycle and return.

8.17   Adjacency List

A graph can also be represented in memory by using adjacency list. The adjacency-list representation of graph G=(V, E) with n nodes consists of an array of pointers 'adj' of order n, each element of which points to a list. For example, adj[i] $(1 \leq i \leq n)$ will point to a list $j_1, j_2, \ldots\ldots\ldots j_k$, such that there exists an edge from i to j_x $(1 \leq x \leq k)$. Consider the following graph:

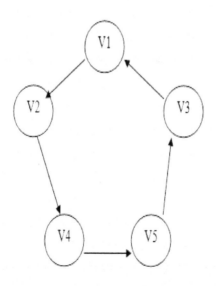

This graph can be represented by the following adjacency list:

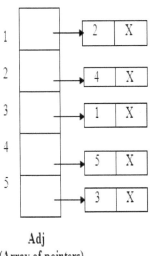

Adj
(Array of pointers)

If there is a weight associated with each edge, then we can declare another field say 'weight' in each node of the list and can store it with vertex v in that list.

****

/* *Implementation of simple directed graph using adjacency list* */

```
#include<stdio.h>
#include<alloc.h>
#define MAX 100

typedef struct graph_type
{
        int vertex;
```

370

```c
        int weight;
        struct graph_type *next;
}graph;

graph *adj[MAX];
int n;

void insert_edge(), delete_edge(), disp();

void main()
{
        int x, i;

        printf("Enter number of nodes in the graph\n");
        scanf("%d",&n);

        if(n>MAX)
        {
        printf("Input size is greater than declared size\n");
                exit();
        }

        for(i=1;i<=n;i++)
        adj[i]=NULL;                    /* Create a NULL graph */

        while(1)
        {
                printf("Enter choice\n");
                printf("1.Insert an edge\n");
                printf("2.Delete an edge\n");
                printf("3.Display the graph\n");
                printf("4.exit\n");
                scanf("%d",&x);

                switch(x)
                {
                        case 1:  insert_edge();        break;
```

371

```
                    case 2:  delete_edge();        break;
                    case 3:    disp();              break;
                    case 4:    exit();
              }          /*   end switch   */
       }          /*    end  while   */
}        /* end main   */

void insert_edge()
{
          int a, b, wt;
          graph *ptr;

          printf("Enter first node\n");
          scanf("%d",&a);
          printf("Enter second node\n");
          scanf("%d",&b);
          printf("enter weight of edge\n");
          scanf("%d",&wt);

          if(a>n || a<1 || b>n || b<1|| a==b)
          {
               printf("error\n");
               return;
          }

          ptr=adj[a];

          while(ptr!=NULL)
          {
               if((*ptr).vertex==b)  /* if there is already an edge */
               {
                     printf("error\n");
                     return;
```

372

```
                }
                ptr=(*ptr).next;

        }  /* end while */
        ptr=(graph *)malloc(sizeof(graph));
        if(ptr==NULL)
        {
                printf("no space\n");
                return;
        }
        (*ptr).vertex=b;
        (*ptr).weight=wt;
        (*ptr).next=adj[a];
        adj[a]=ptr; /* Make 'ptr' as the starting node of list 'adj[a]' */
}  /* end insert_edge */

void delete_edge()
{
        int a, b;
        graph *ptr, *prev;

        printf("Enter first node\n");
        scanf("%d",&a);
        printf("Enter second node\n");
        scanf("%d",&b);

        if(a>n || a<1|| b>n || b<1 || a==b)
        {
                printf("error\n");
                return;
        }

        ptr=adj[a];
```

373

```c
        while(ptr!=NULL && (*ptr).vertex!=b)
        ptr=(*ptr).next;

        if(ptr==NULL)
        {
                printf("error\n");
                return;
        }

        if(ptr==adj[a])
        {
            adj[a]=(*ptr).next;
            free(ptr);
            return;
        }

        prev=adj[a];

        while((*prev).next!=ptr)
        prev=(*prev).next;

        (*prev).next=(*ptr).next;
        free(ptr);

}  /* end delete_edge */

void disp()
{
        graph *ptr;
        int i;

        for(i=1;i<=n;i++)
        {
                ptr=adj[i];

                while(ptr!=NULL)
                {
printf("%d→%d (weight:%d) \n", i, (*ptr).vertex, (*ptr).weight);
```

```
                        ptr=(*ptr).next;
            }

      } /* end for */

} /* end disp */

/*

After executing:

Enter number of nodes in the graph
4
Enter choice
1.Insert an edge
2.Delete an edge
3.Display the graph
4.exit
1
Enter first node
1
Enter second node
2
enter weight of edge
2
Enter choice
1.Insert an edge
2.Delete an edge
3.Display the graph
4.exit
1
Enter first node
2
Enter second node
3
enter weight of edge
3
Enter choice
1.Insert an edge
2.Delete an edge
3.Display the graph
4.exit
1
Enter first node
3
```

Enter second node
4
enter weight of edge
4
Enter choice
1.Insert an edge
2.Delete an edge
3.Display the graph
4.exit
1
Enter first node
4
Enter second node
1
enter weight of edge
5
Enter choice
1.Insert an edge
2.Delete an edge
3.Display the graph
4.exit
3
1-->2 (weight:2)
2-->3 (weight:3)
3-->4 (weight:4)
4-->1 (weight:5)
Enter choice
1.Insert an edge
2.Delete an edge
3.Display the graph
4.exit
2
Enter first node
4
Enter second node
1
Enter choice
1.Insert an edge
2.Delete an edge
3.Display the graph
4.exit
3
1-->2 (weight:2)
2-->3 (weight:3)
3-->4 (weight:4)
Enter choice

376

****

Steps of the program:

void insert_edge():

Consider that the edge 'e' is to be inserted from vertex 'a' to vertex 'b'; perform the following steps to accomplish this:

1) If vertex 'b' is already present in adjacency list of 'adj[a]' i.e. if there exists an edge from 'a' to 'b', then print: error.

2) Else, insert 'b' into a's adjacency list 'adj[a]'.

void delete_edge():

Consider that the edge, which is to be deleted, is from vertex 'a' to vertex 'b'; perform the following steps to delete this edge:

1) If vertex 'b' is not present in adjacency list of 'adj[a]', i.e. an edge from 'a' to 'b' doesn't exist, then print: error.

2) Else, remove it from the adjacency list of 'adj[a]'.

377

8.18   Graph Traversal

For traversing a graph in a systematic order, there are two techniques:

- Depth First Search
- Breadth First Search

Depth First Search(DFS):

Traversing in a graph is the process of exploring all the vertices of the graph one by one in some systematic order. Suppose we start traversing from node A of the graph, then procedure for Depth First Search is as under:

First we examine starting node A. Then we inspect a neighbor of A say B, then a neighbor of B, and so on. When we reach at the dead state that is if no new vertex can be explored, then we backtrack and examine the another neighbor of the previously explored vertex, until all the nodes of the graph have been processed. In Depth First Search, backtracking can take place by maintaining a stack in memory for all the previously processed vertices.

Note: Graph may be directed or undirected.

EXAMPLE:

Consider the following undirected graph G:

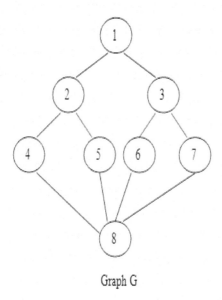

Graph G

For above graph G, if the starting node is 1, then the Depth First Search algorithm will work as follows:

1) Initially print:1 and push it onto the stack.

2) Print first neighbor of vertex:1, which is 2 and push it onto the stack.

   Print: 2, STACK: 1   2

3) Print 4(first neighbor of vertex numbered 2) and push it onto the stack.

   Print: 4, STACK: 1   2   4

4) Now process vertex numbered 8 as above(first neighbor of 4).

Print: 8,   STACK: 1   2   4   8

5) Similarly, process vertex numbered 5(a neighbor of 8).

Print: 5,   STACK: 1   2   4   8   5

6) Now, we will have to use backtracking, because both of the neighbors 2 and 8 of vertex numbered 5 have been explored. So pop the top element 5 from the stack, and process vertex numbered 6, which is another neighbor of top element 8 of the stack.

Print: 6,   STACK: 1   2   4   8   6

7) Process 3(a neighbor of 6) as above:

Print: 3,   STACK: 1   2   4   8   6   3

8) Process 7(a neighbor of 3) as above:

Print: 7,   STACK: 1   2   4   8   6   3   7

Now there is no new vertex possible that we can reach via vertex 7. So start popping each element from the stack, use backtracking, until we get another vertex which has not been explored yet, or stack gets empty. But in our graph G, there is no other vertex that has not been explored. So the stack gets empty. In this way, the Depth First Search starting at node 1 is now complete, and following solution is printed for graph G:

1   2   4   8   5   6   3   7

Breadth First Search(BFS):

Suppose we start traversing from node A of a given graph. Then Breadth First Search algorithm works as follows:

Initially we visit the starting node A. Then we visit all the neighbors of A. Thereafter all the neighbors of neighbors of A and so on. This can be accomplished by using a queue. After examining a node say 'A', insert all of its neighbors into a queue and thereafter delete node 'A' from the queue.

Note: Graph may be directed or undirected.

EXAMPLE:

Consider the following graph:

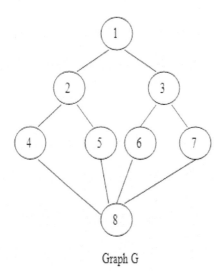

Graph G

For above graph G, if the starting node is 1, then the Breadth First Search algorithm will work as follows:

a) Initially add 1 to the queue.

> Front: 1,   Queue: 1
> Rear: 1

b) Print and remove the front element 1 of the queue and add all its neighbors(2 and 3), to the queue.

> Front: 2,   Queue: ∅ 2 3
> Rear: 3,   Print: 1

c) Again, delete the front element 2 of the queue, print it, and add its neighbors 4 and 5, to the queue.(Note that, here node 1, which is a neighbor of 2, has not been added to the queue, because it has already been processed).

> Front: 3,   Queue: ∅ ∅ 3 4 5
> Rear:5,   Print: 2

d) Print and delete front element 3 of the queue and add its neighbors 6 and 7, to the queue(Again, node 1, a neighbor of 3, has not been added to the queue, because it has already been processed).

> Front: 4,   Queue: ∅ ∅ ∅ 4 5 6 7
> Rear: 7,   Print: 3

e) Now, print and remove front element 4, and add the neighbors of 4 to the queue as follows:

> Front: 5,   Queue: ∅ ∅ ∅ ∅ 5 6 7 8
> Rear: 8,   Print: 4

f) Print and remove front element 5 of the queue. As, all the neighbors of 5 have already been explored, so, there is no other element as of now, which can be appended to the queue.

Front: 6,   Queue: ∅ ∅ ∅ ∅ ∅ 6 7 8
Rear: 8,   Print: 5

g) Also, the neighbors of front element 6 have already been processed. So print and delete it from the queue.

Front: 7,   Queue: ∅ ∅ ∅ ∅ ∅ ∅ 7 8
Rear: 8,   Print: 6

h) Similarly, print and remove front element 7 from the queue.

Front: 8,   Queue: ∅ ∅ ∅ ∅ ∅ ∅ ∅ 8
Rear: 8,   Print: 7

i) Print and remove last element of the queue.

Queue: ∅ ∅ ∅ ∅ ∅ ∅ ∅ ∅
Print: 8

The queue is empty now. So the Breadth First Search starting at node 1 is now complete. Following solution is printed for graph G:

1 2 3 4 5 6 7 8

```
************************************************
/* Implementation of Graph Traversals */

#include<stdio.h>
#include<alloc.h>
#define MAX 100
#define true 1
#define false 0

int visited[MAX];
void depth_first_search(int), breadth_first_search(int);

typedef struct graph_type
{
        int vertex;
        struct graph_type *next;
}graph;

graph *adj[MAX];
int n;

void insert_edge(), delete_edge(), disp();

void main()
{
        int x, i;

      printf("Input the number of vertices in the graph\n");
        scanf("%d",&n);

      if(n>MAX)
      {
      printf("Input size is greater than declared size\n");
            exit();
      }
      for(i=1;i<=n;i++)
      adj[i]=NULL;          /* Create a NULL graph */
```

```c
while(1)
{
        printf("Enter choice\n");
        printf("1.Insert an edge\n");
        printf("2.Delete an edge\n");
        printf("3.Display the graph\n");
        printf("4.Depth first search\n");
        printf("5.Breadth first search\n");
        printf("6.exit\n");
        scanf("%d",&x);

        switch(x)
        {
                case 1:  insert_edge();        break;

                case 2:  delete_edge();        break;

                case 3:  disp();               break;

                case 4:
                        for(i=1;i<=n;i++)
                                visited[i]=false;
                        depth_first_search(1); break;

                case 5:
                        for(i=1;i<=n;i++)
                                visited[i]=false;
                        breadth_first_search(1); break;

                case 6:   exit();

        }       /* end switch */

}       /* end while */

}       /* end main */
```

385

```c
void insert_edge()
{
        int a, b;
        graph *ptr;

        printf("Enter first node\n");
        scanf("%d",&a);
        printf("Enter second node\n");
        scanf("%d",&b);

        if(a>n || a<1 || b>n || b<1|| a==b)
        {
            printf("error\n");
            return;
        }

        ptr=adj[a];

        while(ptr!=NULL)
        {
            if((*ptr).vertex==b)    /* There is already an edge */
            {
                printf("error\n");
                return;
            }

            ptr=(*ptr).next;

        } /* end while */

        ptr=(graph *)malloc(sizeof(graph));

        if(ptr==NULL)
        {
            printf("no space\n");
            return;
        }
```

```
        (*ptr).vertex=b;
        (*ptr).next=adj[a];
        adj[a]=ptr; /* Make 'ptr' as the starting node of list 'adj[a]' */
}  /* end insert_edge */

void delete_edge()
{
        int a, b;
        graph *ptr, *prev;

        printf("Enter first node\n");
        scanf("%d",&a);
        printf("Enter second node\n");
        scanf("%d",&b);

        if(a>n || a<1|| b>n || b<1 || a==b)
        {
            printf("error\n");
            return;
        }

        ptr=adj[a];

        while(ptr!=NULL && (*ptr).vertex!=b)
        ptr=(*ptr).next;

        if(ptr==NULL)
        {
            printf("error\n");
            return;
        }

        if(ptr==adj[a])
        {
            adj[a]=(*ptr).next;
            free(ptr);
```

387

```
            return;
        }
        prev=adj[a];

        while((*prev).next!=ptr)
        prev=(*prev).next;

        (*prev).next=(*ptr).next;
        free(ptr);
}   /* end delete_edge */

void disp()
{
        graph *ptr;
        int i;

        for(i=1;i<=n;i++)
        {
                ptr=adj[i];

                while(ptr!=NULL)
                {
                        printf("%d→%d \n", i, (*ptr).vertex);
                        ptr=(*ptr).next;

                }   /* end while */

        }   /* end for */
}   /* end disp */

void depth_first_search(int v)
{
        graph *ptr;
        int w;
```

```c
            visited[v]=true;
            printf("%d ",v);
            for(ptr=adj[v];ptr!=NULL;ptr=(*ptr).next)
            {
                        w=(*ptr).vertex;
                        if(visited[w]==false)
                        depth_first_search(w);
            } /* end for */
} /* end depth_first_search */

void breadth_first_search(int v)
{
            int rear, front, u, w, queue[MAX];
            graph *ptr;

            u=v;
            rear=front=0;
            visited[v]=true;

            queue[rear++]=v;
            while(1)
            {
                        if(front==rear)
                        break;
                        for(ptr=adj[u];ptr!=NULL;ptr=(*ptr).next)
                        {
                                    w=(*ptr).vertex;
                                    if(visited[w]==false)
                                    {
                                                queue[rear++]=w;
                                                visited[w]=true;
                                    } /* end if */
                        } /* end for */
```

389

```
                    printf("%d ",queue[front++]);
                         /* Remove and print front element of the
                            queue  */

                    u=queue[front];

            }    /*  end while  */

}   /* end breadth_first_search  */
/*
```

After executing:

Input the number of vertices in the graph
4
Enter choice
1.Insert an edge
2.Delete an edge
3.Display the graph
4.Depth first search
5.Breadth first search
6.exit
1
Enter first node
1
Enter second node
3
Enter choice
1.Insert an edge
2.Delete an edge
3.Display the graph
4.Depth first search
5.Breadth first search
6.exit
1
Enter first node
1
Enter second node
2
Enter choice
1.Insert an edge
2.Delete an edge
3.Display the graph
4.Depth first search
5.Breadth first search
6.exit

1
Enter first node
3
Enter second node
4
Enter choice
1.Insert an edge
2.Delete an edge
3.Display the graph
4.Depth first search
5.Breadth first search
6.exit
1
Enter first node
2
Enter second node
4
Enter choice
1.Insert an edge
2.Delete an edge
3.Display the graph
4.Depth first search
5.Breadth first search
6.exit
4
1 2 4 3 Enter choice
1.Insert an edge
2.Delete an edge
3.Display the graph
4.Depth first search
5.Breadth first search
6.exit
5
1 2 3 4 Enter choice
1.Insert an edge
2.Delete an edge
3.Display the graph
4.Depth first search
5.Breadth first search
6.exit
6... ... ...(terminated)

*/

Steps of the program:

void depth_first_search(int v):

1) Print vertex: v, and make visited[v] as true.

2) For each neighbor w of v, if 'visited[w]' is false, which means that if w has not been explored yet, then call 'depth_first_search' with parameter: w.

Recursion is a stack making procedure, so each time when 'depth_first_search(w)' is called, w is pushed onto a stack. When a dead state is reached, top element of the stack is popped out and, loop 'for(ptr=adj[v];ptr!=NULL;ptr=(*ptr).next)' explores the another neighbor of popped out element.

void breadth_first_search(int v):

1) Add vertex: v to the queue, make visited[v] as true, and assign v to u.

2) Perform the following steps until queue becomes empty(rear and front become equal).

    (a) For each neighbor w of u, if visited[w] is false, then add w to the queue.

    (b) Remove and print front element of the queue. Increment 'front' by 1 i.e. make the next available element as the front element of the queue and assign it to 'u'.

8.19   <u>Minimum Cost Spanning Trees</u>

Let G be an undirected graph. Then a sub-graph t of G is a spanning tree iff t is a tree and contains all the vertices of G.

EXAMPLE:

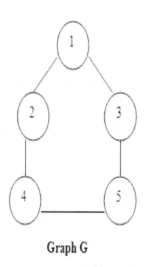

Graph G

Spanning Trees for above graph G:

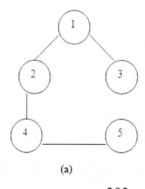

(a)

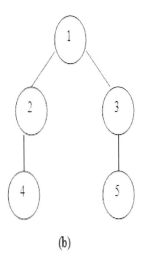

(b)

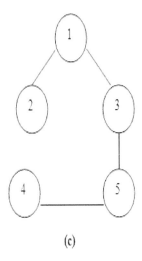

(c)

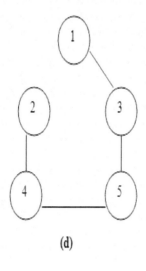

(d)

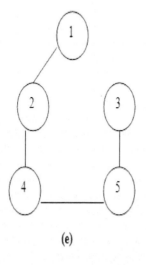

(e)

Let G be a weighted graph then weight of graph G is the sum of the weights of the edges of the graph. A **minimum cost spanning tree** for a weighted graph is a spanning tree with minimum weight.

EXAMPLE:

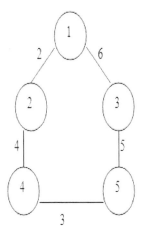

Graph G

Minimum cost spanning tree for the given graph G:

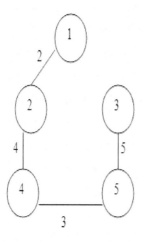

Tree t

Prim's Algorithm:

Prim's algorithm builds a minimum cost spanning tree edge by edge. In the starting, a vertex is chosen randomly, and included in the tree. Then, edges are added one by one. The next edge e(i, j) is added into the tree, such that vertex i stands included in the tree but vertex j does not. And the cost of e(i, j) is minimum among all the edges e'(x, y) of the graph, where vertex x is in the tree but vertex y doesn't belong to the tree, yet.

EXAMPLE:

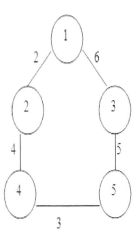

Graph G

Stages in Prim's algorithm:

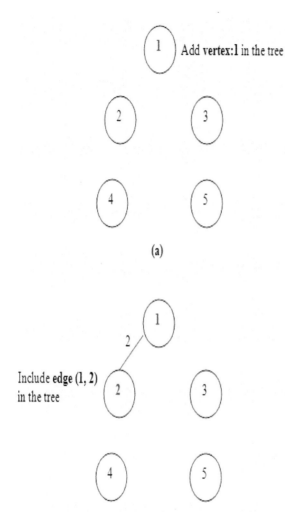

(a)

(b)

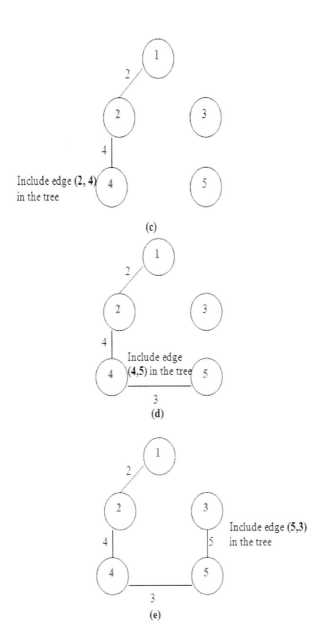

Include edge (2, 4) in the tree

(c)

Include edge (4,5) in the tree

(d)

Include edge (5,3) in the tree

(e)

```
************************************************

/* Implementation of minimum cost spanning tree */

#include<stdio.h>
#include<alloc.h>
#define inf 9999
#define MAX 100
#define true 1
#define false 0

typedef struct graph_type
{
        int vertex;
        int weight;
        struct graph_type *next;
}graph;

graph *adj[MAX];
int n;

void insert_edge(int, int, int), delete_edge(int, int), disp(), spanning_tree();

void main()
{
        int x, i, a, b, wt;

        printf("Enter number of nodes in the graph\n");
        scanf("%d",&n);

        if(n>MAX)
        {
        printf("Input size is greater than declared size\n");
                exit();
        }

        for(i=1;i<=n;i++)
        adj[i]=NULL;        /* Create a NULL graph */
```

```
while(1)
{
        printf("Enter choice\n");
        printf("1.Insert an edge\n");
        printf("2.Delete an edge\n");
        printf("3.Display the graph\n");
        printf("4.Minimum Spanning Tree\n");
        printf("5.exit\n");
        scanf("%d",&x);

        switch(x)
        {
                case 1:
                    printf("Enter first node\n");
                            scanf("%d",&a);
                    printf("Enter second node\n");
                            scanf("%d",&b);
                    printf("enter weight of edge\n");
                            scanf("%d",&wt);

                            insert_edge(a, b, wt);
                            insert_edge(b, a, wt);
                    /* It is an undirected graph, so insert an edge
                       from a to b and also from b to a  */
                            break;

                case 2:
                    printf("Enter first node\n");
                            scanf("%d",&a);
                    printf("Enter second node\n");
                            scanf("%d",&b);

                            delete_edge(a, b);
                            delete_edge(b, a);
                            break;
```

```c
            case 3:  disp();              break;
            case 4:  spanning_tree();     break;
            case 5:  exit();
        }  /* end switch */
    }  /* end while */
}  /* end main */
void insert_edge(int a, int b, int wt)
{
        graph *ptr;
        if(a>n || a<1 || b>n || b<1|| a==b)
        {
                printf("error\n");
                return;
        }
        ptr=adj[a];
        while(ptr!=NULL)
        {
                if((*ptr).vertex==b) /* if there is already an edge */
                {
                        printf("error\n");
                        return;
                }
                ptr=(*ptr).next;
        }  /* end while */
        ptr=(graph *)malloc(sizeof(graph));
        if(ptr==NULL)
        {
                printf("no space\n");
```
403

```c
                return;
        }
        (*ptr).vertex=b;
        (*ptr).weight=wt;
        (*ptr).next=adj[a];
        adj[a]=ptr; /* Make 'ptr' as the starting node of list 'adj[a]' */
}  /* end insert_edge */

void delete_edge(int a, int b)
{
        graph *ptr, *prev;
        if(a>n || a<1|| b>n || b<1 || a==b)
        {
            printf("error\n");
            return;
        }
        ptr=adj[a];

        while(ptr!=NULL && (*ptr).vertex!=b)
        ptr=(*ptr).next;

        if(ptr==NULL)
        {
            printf("error\n");
            return;
        }
        if(ptr==adj[a])
        {
            adj[a]=(*ptr).next;
            free(ptr);
            return;
        }
```

```
                        prev=adj[a];

                        while((*prev).next!=ptr)
                        prev=(*prev).next;

                        (*prev).next=(*ptr).next;
                                free(ptr);

}  /* end delete_edge */

void disp()
{
                        graph *ptr;
                        int i;

                        for(i=1;i<=n;i++)
                        {
                                ptr=adj[i];

                                while(ptr!=NULL)
                                {
printf("%d→%d (weight:%d) \n", i, (*ptr).vertex, (*ptr).weight);
                                        ptr=(*ptr).next;
                                }

                        }  /* end for */
}  /* end disp */

void spanning_tree()
{
                        graph *ptr;
                        int included[MAX], i, j, tree[MAX][3];
                        int mincost, old_vertex, new_vertex;

                        included[1]=true;      /* Add vertex numbered 1 in the tree */

                        for(i=2; i<=n; i++)
                        included[i]=false;
```

```
for(i=1; i<=n-1; i++)    /* n-1 edges have to be added  */
{
        mincost=inf;

        for(j=1; j<=n; j++)
        if(included[j]==true)         /*  If j is in the tree  */
        {
                ptr=adj[j];

                while(ptr!=NULL)
                {
if(included[(*ptr).vertex]==false && mincost>(*ptr).weight)
                        {
                                mincost=(*ptr).weight;
                                old_vertex=j;
                                new_vertex=(*ptr).vertex;

                        }  /*  end if  */

                        ptr = (*ptr).next;

                }   /*  end while  */

        }  /*  end if  */ /*  end for  */

        if(mincost==inf)
        break;

        tree[i][1]=old_vertex;
        tree[i][2]=new_vertex;
        included[new_vertex]=true;

}   /*  end for  */

if(i==n)
for(j=1; j<=n-1; j++)
printf("%d-->%d \n", tree[j][1], tree[j][2]);

}  /*  end spanning_tree  */
```

```
/*    After executing:
Enter number of nodes in the graph
4
Enter choice
1.Insert an edge
2.Delete an edge
3.Display the graph
4.Minimum Spanning Tree
5.exit
1
Enter first node
1
Enter second node
2
enter weight of edge
2
Enter choice
1.Insert an edge
2.Delete an edge
3.Display the graph
4.Minimum Spanning Tree
5.exit
1
Enter first node
2
Enter second node
3
enter weight of edge
3
Enter choice
1.Insert an edge
2.Delete an edge
3.Display the graph
4.Minimum Spanning Tree
5.exit
1
Enter first node
3
Enter second node
4
enter weight of edge
4
Enter choice
1.Insert an edge
2.Delete an edge
```

3.Display the graph
4.Minimum Spanning Tree
5.exit
1
Enter first node
4
Enter second node
1
enter weight of edge
5
Enter choice
1.Insert an edge
2.Delete an edge
3.Display the graph
4.Minimum Spanning Tree
5.exit
3
1-->4 (weight:5)
1-->2 (weight:2)
2-->3 (weight:3)
2-->1 (weight:2)
3-->4 (weight:4)
3-->2 (weight:3)
4-->1 (weight:5)
4-->3 (weight:4)
Enter choice
1.Insert an edge
2.Delete an edge
3.Display the graph
4.Minimum Spanning Tree
5.exit
4
1-->2
2-->3
3-->4
Enter choice
1.Insert an edge
2.Delete an edge
3.Display the graph
4.Minimum Spanning Tree
5.exit
5... ... ...(terminated)

*/

****

408

Steps of the program:

void spanning_tree():

1) Add vertex numbered 1 in the tree that is set the value of included[1] to true. Set the values of all other elements of array 'included' to false.

2) A tree with n vertices have n-1 edges. So outer loop 'for(i=1; i<=n-1; i++)' is used to append n-1 edges in the graph one by one. These n-1 edges should cover all the vertices of the graph. So we will have to add each vertex in the tree one by one.

   a) Choose an edge which has the minimum cost(weight) among all the edges, whose starting point(vertex) is in the tree and ending point(vertex) has not yet been added in the tree.

   b) If such an edge is found, then add its second vertex (which doesn't belong to the tree yet) in the tree. Store the starting and ending vertices of the edge in tree[i][1] and tree[i][2] respectively.

3) If a tree is found, then print all the edges of the tree.

8.20   TOPOLOGICAL SORT

Suppose G is a graph, in which each node N represents a job to be done, and a directed edge e(x, y) (from x to y) shows that without completing the job x, we can not begin job y. Now suppose that G contains a cycle Q:

Q=(a, b, c, a)

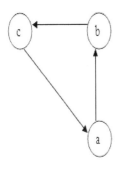

Graph G

From above, it will be seen that we can not begin job 'b' before completing 'a', and we can not begin 'c' before completing 'b', and we can not begin 'a' before completing 'c'. Thus we can not complete any of the jobs in the cycle. **Topological sort**, for a directed graph G, is the linear ordering of the nodes of G, such that if there is an edge e(x, y) (from x to y) then x must appear before y in the linear ordering. This means, **topological sort** for a graph G shows the order of completion of each job. There may be more than 1 topological sorts for a graph. But, there must not be any cycle, while performing the topological sort for a given graph.

Algorithm for topological sort:

1) For each node x, find the indegree of x and store it in 'indeg[x]'.

2) Put in a queue all the nodes with 0 indegree.

3) Repeat this step until queue becomes empty.

   (i) Delete the front element say x from the queue.

   (ii) For each neighbor y of x, do following:

       (a) Set indeg[y]=indeg[y]-1.
       (b) If indeg[y]==0, then add y to the queue.

4) Exit.

****

/* Implementation of Topological Sort */

```
#include<stdio.h>
#include<alloc.h>
#define MAX 100

typedef struct graph_type
{
        int vertex;
        struct graph_type *next;
}graph;

graph *adj[MAX];
int n;
void insert_edge(), delete_edge(), disp(), topological_sort();
int indegree(int);
```

```
void main()
{
        int x, i;
        printf("Enter number of nodes in the graph\n");
        scanf("%d",&n);
        if(n>MAX)
        {
        printf("Input size is greater than declared size\n");
                exit();
        }
        for(i=1;i<=n;i++)
        adj[i]=NULL;    /* Create a NULL graph */
        while(1)
        {
                printf("Enter choice\n");
                printf("1.Insert an edge\n");
                printf("2.Delete an edge\n");
                printf("3.Display the graph\n");
                printf("4.Topological sort\n");
                printf("5.exit\n");
                scanf("%d",&x);

                switch(x)
                {
                        case 1:  insert_edge();      break;
                        case 2:  delete_edge();       break;
                        case 3:   disp();             break;
                        case 4: topological_sort();  break;
                        case 5:   exit();

                }       /* end switch */
        }       /* end while */
}       /* end main */
```

```c
void insert_edge()
{
        int a, b;
        graph *ptr;

        printf("Enter first node\n");
        scanf("%d",&a);
        printf("Enter second node\n");
        scanf("%d",&b);

        if(a>n || a<1 || b>n || b<1|| a==b)
        {
            printf("error\n");
            return;
        }

        ptr=adj[a];

        while(ptr!=NULL)
        {
            if((*ptr).vertex==b) /* if there is already an edge */
            {
                printf("error\n");
                return;
            }

            ptr=(*ptr).next;

        } /* end while */

        ptr=(graph *)malloc(sizeof(graph));

        if(ptr==NULL)
        {
            printf("no space\n");
            return;
        }
```

413

```c
        (*ptr).vertex=b;
        (*ptr).next=adj[a];
        adj[a]=ptr; /* Make 'ptr' as the starting node of list 'adj[a]' */

}  /* end insert_edge */

void delete_edge()
{
        int a, b;
        graph *ptr, *prev;

        printf("Enter first node\n");
        scanf("%d",&a);
        printf("Enter second node\n");
        scanf("%d",&b);

        if(a>n || a<1|| b>n || b<1 || a==b)
        {
            printf("error\n");
            return;
        }

        ptr=adj[a];

        while(ptr!=NULL && (*ptr).vertex!=b)
        ptr=(*ptr).next;

        if(ptr==NULL)
        {
            printf("error\n");
            return;
        }

        if(ptr==adj[a])
        {
            adj[a]=(*ptr).next;
            free(ptr);
```

```
            return;
        }
        prev=adj[a];

        while((*prev).next!=ptr)
        prev=(*prev).next;

        (*prev).next=(*ptr).next;
        free(ptr);

}  /* end delete_edge */

void disp()
{

        graph *ptr;
        int i;

        for(i=1;i<=n;i++)
        {
                ptr=adj[i];

                while(ptr!=NULL)
                {
                        printf("%d→%d \n", i, (*ptr).vertex);
                        ptr=(*ptr).next;
                }

        }  /* end for */

}  /* end disp */

void topological_sort()
{
        int i, queue[MAX], rear, front, x, indeg[MAX], y;
        graph *ptr;
```

```c
rear=front=0;

for(i=1;i<=n;i++)
indeg[i]=indegree(i);    /* Find the indegree of each node */

for(i=1;i<=n;i++)
if(indeg[i]==0)
queue[rear++]=i;    /* Add all the nodes with 0 indegree to
                        the queue */

while(rear!=front)        /* Until queue is empty */
{
        x=queue[front++];    /* Remove the front
                                element of the queue */

        for(ptr=adj[x];ptr!=NULL;ptr=(*ptr).next)
        {
            y=(*ptr).vertex;
            indeg[y]=indeg[y]-1;
            if(indeg[y]==0)
            queue[rear++]=y;
        }    /* Delete the edge from x to y(virtually) and
                decrement the indegree of y by 1 */

}   /* end while */

if(rear==n)
for(i=0;i<n;i++)
printf("%d ", queue[i]);

}  /* end topological_sort */

int indegree(int y)
{
        graph *ptr;
        int i, indeg=0;
```

```
for(i=1;i<=n;i++)
    if(y!=i)
        for(ptr=adj[i];ptr!=NULL;ptr=(*ptr).next)
            if((*ptr).vertex==y)
                indeg++;

    return indeg;
```

} /* end indegree */

/*

After executing:

Enter number of nodes in the graph
4
Enter choice
1.Insert an edge
2.Delete an edge
3.Display the graph
4.Topological sort
5.exit
1
Enter first node
1
Enter second node
2
Enter choice
1.Insert an edge
2.Delete an edge
3.Display the graph
4.Topological sort
5.exit
1
Enter first node
1
Enter second node
3
Enter choice
1.Insert an edge
2.Delete an edge
3.Display the graph
4.Topological sort
5.exit

417

1
Enter first node
2
Enter second node
4
Enter choice
1.Insert an edge
2.Delete an edge
3.Display the graph
4.Topological sort
5.exit
1
Enter first node
4
Enter second node
3
Enter choice
1.Insert an edge
2.Delete an edge
3.Display the graph
4.Topological sort
5.exit
4
1 2 4 3 Enter choice
1.Insert an edge
2.Delete an edge
3.Display the graph
4.Topological sort
5.exit
5……………………………………..(terminated)

*/

****

Steps of the program:

Suppose graph is:

418

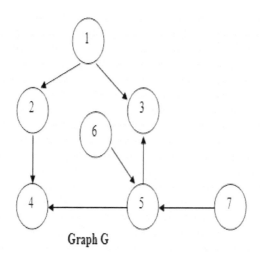

Graph G

Now we will simulate the 'topological_sort' according to this graph:

void topological_sort():

1) Initially all the nodes of 0 indegree will be added to the queue as follows:

   queue: 1   6   7

2) At each iteration of loop 'while(rear!=front)' (i.e. until queue is empty), vertices, which will be added to the queue and edges which will be deleted from the graph are as follows:

Note: Edges will not be deleted from the graph actually, but we will assume that these are being deleted.

419

(a)

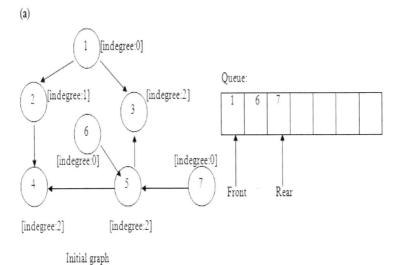

Initial graph

(b) First iteration:

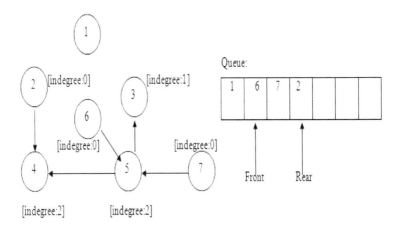

(c) Second iteration:

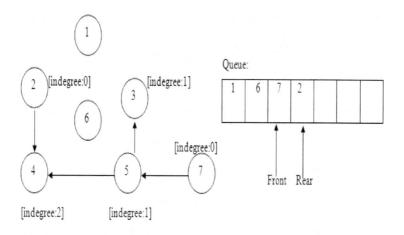

(d) Third iteration:

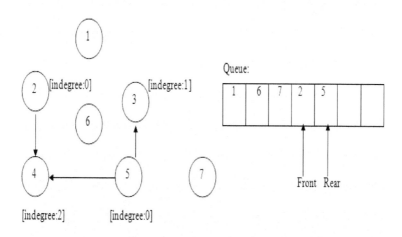

(e) Fourth iteration:

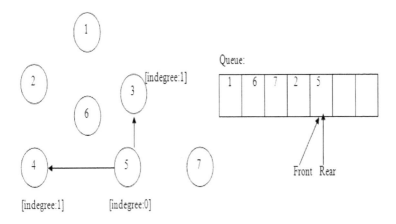

(f) Fifth iteration:

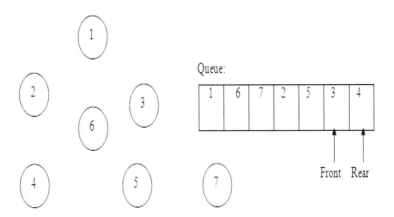

422

(g) Sixth iteration:

Queue:

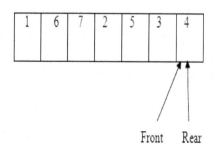

Front   Rear

(h) Seventh iteration:

Queue:

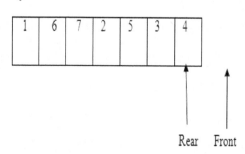

Rear   Front

....(loop terminated)

3) Now all the elements from queue[0] to queue[n-1] are printed. And we get the following output:

    1   6   7   2   5   3   4

SEARCHING

Computer systems are often used to store large amounts of data from which individual records are to be retrieved according to some search criterion. Thus for the efficient storage of data, facilitation of fast searching is an important issue. In this section, we will discuss two searching algorithms.

9.1 Sequential Search

Sequential search is the process of searching an item by comparing it with the various elements of a given array one by one. Suppose A be a given array, may be sorted or unsorted, with N number of elements A_1, A_2, A_3,.........A_N, and we have to search an element say ITEM in the array. Then a simple and common technique is to compare ITEM with each element of the array one by one. That is, first we check whether A_1 = ITEM, then we check whether A_2 = ITEM, and so on. This technique, which traverses array 'A' sequentially to search ITEM, is called a *linear search* or *sequential search*.

The program given below, implements sequential search.

****

```
/* Implementation of Sequential Search */
#include<stdio.h>
#define MAX 100

int SequentialSearch(int[], int, int);
```

```c
void main()
{
        int Numbers[MAX], N, ITEM, I, Pos;

        printf("Enter number of elements\n");
        scanf("%d", &N);

        if(N>MAX)
        {
                printf("Input size is greater than declared size\n");
                exit();
        }

        printf("Enter elements\n");

        for(I=0; I<N; I++)
        scanf("%d", &Numbers[I]);

        printf("Enter element, which has to be searched\n");
        scanf("%d", &ITEM);

        Pos=SequentialSearch(Numbers, N, ITEM);

        if(Pos==-1)
                printf("Element: %d is not found \n", ITEM);
        else
                printf("Element found at position: %d \n", Pos);
} /* end main */

int SequentialSearch(int Numbers[MAX], int N, int ITEM)
{
        int I;

        for(I=0; I<N; I++)
        if(Numbers[I]==ITEM)
        return I+1;
```

```
        return –1;

}  /* end SequentialSearch */

/*

After executing:

Enter number of elements
8
Enter elements
7 1 4 5 2 3 8 9
Enter element, which has to be searched
2
Element found at position: 5

*/
```

****

Steps of the program:

int SequentialSearch(int Numbers[MAX], int N, int ITEM):

(1) In this function, lines:

```
for(I=0; I<N; I++)
if(Numbers[I]==ITEM)
return I+1;
```

have been used to compare each element of array 'Numbers' with ITEM and for returning the position of the ITEM, if it is found in the array.

(2) If ITEM is not found in array 'Numbers', then –1 is returned to main.

9.2   Binary Search

There is a searching algorithm, called *binary search*, which works on a sorted array. Suppose we have an array, sorted in ascending order, comprising elements A_1, A_2, A_3,.........A_N. Then to locate an element in this array, we will first compare the element to be located with the middle item. If there is a match, we can return immediately. However, if the item sought is less than the middle key, then it must lie in the lower half of the array and if it is greater, then it must lie in the upper half of the array. So we repeat the procedure on the lower (or upper) half of the array.

The program mentioned below implements binary search.

****

```
/* Implementation of Binary Search */
#include<stdio.h>
#define MAX 100

int BinarySearch(int[], int, int);

void main()
{
        int Numbers[MAX], N, ITEM, I, Pos;

        printf("Enter number of elements\n");
        scanf("%d", &N);

        if(N>MAX)
        {
            printf("Input size is greater than declared size\n");
                exit();
        }
```

427

```c
        printf("Enter elements in ascending order \n");

        for(I=0; I<N; I++)
        scanf("%d ", &Numbers[I]);

        printf("Enter element, which has to be searched\n");
        scanf("%d ", &ITEM);

        Pos=BinarySearch(Numbers, N, ITEM);
        if(Pos==-1)
                printf("Element %d is not found ", ITEM);
        else
        printf("Element: %d is found at position: %d ", Pos+1);
}   /* end main */

int BinarySearch(int Numbers[MAX], int N, int ITEM)
{
        int Mid, Low, High;

        Low=0;          /* Lower bound of array 'Numbers' */
        High=N-1;       /* Upper bound of array 'Numbers' */

        while(Low<=High)
        {
                Mid=(Low+High)/2;

                if(ITEM==Numbers[Mid])
                  return Mid;
                else
                  if(ITEM<Numbers[Mid])
                    High=Mid-1;
                  else
                    Low=Mid+1;

        }   /* end while */
```

```
        return –1;

}   /*  end BinarySearch  */

/*

After executing:

Enter number of elements
9
Enter elements in ascending order
2 9 12 16 23 45 56 67 78
Enter element, which has to be searched
78
Element: 78 is found at position: 9   .........................(output)

*/
```

****

Steps of the program:

int BinarySearch(int Numbers[MAX], int N, int ITEM):

(1) In loop 'while(Low<=High)', element to be searched is compared with middle item of array 'Numbers'. If both are equal, position 'Mid' is returned to 'main' as the location of the item, which is to be searched. Else, upper bound ('High') is changed to Mid-1 or lower bound ('Low') is changed to Mid+1, depending upon whether ITEM lies in lower half of the array or upper half of the array. Execution of the loop is continued until ITEM is seen in the array or lower bound exceeds the upper bound.

(2) If ITEM is not found then –1 is returned to 'main'.

SORTING

Arranging of data or information in a computer is one of the basic function, which has its own importance. The process of arranging the data or information in some logical order is known as `sorting`. This logical order may be either ascending or descending in case of numeric values, or dictionary order in the case of alphanumeric values. Let A be a list of N elements A_1, A_2, A_3......A_n in memory. Sorting A, in ascending order refers to the operation of rearranging the contents of A so that they are in increasing order as given below:

$A_1 <= A_2 <= A_3 <= \ldots\ldots <= A_n$.

For example, suppose array A contains 8 elements as follows :

7, 48, 56, 9, 43, 37, 21, 58

After sorting, in ascending order, 'A' must appear in memory as follows:

7, 9, 21, 37, 43, 48, 56, 58

SORTING ALGORITHMS

10.1   BUBBLE SORT

Suppose the list of numbers A[1], A[2], A[3] …….. A[N] is in memory and we have to sort these elements in ascending order. Then bubble sort algorithm works as follows :

Pass 1:
> Compare A[1] and A[2] and arrange them in order, so that A[2]>A[1]. Then   compare A[2] and A[3] and arrange them so that A[3]>A[2]. Continue until we compare A[N-1] with A[N] and arrange them so that A[N]>A[N-1].

Above pass involves n-1 comparisons. When this pass is completed, the largest element is placed at the N_{th} position. In other words, after this pass, the largest element of the array will occupy the position A[N].

Pass 2:
> Now the largest element is at its right position in the array. So, now repeat this procedure for remaining N-1 elements i.e. now we will stop after we compare and rearrange A[N-2] and A[N-1]. Pass 2 involves N-2 comparisons and, when this pass is completed; the second largest element will occupy the position A[N-1].

Pass 3:

      Repeat above process for remaining N-2 elements. This time third largest element will occupy the position A[N-2].

....
....
....
....
....
....

Pass N-1 :

      Compare last two elements A[1] and A[2] and arrange them in order, so that A[2]>A[1].

After N-1 passes, the list will be sorted in increasing order.

Note: The process of sequentially traversing a list or a part of a list is called a **pass.**

To illustrate working of bubble sort, consider the following example :

Consider the sorting of following array in ascending order.

8, 12, 2, 4, 11

The sorting algorithm functions as follows:

Pass 1:

8	12	2	4	11	Arrange 8 & 12
8	2	12	4	11	Arrange 12 & 2
8	2	4	12	11	Arrange 12 & 4
8	2	4	11	12	Arrange 12 &11

Pass 2:

2	8	4	11	*12*	Arrange 8 & 2
2	4	8	11	*12*	Arrange 8 & 4
2	4	8	11	*12*	Arrange 8 & 11

Pass 3:

2	4	8	*11*	*12*	Arrange 2 & 4
2	4	8	*11*	*12*	Arrange 4 & 8

Pass 4:

2	4	*8*	*11*	*12*	Arrange 2 & 4

Illustration of Bubble Sort

```
*************************************************
```

/* *Implementation of Bubble Sort* */

```c
#include<stdio.h>
#define MAX 100

void main()
{
        int element[MAX],n,temp,i,j;
        int sorted=0;

        printf("enter number of elements\n");
        scanf("%d",&n);

        if(n>MAX)
        {
        printf("Input size is greater than declared size\n");
            exit();
        }
        printf("enter elements\n");
        for(i=1;i<=n;i++)
        scanf("%d",&element[i]);

        for(i=1;i<=n-1 && !sorted;i++)
```
                /* *This loop is used to execute passes 1 to N-1 and variable 'sorted' is used to check whether array 'element' has been sorted. If not then do following:* */
```c
        {
                sorted=1;
```
                /* *Change the value of 'sorted' to 1 by considering that the array 'element' is sorted now* */
```c
                for(j=1;j<=n-i;j++)
```
                        /* *This loop is used to make comparisons. At each ith execution of above loop, n-i comparisons will take place* */
```c
                {
```

434

```
                    if(element[j]>element[j+1])
                    {
                            temp=element[j];
                            element[j]=element[j+1];
                            element[j+1]=temp;
                            sorted=0;
                                    /*  If control comes in above
                                        'if' statement, then it means
                                        that array 'element' is not
                                        sorted yet, so change the
                                        value of 'sorted' to 0  */

                    }   /* end if */

                }   /* end for */

            }   /* end for */

            for(i=1;i<=n;i++)
            printf("%d ",element[i]);

        }  /* end main */


        /*

        After executing:

        enter number of elements
        8
        enter elements
        4 65 323 76 65 8 9 4
        4 4 8 9 65 65 76 323 .......................(output)


        */


        ************************************************
```

435

Steps of the program:

1) Input the unsorted elements in array 'element'.

2) Here 'for(i=1;i<=n-1 && !sorted ; i++)' loop is used to execute passes 1 to N-1.

3) Initially, variable 'sorted' is taken as 0, which denotes that the array 'element' is not sorted initially.

4) At each iteration of loop 'for(i=1;i<=n-1 && !sorted; i++)', we have to make n-i comparisons. So loop 'for(j=1;j<=n-i;j++)' is used to perform comparisons.

5) Condition 'if(element[j]>element[j+1])' checks, whether element next to 'element[j]' is smaller than 'element[j]'. If it is so, interchange both of them.

6) For each j, where 1 < j < n-i, if control doesn't come in 'if' statement, then it means that array is fully sorted now. So there is no need to execute more passes. But, if control comes in 'if' statement, then change the value of variable 'sorted' to 0 so that further passes of bubble sort can be carried out.

10.2 Selection Sort

Suppose an array comprising n elements A[0], A[1], A[2]...............A[N-1] is in memory. For sorting this array by Selection Sort method, first, find the smallest element in the entire array and exchange it with the element at the first position. Second, find the smallest element from the remaining array i.e. from elements A[1], A[2], A[3] ....A[N-1], and interchange it with the second element and so on. More precisely :

Pass 1.   Find the location of the smallest element in the array of N elements A[0], A[1], A[2].........A[N-1]. Let it be named as LOC. Now interchange A[LOC] with A[0]. Then : A[0] is sorted.

Pass 2.   Find the location LOC of the smallest element in sub array A[1], A[2], A[3].........A[N-1], and then interchange A[1] with A[LOC]. Then : A[0], A[1] are sorted, since A[0] ≤ A[1].

Pass 3.   Find the location LOC of the smallest element in sub array A[2], A[3], A[4].........A[N-1], and then interchange A[2] with A[LOC]. Then : A[0], A[1], A[2] are sorted, since A[0] ≤ A[1] ≤ A[2].

:
:
:
:
:
:
:
:

Pass k.   Find the location LOC of the smallest element
               in sub array A[k-1], A[k], A[k+1],
               A[k+2]................A[N-1], and interchange
               A[k-1] with A[LOC]. Then : A[0], A[1],
               A[2]...........A[k-1]   are   sorted,   since
               A[0]≤A[1] ≤A[2]...........≤ A[k-2] ≤ A[k-1].

     :
     :
     :
     :
     :
     :
     :
     :

Pass N-1.   Find the location LOC of the smallest element in
               sub array A[N-2], A[N-1], and interchange
               A[N-2] with A[LOC]. Then : A[0], A[1],
               A[2]...............A[N-1] are sorted. So after N-
               1 passes, the array will be sorted in ascending
               order.

EXAMPLE:

Suppose an array A contains 9 elements as follows:

67, 59, 47, 35, 72, 31, 25, 7, 89

Applying the selection sort algorithm to A, the data yield
will be as per the following figure. Here LOC is the location
of smallest element among A[k-1], A[k], A[k+1]....... A[N-
1] during pass k. At each pass k, elements given in circles
are interchanged.

Pass K	A[0]	A[1]	A[2]	A[3]	A[4]	A[5]	A[6]	A[7]	A[8]
K=1, LOC=7	67	59	47	35	72	31	25	7	89
K=2, LOC=6	7	59	47	35	72	31	25	67	89
K=3, LOC=5	7	25	47	35	72	31	59	67	89
K=4, LOC=3	7	25	31	35	72	47	59	67	89
K=5, LOC=5	7	25	31	35	72	47	59	67	89
K=6, LOC=6	7	25	31	35	47	72	59	67	89
K=7, LOC=7	7	25	31	35	47	59	72	67	89
K=8, LOC=7	7	25	31	35	47	59	67	72	89
Sorted:	7	25	31	35	47	59	67	72	89

****

```c
/*  Implementation of Selection Sort  */
#include <stdio.h>
#define MAX 100

void SelectionSort(int[], int);

void main()
{
    int I, N, Numbers[MAX];
```

439

```
      printf("Enter number of elements\n");
      scanf("%d", &N);

      if(N>MAX)
      {
          printf("Input size is greater than declared size\n");
             exit();
      }

      printf("Enter numbers\n");
      for(I=0; I<N; I++)
      scanf("%d", &Numbers[I]);

      SelectionSort(Numbers, N);
      printf("Sorted numbers are\n");
      for(I=0; I<N; I++)
      printf("%d ", Numbers[I]);

}    /* end main */

void SelectionSort(int Numbers[MAX], int N)
{
      int K, J, TEMP, LOC;

      for(K=1; K<=N-1; K++)          /* This loop is used to execute N-1
                                         passes */
      {
          LOC=K-1;

          for(J=K; J<N; J++)
             if(Numbers[LOC]>Numbers[J])
                LOC=J;

      /* Above steps are used to find the location of the smallest element
         in sub array Numbers[K-1], Numbers[K],
         Numbers[K+1]...........Numbers[N-1]. Here 'LOC' is the
         variable, which denotes the location of the smallest element in
         this sub array */
```

```
            if(LOC!=K-1)
            {
                    TEMP=Numbers[K-1];
                    Numbers[K-1]=Numbers[LOC];
                    Numbers[LOC]=TEMP;

            }   /* Interchange 'Numbers[K-1]' with 'Numbers[LOC]' */

        }   /* end for */
}   /* end SelectionSort */

/*

After executing:

Enter number of elements
7
Enter numbers
20 25 7 45 15 9 4
4 7 9 15 20 25 45          ........................(Output)

*/
```

****

Steps of the program:

We will simulate this program by using the following array of elements:

20 25 7 45 15 9 4

void SelectionSort(int Numbers[MAX], int N)

1. In this function, loop 'for(K=1; K<=N-1; K++)' is used to carry out N-1 passes.

441

2. Initially, store 'K-1' in 'LOC' i.e. consider 'Numbers[K-1]' is the smallest of sub array Numbers[K-1], Numbers[K], Numbers[K+1]..............Numbers[N-1].

3. Loop 'for(J=K; J<N; J++)' checks the smallest number in sub array Numbers[K-1], Numbers[K], Numbers[K+1]..............Numbers[N-1], and stores its location in variable 'LOC'.

4. Condition 'if(LOC!=K-1)' is used to verify that if location of the smallest element is not equal to K-1, then swap 'Numbers[LOC]' with 'Numbers[K-1]'.

In the beginning 'K-1' is 0 and location of the smallest number is 6 i.e. 'Numbers[6]' is the smallest number, which is 4.

So 'Numbers[6]' and 'Numbers[0]' ('Numbers[LOC]' and 'Numbers[K-1]') will be interchanged at first iteration of 'for(K=1; K<=N-1; K++)'. Thus array 'Numbers' will become:

4 25 7 45 15 9 20

At second iteration of loop 'for(K=1; K<=N-1; K++)', 'K' is 2. This time location of the second smallest number is 2. So now 'Numbers[2]' and 'Numbers[1]' are interchanged and order of elements in array 'Numbers' becomes as under:

4 7 25 45 15 9 20

Thus after $(N-1)_{th}$ iteration of loop 'for(K=1; K<=N-1; K++)', array 'Numbers' will be completely sorted.

10.3   Insertion Sort

In insertion sort, the whole list is divided into two sublists such that, one sublist is sorted and the other is unsorted. Initially, the sorted sublist comprises of the first element of the list and the unsorted sublist consists of the remaining elements. Each element of the unsorted sublist is inserted into the sorted sublist, at its proper position, till it is empty. Suppose we have to sort an array A with n elements : A[0], A[1], A[2]..............A[N-1].

Then, insertion sort algorithm scans array A from A[1] to A[N-1] and inserts each element A[k] into its proper position in the previously sorted sub-array A[0], A[1], A[2].........A[k-1], where $1 \leq k \leq N-1$.

Let us take an example. Suppose array A contains following 5 elements:

8, 4, 6, 2, 1.

Criteria to sort these numbers is as following:

A[0]	A[1]	A[2]	A[3]	A[4]
8	4	6	2	1

A[0]	A[1]	A[2]	A[3]	A[4]
4	8	6	2	1

Insert A[2] i.e. 4 at its proper position to previously sorted array.

4	6	8	2	1

Insert A[3] i.e. 6 at its proper position to previously sorted array.

2	4	6	8	1

Insert A[4] i.e. 2 at its proper position to the previously sorted array.

1	2	4	6	8

Insert A[5] i.e. 1 at its proper position to the previously sorted array.

Note that, A[0] is sorted by itself, being the only number.

****

/* *Implementation of Insertion Sort* */

```c
#include <stdio.h>
#define MAX 100
void InsertionSort(int[], int);
```

```c
void main()
{
        int I, N, Numbers[MAX];

        printf("Enter number of elements\n");
        scanf("%d", &N);

        if(N>MAX)
        {
            printf("Input size is greater than declared size\n");
            exit();
        }

        printf("Enter numbers\n");
        for(I=0; I<N; I++)
        scanf("%d", &Numbers[I]);

        InsertionSort(Numbers, N);

        printf("Sorted numbers are\n");
        for(I=0; I<N; I++)
        printf("%d ", Numbers[I]);

}   /* end main */

void InsertionSort(int Numbers[MAX], int N)
{
        int I, J, TEMP;

        for(I=1; I<=N-1; I++)
        {
                TEMP=Numbers[I];
                J=I-1;

                while(J>=0 && Numbers[J]>TEMP)
                {
                        Numbers[J+1]=Numbers[J];
                        J--;
```

```
}    /* end while */
                        /* Above 'while' loop is used to move each element
                           one position backward from the sorted sublist
                           until we get an element less than 'TEMP' */

    Numbers[J+1]=TEMP;          /* Insert 'TEMP' at
                                   position J+1 */

    }    /* end for */
}    /* end InsertionSort */

/*

After executing:

Enter number of elements
7
Enter numbers
5 6 8 9 0 3 2
0 2 3 5 6 8 9 ...............(Output)

*/
```

****

Steps of the Program:

We will simulate this sorting procedure by using the list of numbers given below:

8, 4, 6, 2, 1.

void InsertionSort(int Numbers[MAX], int N):

1) In this function, loop 'for(I=1; I<=N-1; I++)' is used to scan the elements from 'Numbers[1]' to 'Numbers[N-1]'. In our case, these elements are 4, 6,

446

2 and 1 respectively. Consider the execution of each statement in the first iteration of this loop.

➢ Statement 'TEMP=Numbers[I]' has been used to assign the value of 'Numbers[I]' to 'TEMP'. So, in first iteration of loop 'for(I=1; I<=N-1; I++)', Numbers[1], which is 4, is assigned to variable 'TEMP'.

➢ In loop 'while(J>=0 && Numbers[J]>TEMP)', each element starting from 'Numbers[I-1]' to 'Numbers[0]', is shifted one position backward, until we get an element less than 'TEMP'. At this time, value of 'I' is 1 and also 'Numbers[0] > TEMP' (8>4).

Therefore 'Numbers[0]', which is 8, is shifted to the second position. So elements in array 'Numbers' becomes:

8, 8, 6, 2, 1

Now there is no element, which can be shifted backward. So control will come out of the 'while' loop. And then 'TEMP' is assigned to 'Numbers[J+1]', where value of 'J' is -1, and value of 'TEMP' is 4 at present. So 4 is assigned to 'Numbers[0]'. Now order of elements of array 'Numbers' is changed into the following order:

4, 8, 6, 2, 1

2) Similarly, after second iteration of loop 'for(I=1; I<=N-1; I++)', 6 will be inserted at the second position of array 'Numbers' i.e. after second

447

iteration, elements of array 'Numbers' will be in the following order:

4, 6, 8, 2, 1

So after the last iteration, array 'Numbers' will be completely sorted and will be in the following order:

1, 2, 4, 6, 8

10.4   Shell Sort

By "Shell Sort" method, elements of the original file are distributed into several separate subfiles, and these subfiles are sorted first before the original file. Suppose the original file is divided into k subfiles, where, each of these subfiles contain every k^{th} element of the original file. Then this method sorts each subfile one by one, separately. The value of k is called an increment. For example, if k is 5, then, subfiles comprising one fifth of the elements of the original file are sorted in the following manner:

Subfile 1: x[1]   x[6]   x[11]..........................

Subfile 2: x[2]   x[7]   x[12]..........................

.

.

.

.

.

.

.

subfile 5: x[5]   x[10]   x[15]..........................

After these subfiles are sorted (by simple insertion method), a new smaller value of k is chosen and the procedure is repeated again and again by taking smaller values of k till its value is set to 1. Now, the sub-file consisting of the entire file is sorted. The decreasing sequence of increments is fixed at the starting of the entire process. The last value in this sequence must be 1.

Simple insertion sort is very efficient on an array, which is almost in sorted order. Since the first increment used by shell sort is large, so the sizes of the individual subfiles are quite small. Thus the simple insertion sort on these subfiles is fast. Sorting of every subfile one by one causes the entire array to be nearly sorted. After each successive pass of shell sort, smaller value of increment is used. So further successive passes of the shell sort deal with the larger subfiles. But these larger subfiles are almost in sorted order due to the action of previous passes. Thus the insertion sort on these subfiles is quite efficient.

EXAMPLE:

Suppose an array contains following numbers:

5	50	25	38	7	15	22	31

Original file

Then:

Pass 1:
Increment k = 4

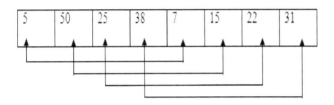

5	15	22	31	7	50	25	38

Sort four subfiles: (5, 7), (50, 15), (25, 22) and (38, 31) independently.

Pass 2:
Increment k=2

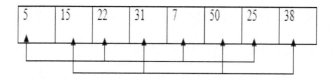

Sort two subfiles: (5, 22, 7, 25) and (15, 31, 50, 38) independently.

Pass 3:
Increment k=1

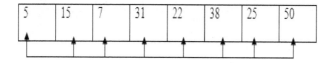

5	7	15	22	25	31	38	50

Sorted file

In the last, sort the entire file.

```
*************************************************
```

/* *Implementation of Shell Sort* */

```c
#include<stdio.h>
#define MAX 100
#define INCR 10
void buildincrements(int);
void shellsort();

int x[MAX], n, increments[INCR], num_of_inc;

void main()
{
            int i;

            printf("Input the size of array\n");
            scanf("%d",&n);

            if(n>MAX)
            {
      printf("Input size is greater than declared size\n");
                  exit();
            }

            printf("enter numbers\n");
            for(i=1;i<=n;i++)
            scanf("%d",&x[i]);

            increments[1]=1;   /* Last value of increments
                                  should be 1 i.e. last subfile
                                  should include all the elements
                                  of array 'x' */

            buildincrements(1);  /* This function is used to build
                                    the sequence of increments.
                                    Initially pass the value of
                                    last increment */

            shellsort();
```

452

```
                for(i=1;i<=n;i++)
                printf("%d ",x[i]);

}   /* end main */


void buildincrements(int i)
{
        if(increments[i]<n)
        {
                increments[i+1]=2*increments[i];
                        /* Next increment= 2* (Previous increment) */
                buildincrements(i+1);   /* Call this function
                                        again to generate the
                                        next increment */
        }
        else
        num_of_inc=i-1;   /* 'num_of_inc' contains total
                            number of increments */

}   /* end buildincrements */


/* In above function, we will get a sequence of increments: 1, 2, 4, 8...........
But we will have to use this sequence in opposite order: .............8, 4, 2, 1
i.e. first we will sort a subfile, that contains every 'increments[num_of_inc]th'
element of the original file and thereafter every 'increments[num_of_inc-1]th'
element, 'increments[num_of_inc-2]th' element, ........................ and so on.   */


void shellsort()
{
                int i, j, temp, span;

                for(; num_of_inc>=1;num_of_inc--)
                {
                        /* 'num_of_inc' is used as an index to
                            array 'increments' */

                span=increments[num_of_inc];
```

```
                    for(i=span+1;i<=n;i++)
                    {
                            temp=x[i]; /* Insert element x[i]
                                          into its proper
                                          position within its
                                          subfile */

                    for(j=i-span;j>=1&&x[j]>temp;j-=span)
                            x[j+span]=x[j];
                            x[j+span]=temp;

                    }  /*  end for  */

            }  /*  end for  */

}  /* end shellsort */

/*
```

After executing:

Input the size of array
6
enter numbers
15   7   25   14   16   21
7   14   15   16   21   25.......................(output)

*/

∗∗∗

Steps of the Program:

We will illustrate this program by using the list of numbers taken in the example at the start of shell sort:

5,   50,   25,   38,   7,   15,   22,   31

454

void main():

1) 'increments[1]' is initialized with 1. As, in last, we will have to sort the subfile, that contains each and every element of 'x'.

2) 'buildincrements' is called with parameter 1. This value is collected in variable 'i' in function 'buildincrements'.

void buildincrements(int i):

1) Initially 'i' is 1, and increments[1]=1, i.e. increments[i]<n (1<8), hence

   increments[i+1]=2 * increments[i];

   Logic to build the next increment is: Next increment= 2*(Previous increment). So increments[2]=1*2=2.

2) Now 2 is passed to generate increments[3]. Increments[2]<n (2<8), so:

   increments[3]=2*increments[2]=4.

   Similarly
   increments[4]=2*4=8.

3) When 4 is passed to generate increments[5], condition 'increments[4]<n' (8<8) becomes false. So 'else' part of condition 'if(increments[i]<n)' is executed this time.

   num_of_inc=i-1=4-1=3.

Therefore only three increments: (1, 2, 4) will be used in opposite order.

455

void shellsort():

1) At first iteration of loop 'for(;num_of_inc>=1;num_of_inc--)', subfiles: (x[1], x[5]), (x[2], x[6]), (x[3], x[7]) and (x[4], x[8]) will be sorted, because num_of_inc=3, and span=increments[3]=4.

So if span=4, then at first iteration of loop 'for(i=span+1;i<=n;i++)', 'x[i]' will be placed at its proper position within its subfile. After first iteration of this loop, array 'x' becomes:

$\boxed{5}$, 50, 25, 38, $\boxed{7}$, 15, 22, 31

[7 will occupy its proper position within its subfile]

After second iteration:

5, $\boxed{15}$, 25, 38, 7, $\boxed{50}$, 22, 31

[15 will occupy its proper position within its subfile]

After third iteration:

5, 15, $\boxed{22}$, 38, 7, 50, $\boxed{25}$, 31

[22 will occupy its proper position within its subfile]

After fourth iteration:

5, 15, 22, $\boxed{31}$, 7, 50, 25, $\boxed{38}$

[31 will occupy its proper position within its subfile]

456

2) Similarly at second iteration of loop 'for(;num_of_inc>=1;num_of_inc--)', subfiles containing every second element will be sorted. And in last iteration, whole array is sorted.

As "Shell Sort" sorts a number of subfiles first, before sorting the actual file, so this technique can also be applied to improve bubble sort. In "Shell Sort", we have used "Insertion sort" to sort the individual subfiles. In place of insertion sort, we can also use "Bubble Sort" to sort the individual subfiles. Initial bubble sorts will be on small files and thereafter on nearly sorted files, in which few interchanges will be necessary. The basic difference between the two techniques is that in shell sort we used insertion sort on every subfile, but in this type of sorting technique, we use bubble sort to sort each subfile.

****

/* Bubble sort on number of subfiles first, and thereafter on actual file */

```
#include<stdio.h>
#define MAX 100
#define INCR 10

#define SIZE 50
#define UNSORTED 0
#define SORTED 1

void buildincrements(int);
void bubblesort();

int n, x[MAX], increments[INCR], num_of_inc;
```

457

```c
void main()
{
              int i;
              printf("Input the size of array\n");
              scanf("%d",&n);

              if(n>MAX)
              {
       printf("Input size is greater than declared size\n");
              exit();
              }

              printf("enter numbers\n");
              for(i=0;i<n;i++)
              scanf("%d",&x[i]);

              increments[1]=1;

              buildincrements(1);
              bubblesort();

              for(i=0;i<n;i++)
              printf("%d ",x[i]);
}   /* end main */

void buildincrements(int i)
{
              if(increments[i]<n)
              {
                     increments[i+1]=2*increments[i];
                     buildincrements(i+1);
              }
              else
              num_of_inc=i-1;
}   /* end buildincrements */
```
458

```
void bubblesort()
{
        int span, temp, i, j, k, all, prev, sublist[SIZE];
        for(;num_of_inc>=1;num_of_inc--)
        {
                span=increments[num_of_inc];

                for(k=0; k<span && k<n-span; k++)
                    sublist[k] = UNSORTED;

                all = 0;

                for(i=0; i<n-span && all < span; i++)
                {
                        if(sublist[i%span]==SORTED)
                            continue;

                        prev=all;

                        sublist[i%span]=SORTED;
                        all++;

                for(j=i%span; j+span<n-(i/span)*span;j+=span)
                        if(x[j]>x[j+span])
                        {
                                temp=x[j];
                                x[j]=x[j+span];
                                x[j+span]=temp;
                                all = prev;
                                sublist[i%span]=UNSORTED;
                        }
                }   /* end for */
        }   /* end  for   */
}   /* end bubblesort  */
```

459

/*

After executing:

Input the size of array
7
enter numbers
15   25   5   45   16   18   24
5   15   16   18   24   25   45…………………………(output)

*/

****

Steps of the Program:

We will simulate this program with the following array:

5,   50,   25,   38,   7,   15,   22,   31

void buildincrements(int i):

'buildincrements' generate (1,   2,   4) as the sequence of increments.

void bubblesort():

1) At   first   iteration   of   loop:
   'for(;num_of_inc>=1;num_of_inc--)', subfiles: *(x[1],*
   x[5]), (x[2], x[6]), (x[3], x[7]) and *(x[4], x[8])* will
   be sorted, because span=4.

   After first iteration of this loop array 'x' becomes:

   5,   15,   22,   31,   7,   50,   25,   38

460

2) We consider second iteration of loop 'for(;num_of_inc>=1;num_of_inc--)', i.e. at present span=2.

   a) So if span=2, then at first iteration of loop 'for(i=0;i<n-span && all<span;i++)',largest element of first subfile will be properly placed at its position within its subfile.

      (i)   First iteration (i=0):

        Before first iteration:

$$\boxed{5}, \; 15, \; \boxed{22}, \; 31, \; \boxed{7}, \; 50, \; \boxed{25}, \; 38$$

        After first iteration:

5,   15,   7,   31,   22,   50,   25,   38

[25 will occupy the last position of its subfile]

      (ii)   Second iteration (i=1):

        Largest element of second subfile is properly placed at its position within its subfile as following:

        Before second iteration:

$$5, \; \boxed{15}, \; 7, \; \boxed{31}, \; 22, \; \boxed{50}, \; 25, \; \boxed{38}$$

        After second iteration:

5,   15,   7,   31,   22,   38,   25,   50

[50 will occupy the last position of its subfile]

(iii)   Third iteration (i=2):

Second largest element of first subfile will be properly placed at its position:

.

.

.

.

.

.

.

.

After last iteration, both of the subfiles are completely sorted.

3) At the last iteration of loop 'for(;num_of_inc>=1;num_of_inc--)', entire file (whole array 'x') is bubble sorted.

10.5   Merging of two sorted arrays

Merging of two sorted arrays is the process of combining the elements of arrays into a third sorted array. Consider an example, suppose an array 'A' contains following 5 elements:

5, 11, 13, 19, 20

And an array 'B' contains following 4 elements:

1, 7, 22, 24

Our job is to combine these sorted arrays into a third sorted array 'C'. This process of merging is mentioned below:

Take two pointers 'P1' and 'P2', which are initially pointing to the first element of arrays 'A' and 'B' respectively. Take another pointer 'TOP', which is pointing to the topmost vacant position of array 'C'. Initially, this pointer will point to the first location.

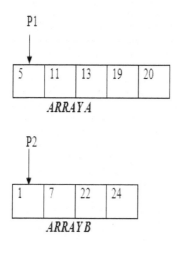

ARRAY A

ARRAY B

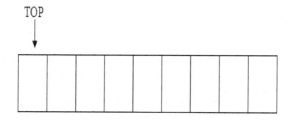

ARRAY C

Compare A[P1] and B[P2]. Place the smaller element in array 'C'. In our case, smaller element is B[P2], which is 1. So put it in array 'C', and increment the value of P2 and

TOP by 1. Now P2 is pointing to 7. Pictorial representation of this will be as follows :

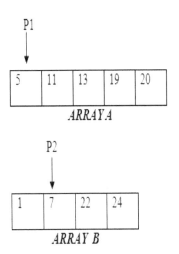

P1

| 5 | 11 | 13 | 19 | 20 |

ARRAY A

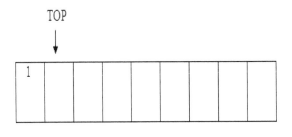

P2

| 1 | 7 | 22 | 24 |

ARRAY B

TOP

| 1 | | | | | | | | |

ARRAY C

Again compare A[P1] with B[P2], and place the smaller element in array 'C'. This time, smaller element is A[P1], which is 5. So place it in array 'C' and increment the value of P1 and TOP by 1. Now P1 will point to 11, which is the second element of array 'A'. Repeat this procedure again and again, until one of the pointers, either 'P1' reaches at the end of 'A' or 'P2' reaches at the end of 'B'. In our case, 'P1' will reach at the end of 'A', first. So after executing above procedure, array 'C' will contain following elements.

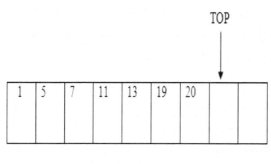

ARRAY C

Now place the remaining elements of second array in array 'C'. In our situation, this second array is 'B'. So move numbers 22 and 24 in array 'C'.

Now array 'C' contains all the elements of arrays 'A' and 'B', both of which stand completely merged into array 'C'.

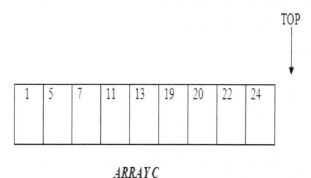

ARRAY C

Arrays 'A' and 'B' are completely merged into array 'C'.

465

****

/* *Merging of two sorted arrays* */

```c
#include<stdio.h>
#define MAX 100
#define HIGH 200

void Merge(int [], int [], int, int, int []);

void main()
{
        int N1, N2, A[MAX], B[MAX], C[HIGH], I;

        printf("Enter number of elements in first array\n");
        scanf("%d", &N1);

        if(N1>MAX)
        {
            printf("Input size is greater than declared size\n");
                exit();
        }

        printf("Enter elements in ascending order\n");

        for(I=0; I<N1; I++)
        scanf("%d", &A[I]);

        printf("Enter number of elements in second array\n");
        scanf("%d", &N2);

         if(N2>MAX)
        {
            printf("Input size is greater than declared size\n");
                exit();
        }

        printf("Enter elements in ascending order\n");
```

```
for(I=0; I<N2; I++)
    scanf("%d", &B[I]);

Merge(A, B, N1, N2, C);     /* Invoke 'Merge' function to merge
                               the elements of arrays 'A' and 'B'
                               in array 'C' */

printf("Merged elements are\n");

for(I=0; I<N1+N2; I++)
    printf("%d ", C[I]);

}    /* end Merge */

void Merge(int A[MAX], int B[MAX], int N1, int N2, int C[HIGH])
{
    int P1=0, P2=0, TOP=0;

    while(P1<N1 && P2<N2)
    {
        if(A[P1]<B[P2])
            C[TOP++]=A[P1++];
        else
            C[TOP++]=B[P2++];
                        /* If A[P1] is smaller, then assign it to
                           C[TOP] otherwise assign B[P2] to
                           C[TOP] */
    }   /* end while */

    while(P1<N1)
        C[TOP++]=A[P1++];     /* If 'P1' hasn't attained its
                                 limit, then copy rest of the
                                 elements of array 'A' in
                                 array 'C' */

    while(P2<N2)
        C[TOP++]=B[P2++];     /* Else, if 'P2' hasn't arrived
                                 at its end, then copy rest of
                                 the elements of array 'B' in
                                 array 'C' */

}    /* end Merge */
```

```
/*
```

After executing:

Enter number of elements in first array
5
Enter elements in ascending order
1 6 9 23 56
Enter number of elements in second array
5
Enter elements in ascending order
2 4 6 7 8
Merged elements are
1 2 4 6 6 7 8 9 23 56 ....(Output)

```
*/
```

****

Steps of the program:

void Merge(int A[MAX], int B[MAX], int N1, int N2, int C[HIGH]):

> ➢ At the beginning, P1, P2 and TOP are initialized with 0. Now A[P1] and B[P2], both contain the first element of 'A' and 'B', respectively. Variable 'TOP' points to the first empty location of array 'C'.

> ➢ In loop 'while(P1<N1 && P2<N2)', 'A[P1]' and 'B[P2]' are compared. If 'A[P1]' is smaller than 'B[P2]', then 'A[P1]' is assigned to 'C[TOP]' and 'P1' & 'TOP' are incremented by 1. Else 'B[P2]' is assigned to 'C[TOP]', and 'P2' & 'TOP' are incremented by 1. This step is repeated until either 'P1' reaches 'N1' or 'P2' reaches 'N2', where 'N1' and 'N2' denote the size of arrays 'A' and 'B' respectively.

> If 'P1 != N1', then, all the elements starting from 'A[P1]' to 'A[N1]' are moved in array 'C'.

> If 'P2 != N2', then, all the elements starting from 'B[P2]' to 'B[N2]' are placed in array 'C', one by one.

10.6 <u>Merge Sort</u>

Merge Sort apply 'merging' technique to sort an array. But, as we have seen in merging, it requires 2 sorted lists to create a third one. So, we divide our list into 2 sub-lists and, if these are in sorted order then we apply merging on them. But, if these are not, then we will have to divide each sub-list into further sub-lists, until we find two sorted lists. And, our search for finding two sorted lists is completed, if each of these lists contain 1 element only. Suppose we have to sort array 'A', which contains following 6 numbers:

<u>5</u>, <u>15</u>, <u>3</u>, <u>8</u>, <u>14</u>, <u>11</u>

Note that each of these numbers is individually sorted. So, if we consider that these 6 numbers form 6 sub-lists containing one item only, then it will be possible to merge them in pairs. So, apply merging on these sub-arrays in pairs, as given below:

Apply merging on:

    5   and 15
    3   and 8
    14 and 11

469

After merging in pairs, array 'a' will contain the elements in the following
order :

5, 15,   3, 8,   11, 14

Now divide this array into 3 subarrays considering that each subarray contains 2 numbers. Now there will be following sub-arrays:

5, 15
3, 8
11, 14

Again merge in pairs. But this time, we can have only one pair, since the total sub-arrays are 3. So apply merging on first pair. After merging, array 'a' will contain numbers in the following order :

3, 5, 8, 15,   11, 14

This time, divide this array into subarrays, so that each subarray contains 4 numbers. But in our case, we have only 2 subarrays, out of which first subarray contains 4 numbers and second contains 2 numbers. So merge these two subarrays. Now, after merging, array 'a' will be completely sorted :

3, 5, 8, 11, 14, 15

These numbers are fully sorted now.

```
***********************************************
/* Implementation of Merge Sort */

#include<stdio.h>
#define MAX 100

void mergesort(int x[MAX], int n);

void main()
{
        int n, x[MAX], i;

        printf("enter size of the array \n");
        scanf("%d",&n);

        if(n>MAX)
        {
            printf("Input size is greater than declared size\n");
            exit();
        }

        printf("enter elements \n");
        for(i=1;i<=n;i++)
        scanf("%d",&x[i]);

        mergesort(x,n);

}  /* end main */

void mergesort(int x[MAX], int n)
{
        int l1, l2, u1, u2, aux[MAX], size, i, j, k;

        size=1;        /* Initially size of each subarray is 1 */

        while(size<n)
        {
            l1=1;        /* set lower bound of first set of elements to 1 */
```

471

```
k=1;
while(l1+size<=n)
{
    u1=l1+size-1;        /* upper bound of first set of
                            elements */
    l2=u1+1;             /* lower bound of second set of
                            elements */

    u2=(l2+size-1<n)?l2+size-1:n;
                         /* upper bound of second set of elements */
    i=l1; j=l2

    while(i<=u1 && j<=u2)
        if(x[i]<x[j])
            aux[k++]=x[i++];
        else
            aux[k++]=x[j++];

    while(i<=u1)
        aux[k++]=x[i++];

    while(j<=u2)
        aux[k++]=x[j++];  /* now use merging and store
                             the merged elements in 'aux'
                             array */

    l1=u2+1;             /* Change lower bound of first set to
                            u2+1, so that the next pair of sets
                            could be merged */

}   /* end while */

for(i=1;i<k;i++)
    x[i]=aux[i];         /* store merged elements of 'aux' array into
                            array 'x' */

size*=2; /* now multiply the size of the set of elements by 2 */

}   /* end while */
```

472

```
        for(i=1;i<=n;i++)
        printf("%d ",x[i]);
}
```

```
/*

After executing:

enter size of the array
6
enter elements
7 4 0 9 7 5
0 4 5 7 7 9.................(output)

*/
```

****

Steps of the program:

void mergesort(int x[MAX], int n):

Suppose array entered by user is :

     5,   15,   3,   8,   14,   11

1) Initially consider that there are n sets of elements and the size of each set of elements is 1, and we have to merge these in pairs. In a pair, consider '11' and 'u1' as the lower and upper bound of first set of elements, and '12' and 'u2' as the lower and upper bound of second set of elements.

   At first iteration of loop 'while(size<n)', following steps are executed:

a) In the beginning, first pair of set of elements is taken i.e. 5 and 15 . Merging is applied on this pair and merged elements are stored in array 'aux'.

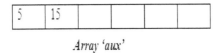

Array 'aux'

b) Now a new pair of set of elements is taken and merging is applied on this pair. And again result is pushed in array 'aux'. At present, this new pair is: 3 and 8.

After merging, array 'aux' will contain following 4 numbers :

Array 'aux'

c) After that, third pair is taken and again elements are merged. Now 'aux' contains all the 6 numbers in the following order :

| 5 | 15 | 3 | 8 | 11 | 14 |

Array 'aux'

Now each and every element of array 'aux' is assigned to 'x'. Note that, now each adjacent 2 numbers are in sorted order. So, now, there are 3 pairs on which same technique will be applied.

2) 'size' is multiplied by 2, and above procedure is repeated in further iterations of loop 'while(size<n)' again and again until size of the set of elements ('size') reaches n.

10.7   Merge Sort Using Recursion

The basic concept behind Merge Sort is to merge two sorted arrays or we can say that before merging, both the arrays must be sorted. Procedure to sort a list using Merge Sort is to split the list into two halves, and if both of the sub-lists are in sorted order, then merge them. But, if these are not in sorted order, then again split each of the sublists into two halves and repeat this process until we get sorted sublists. Key point is that if your list is 1 item long, then it is sorted. Now the above mentioned steps can be performed recursively as given below:

1) Split the list into two halves.
2) Keep on dividing the each list into two sub-lists until we get a bunch of lists containing 1 item only.
3) Now each individual list is sorted. Start merging them to create one sorted list.

Example:

Consider a list, which contains 8 elements:

a) Split the above list into two halves, as follows:

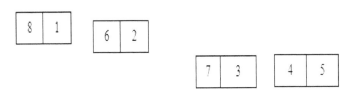

First half   Second half

b) Each list is again split into two halves:

c) Again split each list into two halves:

Now each list contains one element only. So each list is individually sorted. Start merging the lists.

d) Merge the following lists:

476

(8) and (1),   (6) and (2),   (7) and (3),   (4) and (5)

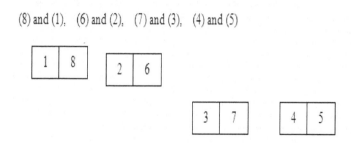

After merging the lists, which were split in step: (c), there are 4 lists formed that are sorted individually. These are the same sub-lists that were split in step: (b). The difference is that now these sub-lists are sorted.

e) Now merge the following lists:

(1, 8) and (2, 6),   (3, 7) and (4, 5)

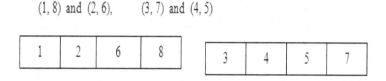

The above two lists formed are the sorted versions of the two sub-lists, which were split in step: (a).

f) Now merge the above two sub-lists.

1	2	3	4	5	6	7	8

The above list formed is the sorted version of the actual list provided as an input for sorting.

```
***********************************************
/* Program to implement Merge Sort using Recursion */
#include <stdio.h>
#define MAX 80

void MergeSort(int [], int [], int, int);
void Merge(int [], int [], int, int, int, int);

void main()
{
        int Numbers[MAX], Queue[MAX], N, I;

        printf("Enter number of elements\n");
        scanf("%d", &N);

        if(N>MAX)
        {
            printf("Input size is greater than declared size\n");
            exit();
        }

        printf("Enter numbers\n");
        for(I=0; I<N; I++)
        scanf("%d", &Numbers[I]);

        MergeSort(Numbers, Queue, 0, N-1);

        printf("Sorted numbers are\n");
        for(I=0; I<N; I++)
        printf("%d ", Numbers[I]);

}   /* end main */

void MergeSort(int Numbers[], int Queue[], int Start, int End)
{
        int Mid, i;
```

```
            if(Start<End)
            {
                    Mid = ( Start + End ) / 2;
                    MergeSort(Numbers, Queue, Start, Mid);
                                            /* First half */
                    MergeSort(Numbers, Queue, Mid+1, End);
                                            /* Second half */
                    Merge(Numbers, Queue, Start, Mid, Mid+1, End);
                                    /* Merge the sorted sub-lists */
                    for(i=Start; i<=End; i++)
                            Numbers[i] = Queue[i];

            }       /* end if */

}       /* end MergeSort */

void Merge(int Numbers[], int Queue[], int l1, int u1, int l2, int u2)
{
            int q=l1;

            while(l1<=u1 && l2<=u2)
            {
                    if(Numbers[l1]<Numbers[l2])
                            Queue[q++] = Numbers[l1++];
                    else
                            Queue[q++] = Numbers[l2++];
            }

            while(l1<=u1)
                    Queue[q++] = Numbers[l1++];

            while(l2<=u2)
                    Queue[q++] = Numbers[l2++];

}       /* end Merge */
```

****

479

Steps of the Program:

void MergeSort(int Numbers[], int Queue[], int Start, int End):

Note:

This function is a recursive function, which create stacks. In each stack, variables 'Start' and 'End' will denote the starting and ending locations of the individual sub-lists. These sub-lists will not reside in different locations but will be the partitions of array 'Numbers' only, and are identified by variables 'Start' and 'End'.

> Variables 'Start' and 'End' denote the starting & ending positions of the list.

> In this recursive function, 'Mid' is the variable taken to indicate the middle position of the list.

> Condition 'if(Start<End)' checks whether list contains more than one element or not i.e. if it cannot be divided into further sub-lists then control returns to the previous function.

> Statement 'MergeSort(Numbers, Queue, Start, Mid);', calls this function again with values of 'Start' and 'End' as the starting and ending positions of first half of the list, which has been passed previously in this function.

> Statement 'MergeSort(Numbers, Queue, Mid+1, End);', calls this function again with values of 'Start' and 'End' as the starting and ending

positions of second half of the list, which has been passed previously in this function.

> Function 'Merge' is invoked to merge the two lists whose starting and ending locations are 'Start', 'Mid' and 'Mid+1', 'End' respectively.

> Loop 'for(i=Start; i<=End; i++)' inserts the merged numbers in array 'Numbers'. Now all the elements in array 'Numbers' from location 'Start' to 'End' are in sorted order.

void Merge(int Numbers[], int Queue[], int l1, int u1, int l2, int u2):

This function is used to merge the two lists; whose starting and ending locations are 'l1', 'u1' and 'l2', 'u2' respectively, and are the parts of array 'Numbers' only. These merged numbers are stored in array 'Queue'.

10.8   Quicksort

In a given list of elements, Quicksort algorithm finds the final position of each element one by one. Placing an element say 'N' at its final position means to locate it at a place such that the elements to the left of N are less and elements to right of N are greater than N. This technique requires the partitioning of list into two sublists so that the same procedure can be employed on both of these. After placing N at its final position, list is divided into two halves (left sublist & right sublist), left sublist consists of the elements, which are positioned to the left of N and right sublist consists of the elements, which are placed to the right of N. Each of these sublists is sorted individually by

481

following the same technique. We may illustrate "Quicksort" by means of a specific example.

Suppose A is an array, which contains following 10 numbers:

(40), 27, 14, 58, 85, 89, 35, 65, 91, 60

Starting from the last number, 60, we pass through the array from right to left and comparing each number with the first number, 40, of the array. The moment we get a number less than 40, we stop scanning the list. Here the number is 35. Interchange 35 and 40 to obtain the list:

(35) , 27, 14, 58, 85, 89, (40) , 65, 91, 60

Notice that the numbers 65, 91 and 60 to the right of 40 are greater than 40. Now starting from number 35, go through the array from left to right and compare each number with 40. Stop scanning the list if we get a number greater than 40. The number is 58. Interchange 40 and 58. Now array contains numbers in the following order:

35, 27, 14, (40) , 85, 89, (58) , 65, 91, 60

Now observe that the numbers 35, 27 and 14 to the left of 40 are less than 40. Beginning this time with 58, scan array from right to left, until we get a number less than 40. But this time we don't find any number less than 40. It means 40 is correctly placed in its final position. All numbers less than 40, are now placed to the left of 40, and numbers greater than 40, are at the right of 40. Basically these two sets of numbers form two sublists, as shown below:

35, 27, 14, (40), 85, 89, 58, 65, 91, 60

First sublist   second sublist

Now our task of sorting on array A has been reduced to the task of sorting both of the above subarrays. So apply the same procedure on both of these, one by one.

Basically, the procedure of reducing the list into smaller sublists is repeated until we get a sublist, which contains only one number. Finally, all of these sublists are combined to form one sorted list.

****

```
/* Implementation of Quicksort */
#include<stdio.h>
#define MAX 100

void QuickSort(int[], int, int, int);

void main()
{
        int I, N, Numbers[MAX];

        printf("Enter number of elements\n");
        scanf("%d", &N);

        if(N>MAX)
        {
        printf("Input size is greater than declared size\n");
```

```c
            exit();
    }

    printf("Enter numbers\n");
    for(I=0; I<N; I++)
    scanf("%d", &Numbers[I]);

    QuickSort(Numbers, N, 0, N-1);

    printf("Sorted numbers are\n");
    for(I=0; I<N; I++)
    printf("%d ", Numbers[I]);

}   /* end main */

void QuickSort(int Numbers[MAX], int N, int Start, int End)
{
    int Litem=Start, Ritem=End, LOC=Start, Temp;

    while(1)
    {
while(Numbers[LOC]<=Numbers[Ritem] && LOC!=Ritem)
            Ritem--;
                        /* Scan right to left until we get a
                           number less than 'Numbers[LOC]' */
            if(LOC!=Ritem)
            {
                Temp=Numbers[LOC];
                Numbers[LOC]=Numbers[Ritem];
                Numbers[Ritem]=Temp;
                LOC=Ritem;
            }
            else
                break;
                    /* If we get a number less than
                       'Numbers[LOC]', swap both of them and
                       assign 'Ritem' to 'LOC'. Otherwise break
                       the infinite 'while' loop */
```

```
            while(Numbers[LOC]>=Numbers[Litem] && LOC!=Litem)
                    Litem++;
                            /* Now scan the array from 'Litem' to
                               'LOC' (left to right) until we get a
                               number greater than 'Numbers[LOC]' */
                    if(LOC!=Litem)
                    {
                            Temp=Numbers[LOC];
                            Numbers[LOC]=Numbers[Litem];
                            Numbers[Litem]=Temp;
                            LOC=Litem;
                    }
                    else
                            break;
                            /* If a number greater than 'Numbers[LOC]' is found,
                               exchange both of them and assign 'Litem' to
                               'LOC'. Otherwise break the infinite 'while' loop */
            }   /* end while */
            /* After execution of above 'while' loop, the first element of the array
               will be correctly placed at its position */

            if(LOC-1>Start)
                    QuickSort(Numbers, N, Start, LOC-1);

            if(LOC+1<End)
                    QuickSort(Numbers, N, LOC+1, End);
                            /* Now break the array into two unsorted subarrays and
                               invoke the recursive function 'QuickSort' by passing
                               the parameters of both of these subarrays */
    }   /* end QuickSort */
    /*

    After executing:

    Enter number of elements
```

485

9
Enter numbers
1 87 56 43 56 76 39 9 98
1 9 39 43 56 56 76 87 98   ....(Output)

*/

****

Steps of the program:

We will simulate the above program with the list of numbers taken as under:

40, 27, 14, 58, 85, 89, 35, 65, 91, 60...(Unsorted array)

1. From function 'main', the following parameters are passed to function 'QuickSort':

    (a) Base address of array 'Numbers'.

    (b) Total number of elements in array 'Numbers'.

    (c) Lower bound of the array.

    (d) Upper bound of the array.

2. In function 'QuickSort', 'LOC' is the position of the item, which we have to place at its final position. 'Litem' is the location of starting item of the array and 'Ritem' is the position of the ending element of the array, from where we have to start scanning the list.

3. Loop 'while(1)' is an infinite loop, which is terminated in between, if item 'Numbers[LOC]' occupies its final position in the array. Consider the first iteration of this loop:

486

➢ Loop
'while(Numbers[LOC]<=Numbers[Ritem]
&& LOC!=Ritem)' scans the array from
right to left ('Ritem' to 'LOC') until we get
a number less than 'Numbers[LOC]'. In our
case, the number is 35.

➢ As condition 'if(LOC!=Ritem)' becomes
true, so 'Numbers[LOC]' is swapped with
'Numbers[Ritem]' i.e. 35 and 40 are
interchanged and 'Ritem' is assigned to
'LOC', because location of
'Numbers[LOC]' (40) has now been
changed. Now array 'Numbers' in memory
becomes:

35, 27, 14, 58, 85, 89, 40, 65, 91, 60

➢ Now the list has to be scanned from 'Litem'
to 'LOC' (from left to right) i.e. from 35 to
40. Loop
'while(Numbers[LOC]>=Numbers[Litem]
&& LOC!=Litem)' do the same until we get
a number greater than 40. The number is 58.
Condition 'if(LOC!=Litem)' becomes true,
so 40 and 58 are exchanged and 'Litem' is
assigned to 'LOC' as location of
'Numbers[LOC]' (40) has been changed
once again.

In the second iteration of the infinite 'while'
loop, control will come at the starting statement
and list will be scanned from 58 to 40. But this
time, we don't get any number less than 40 i.e.

487

40 has correctly been placed at its final position. So condition 'if(LOC!=Ritem)' becomes false and 'else' part of this statement gets executed, which breaks the 'while' loop.

4. After the termination of loop 'while(1)', array is divided into two subarrays, and function 'QuickSort' is again invoked by passing the parameters of both of these one by one. Note that, these subarrays do not reside in different locations but are the parts of array 'Numbers' only. Variables 'Start' and 'End' are used to indicate the starting and ending locations of these subarrays by which they can be distinguished. Same strategy is applied on these subarrays individually.

10.9   Radix Sort

Suppose a list of N elements is to be sorted and x is the total number of digits of the largest number among all the numbers in the list. Then this sorting technique sorts the list x times, according to each possible digit starting from the least significant digit. Suppose we have some cards, where each card contains a 3-digit number. Then these cards can be sorted with the following procedure:

(a) Cards are first sorted according to the unit's digit.

(b) On the second pass, the cards are sorted according to the ten's digit.

(c) On the third pass, the cards are sorted according to the hundred's digit.

We may illustrate this with an example. Suppose we have nine cards containing three digits numbers as follows:

615, 301, 549, 341, 440, 20, 521, 628, 123

(a) In the first pass, the unit's digits are sorted. The sorted numbers are reinput for the second pass.

(b) In the second pass, the ten's digits are sorted. Again sorted numbers are reinput for the third pass.

(c) In the last pass, numbers are sorted according to the hundred's digit.

Input	0	1	2	3	4	5	6	7	8	9
615						615				
301		301								
549										549
341		341								
440	440									
220	220									
521		521								
628									628	
123				123						

SORTING ACCORDING TO UNITS DIGIT(FIRST PASS)

After sorting according to units digits, the order of numbers in the list will be as follows:

Sorted numbers:	440	220	301	341	521	123	615	628	549	

Input	0	1	2	3	4	5	6	7	8	9
440					440					
220			220							
301	301									
341					341					
521			521							
123			123							
615		615								
628			628							
549					549					

SORTING ACCORDING TO TENS DIGIT(SECOND PASS)

After sorting according to tens digits, the order of numbers in the list will be as follows:

Sorted numbers:	301	615	220	521	123	628	440	341	549	

Input	0	1	2	3	4	5	6	7	8	9
301				301						
615							615			
220			220							
521						521				
123		123								
628							628			
440					440					
341				341						
549						549				

SORTING ACCORDING TO HUNDREDS DIGIT(THIRD PASS)

When the list is collected after sorting according to hundreds digit, it will be completely sorted:

Sorted numbers:	123	220	301	341	440	521	549	615	628	

****

/* Implementation of Radix Sort */

```
#include<stdio.h>
#include<math.h>
#define MAX 100
```

```c
void RadixSort(int[], int);
int FindMaxNumberOfDigits(int[], int);

void main()
{
        int Numbers[MAX], N, I;

        printf("Enter number of elements\n");
        scanf("%d", &N);

        if(N>MAX)
        {
            printf("Input size is greater than declared size\n");
                exit();
        }

        printf("Enter numbers\n");
        for(I=0; I<N; I++)
        scanf("%d", &Numbers[I]);

        RadixSort(Numbers, N);

        printf("Sorted numbers are\n");
        for(I=0; I<N; I++)
        printf("%d ", Numbers[I]);

}   /* end main */

void RadixSort(int Numbers[MAX], int N)
{
        int NumDigits, I, J, K, Queue[MAX], Q, P, Pth_digit;

        NumDigits = FindMaxNumberOfDigits(Numbers, N);

        for(I=0; I<NumDigits; I++)
            {       /* Suppose the highest number in array 'Numbers' is
                    2948 i.e. a 4 digit number, then this loop will execute
                    4 times */
```

```
Q=0;        /* 'Q' is an index to array 'Queue' */

P=pow(10, I);

/* Here 'P' denotes the digit, according to which array
   'Numbers' will be sorted. Value 1 in 'P' stands for unit's
   digit, 10 stands for ten's digit, 100 for hundred's digit and
   so on... */

for(J=0; J<=9; J++)        /* Every digit can take a value
                              in between 0 to 9 only */
    for(K=0; K<N; K++)

    {          /* For each number, carry out the
                  following steps: */

        Pth_digit=(Numbers[K] / P) % 10;

        /* Here 'Pth_digit' is the digit at position P of
           element 'Numbers[K]'. (Note: Position 1
           stands for unit's place, 10 for ten's
           place......... and so on) */

            if(Pth_digit==J)
                Queue[Q++]=Numbers[K];

            /* All the elements, which are sorted
               according to Pth digit, are collected in
               array 'Queue' */

    }   /* end for */

    for(K=0; K<N; K++)
        Numbers[K]=Queue[K];
                            /* Re input the numbers */

}   /* end for */

}   /* end RadixSort */

int FindMaxNumberOfDigits(int Numbers[MAX], int N)
{
    int Max, MaxNumberOfDigits=0, I;
```

493

```
       Max=Numbers[0];

       for(I=0; I<N; I++)
               if(Numbers[I] > Max)
                       Max=Numbers[I];
```
                       /* Above steps are used to find out the
                          number, which has the maximum value   */
```
       While(Max!=0)
       {
               Max=Max/10;
               MaxNumberOfDigits++;
```
       }   /* These steps are used to count the number of digits in 'Max' and
               for storing the same in variable 'MaxNumberOfDigits' */
```
           return MaxNumberOfDigits;
```
} /* end FindMaxNumberOfDigits */

/*

After executing:

Enter number of elements
8
Enter numbers
1 10 7 348 54 172 2948 5
1 5 7 10 54 172 348 2948   ....(Output)

*/

****

Steps of the Program:

We will simulate this program with the following list of
unsorted numbers:

       38, 72, 56, 345, 106, 249

494

int FindMaxNumberOfDigits(int Numbers[MAX], int N):

This function has been used to find out the number, which has the maximum value among all the numbers in the array and for returning the number of digits that this number holds.

void RadixSort(int Numbers[MAX], int N):

1) Outer loop 'for(I=0; I<NumDigits; I++)' will execute 3 times, because largest number in our case is 345, which contains 3 digits. Now consider the first iteration of this loop:

   ➢ At first iteration of this loop, I=0 and P=pow(10,0)=1.

   ➢ Loop 'for(J=0; J<=9; J++)' is used for every possible value of a digit that it may contain.

   ➢ Inner loop 'for(K=0; K<N; K++)' will execute 6 times.

   ➢ Presently, value of P is 1, so statement 'Pth_digit=(Numbers[K] / P) % 10' will assign unit's digit of 'Numbers[K]' to 'Pth_digit'. At each iteration of 'for(K=0; K<N; K++)', Pth_digit is compared with J, where J varies from 0 to 9. If found equal, then 'Numbers[K]' is appended to array 'Queue'. So every number that contains 0 at its unit place will be added in array 'Queue', thereafter numbers that contain 1 at its unit place are added, ...and so on.

   ➢ After execution of first iteration of outer loop, array 'Numbers' will be sorted according to unit's digit, and order of array 'Numbers' will become as under:

72, 345, 56, 106, 38, 249

2) In the second iteration, value of I is 1. So P = pow(10, I) = 10. This time, by the statement 'Pth_digit=(Numbers[K] / P) % 10', ten's digit of 'Numbers[K]' is assigned to 'Pth_digit'. So now list will be sorted according to ten's digit.

3) After third and final iteration, array 'Numbers' will be completely sorted.

10.10 Heap sort

Suppose H is a complete binary tree with n number of elements. Then H is called a **heap**, or a **maxheap**, if value at each node N of H is less than or equal to the value of its parent node. For example, following tree is a maxheap:

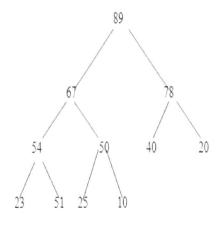

HEAP

496

If H is a heap, then it means that largest element in H appears at the "top" of the heap.

Inserting an Element into the Heap:

In a heap, a new element can be inserted by making it as the last child of the original heap, so that the heap remains a complete binary tree, but inserting an element in this way may violate the order of the heap. So the last inserted element is moved up from its position until it acquires its proper place in the heap. This operation works as follows:

If the value of the last inserted element is greater than the value of its parent node, then interchange both of them. Repeat the same procedure from its parent node, until the newly inserted element obtains its proper place and the tree is converted back into the heap.

Suppose we want to build up a heap from the following list of numbers:

35, 11, 40, 50, 45, 10, 36

Consider a heap, initially having no element in it.

1) Now take the first element and insert it into this empty heap:

35

Heap H

Now heap H contains one element, 35.

2) Take the second element and insert it into the heap such that the heap remains a complete binary tree but not necessarily be a heap.

Heap H

Now adjust the position of 11 in H so that H becomes a heap again. But in this case, 11 is at its proper place in the heap. So, there is no need to bother about it.

3) Insert the third element in the similar fashion:

Figure (a)

Above figure shows a complete binary tree, but it is not a heap. So adjust the position of 40 so that the above tree is converted back into the heap. Pictorial representation of converting it into the heap is shown below:

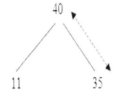

Figure (b) [HEAP H]

498

Compare newly inserted element, 40, with its parent element, 35. 40 is greater than 35, so interchange both of them. Now H is again a heap.

4) Apply the same procedure for inserting element 50 in heap H.

Figure (c)

Above figure shows a complete binary tree, in which, position of 50 has to be adjusted for making it a heap again. See the following figures:

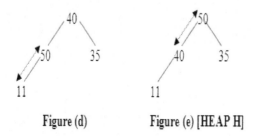

Figure (d)   Figure (e) [HEAP H]

Compare 50 with its parent element, 11, and interchange both of them because 50>11. Again swap 50 with its parent element, 40, because 50>40. Now H is again a heap.

5) Insert 45 in Heap H.

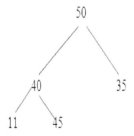

Figure (f)

Make it a heap again:

Figure (g) [HEAP H]

6) Insert 10 in heap H:

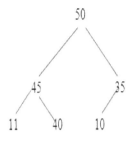

Figure (h) [HEAP H]

In this case, insertion of 10 has not violated the order of heap. So continue inserting elements.

7) Insert 36 in heap H.

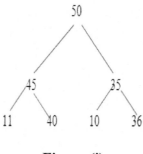

Figure (i)

Make it a heap again:

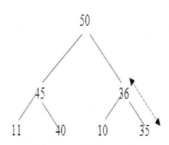

Figure (j) [HEAP H]

Heap made by these numbers is as following:

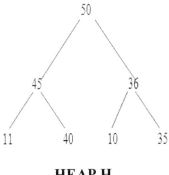

HEAP H

Heap sorting is to extract the elements of this tree in a sorted order. This can be accomplished as follows:

(1) Print(delete) the root R of heap H.

(2) Replace the deleted node R by the last node L of H, so that H is still a complete tree but not necessarily a heap.

(3) If L is not at its proper position in heap H, then interchange the value at node L with the value of one of its child, which is the largest among both of its children. This operation for reheaping the tree H is repeated again and again until L occupies its proper position in heap H.

Procedure for reheaping:

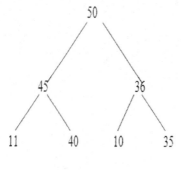

(a) HEAP H

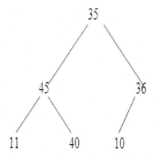

(b) Delete 50 and replace it by 35

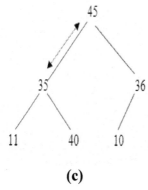

(c)

Root of the tree is not at its proper position in the heap, so compare root with root[left] & root[right] and interchange root with the largest node. In our case, largest node is root[left], which is 45. Swap root with root[left]. Now, 35 is the left child of 45. We name the location of 35 as 'loc'.

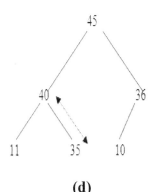

(d)

Compare loc with loc[left] & loc[right] and interchange 'loc' with the largest node. Now, largest node is loc[right], which is 40. Swap 35 and 40. So, element '35' is properly placed at its position now, and again H is finally a heap.

By following this way of extraction of elements from a heap, all the elements of heap H can be taken out in sorted order, one by one.

As, it has been defined that **heap** is a complete binary tree, so, we have to maintain a complete binary tree in memory, but, instead of allocating a new memory space for the tree elements, we may create a logical (virtual) tree in the array itself and can be represented by the following way:

Take first element of the array as the root of the tree, second and third element as the children of first (root) element, and fourth and fifth element as the children of second element and so on. Basically each node 'i' has two children: '2*i' and '2*i + 1', where 'i' can vary from 1 to n/2 only. Here 'n' is the total number of elements.

Please note that if there are n elements in a complete binary tree then there will be n/2 parent (non-leaf) nodes, and the rest will be the leaf nodes.

It requires $\log_2(n)$ comparisons to insert a new element in a heap or to reheapify a tree.

Note: The depth of a complete binary tree is $\log_2(n)$.

****

```
/* Implementation of heap sort */
#include<stdio.h>
#define MAX 20

int x[MAX], n;
void heap(), reheap(int);

void main()
{
            int i;

            printf("Input the size of array\n");
            scanf("%d",&n);

            if(n>MAX)
            {
            printf("Input size is greater than declared size\n");
                    exit();
            }

            printf("enter numbers\n");
```

505

```c
for(i=1;i<=n;i++)
scanf("%d",&x[i]);

heap();          /* heapify the tree */

while(n>=1)
{
        printf("%d ",x[1]);      /* print the largest
                                     element */
        x[1]=x[n];               /* assign last element
                                     of array to x[1] */
        n--;                     /* Now array 'x' contains
                                     'n-1' elements */
        reheap(1);               /* Reheapify the tree and
                                     adjust the root element of the
                                     tree at its proper position */
}  /* end while */

}  /* end main */

void heap()
{
        int i, depth, temp, left, right;

        depth=n;

        while(depth>1)
        {
                depth=depth/2;   /* After each iteration
                                     of this loop, divide
                                     depth by 2 */
                for(i=1;i<=n/2;i++)
                {
                        x[n+1]=x[(n+1)/2];
/* Make right child of x[(n+1)/2] equal to x[(n+1)/2]
   because it will not satisfy the following 'if' condition
   at i=n/2 (if n is even). If we don't do so then by the
   following statement 'right=2*i+1', 'x[right]' will
   take the garbage value at i=n/2 */
```

506

```
                    left=2*i;
                        /* for each 'i' (1< i <n/2), left
                           child of 'x[i]' is x[2*i] */

                    right=2*i + 1;
                        /* and right child of 'x[i]' is
                           'x[2*i +1]' */

                    if(x[i]<x[right])
            /* If value in parent element is less than the
               value of right child, then interchange both of
               them */
                        {
                            temp=x[i];
                            x[i]=x[right];
                            x[right]=temp;
                        }

                    if(x[i]<x[left])
                /* Similarly if left child is greater than parent,
                   then interchange it with parent element */
                        {
                            temp=x[left];
                            x[left]=x[i];
                            x[i]=temp;
                        }
                }  /* end for */
        }  /* end while */
}  /* end heap */

void reheap(int loc)
{
            int left, right, temp;

            if(loc<=n/2)
                {
                    x[n+1]=x[(n+1)/2];    /* If we don't do so, then
                                x[right]will take the garbage value at loc=n/2 */
```
507

```
left=2*loc;
right=2*loc+1;

if(x[left]>x[loc] && x[left]>=x[right])
{
            temp=x[loc];
            x[loc]=x[left];
            x[left]=temp;
            reheap(left);
```

}   /* if 'x[left]>x[right]' then interchange 'x[loc]'
       with 'x[left]'. Now 'x[loc]' is at position 'left',
       so explore left subtree of 'loc' until we get a
       proper position to place 'x[loc]' */

```
else
if(x[right]>x[loc] && x[right]>=x[left])
{
            temp=x[loc];
            x[loc]=x[right];
            x[right]=temp;
            reheap(right);
```

}   /* if 'x[right]>x[left]' then interchange 'x[loc]'
         with 'x[right]'. After doing that 'x[loc]' will
         be placed at position 'right', so this time
         explore right subtree of node 'loc', until
         'x[loc]' acquire its proper position. */

}   /* end if */

} /* end reheap */

/*

After executing:

Input the size of array
6
enter numbers
3 6 8 2 1 0

508

8 6 3 2 1 0..................(output)

*/

****

Steps of the Program:

We will simulate this program with the previous list of numbers:

35, 11, 40, 50, 45, 10, 36

void heap():

1) To heapify a tree we have to make n*log(n) comparisons. So in function 'heap', outer loop 'while(depth>1)' will execute log(n) times and inner loop 'for(i=1;i<=n/2;i++)' will execute n/2 times, and each time 2 comparisons are made. In this way, total comparisons which will be made by this function are n/2 * 2 * log(n). In our case n is 7, and is assigned to 'depth'. After first iteration of outer loop: depth=7/2=3. After second iteration: depth= 3/2=1. So this loop will execute 2 times, as depth of our tree is 2.

2) Inner loop 'for(i=1;i<=n/2;i++)' will execute 3 times, because there are only 3 parent nodes.

3) x[(n+1)/2] is assigned to x[n+1]. Because

   Suppose that we have 6 nodes (even number of nodes). Then n/2 is 3. Right child of this node is x[2*i+1] i.e. x[2*3+1]=x[7]. But x[7] is the 7th

509

element of array 'x', which doesn't belong to this array. So make the value of x[7] equal to its parent element, otherwise it will take the garbage value and in that case, condition 'if(x[i]<x[right])' will fail at i=3.

4) Left and right child of each node 'i' is taken as '2*i' and '2*i+1'.

5) Right child of node 'i' is compared with its parent element 'i' and both of them are interchanged, if right child is greater than its parent node.

6) Similarly, if left child is greater than its parent node, then it is interchanged with its parent node.

void reheap(int loc):

1) We have to reheapify the tree i.e. we have to place the root element of the tree at its proper position in the heap. So from function main, 1 is passed to function 'reheap' i.e. location of the root element of the tree.

2) Location of root element is collected in variable 'loc'.

3) If 'loc<=n/2' i.e. if node at location 'loc' is not the leaf node of the tree, then following steps are executed:

   (a) If 'loc' is not at its proper position in the heap, then left child of x[loc] is compared with its right child. If left child is greater than the right child, then 'x[loc]' is interchanged with its left child. Now element 'x[loc]' is at position 'left'. So function 'reheap' is again called by passing the location of 'x[loc]' as 'left'.

(b) Else, if right child is greater than the left child, then 'x[loc]' is interchanged with 'x[right]', and again function 'reheap' is called with parameter 'right', which is the new location of 'x[loc]'.

4) After few recursive calls 'x[loc]' will be properly placed at its position in the heap.

10.11 Binary Tree Sort

This method involves scanning each element of the array and placing it into its proper position in a binary search tree. Once each input element is in its proper position in the tree, the sorted file can be retrieved by an inorder traversal of the tree.

****

```
/* Implementation of binary tree sort */

#include<stdio.h>
#include<alloc.h>
#define MAX 20

typedef struct tree_type
{
    struct tree_type *left;
    int info;
    struct tree_type *right;
}tree;
```

511

```c
tree *root=NULL;

void inorder(tree *);
void maketree(int item);

void main()
{
        int key, n, i;

        printf("enter number of elements\n");
        scanf("%d",&n);

        if(n>MAX)
        {
        printf("Input size is greater than declared size\n");
                exit();
        }
        printf("enter numbers\n");

        for(i=1;i<=n;i++)
        {
            scanf("%d",&key);
            maketree(key);

        }       /* Make a binary search tree from scanned numbers */

        inorder(root);
}  /* end main */

void maketree(int item)
{
        tree *ptr, *loc, *daddy;

        ptr=(tree *)malloc(sizeof(tree));
```

```
                if(ptr==NULL)
                {
                        printf("no space\n");
                        return;
                }

        (*ptr).info=item;
        (*ptr).left=(*ptr).right=NULL;

        if(root==NULL)        /* if tree is empty then create 'root' of the
                                  tree */
        {
                root=ptr;
                return;
        }

        loc=root;

        while(loc!=NULL)      /* search for the empty subtree, where
                                 'item' can be inserted */
        {
                daddy=loc;

                if(item<(*loc).info)
                loc=(*loc).left;
                else
                loc=(*loc).right;

        }       /*  store the location of parent node of  empty subtree in
                     pointer 'daddy'  */

        if(item<(*daddy).info)
        (*daddy).left=ptr;    /* if 'item' is less than 'info' part of parent
                                 node, then insert 'ptr' at 'daddy->left' */
        else
        (*daddy).right=ptr;        /* else insert it at 'daddy->right' */

}  /* end maketree */
```

513

```
void inorder(tree *ptr)
{
        if(ptr!=NULL)
        {
            inorder((*ptr).left);      /* call recursively with left child of
                                           'ptr' */
            printf("%d ",(*ptr).info);

            inorder((*ptr).right);         /* call this function again with
                                              right child of 'ptr' */
        }

}       /* print 'info' part of left child of 'ptr', 'info' part of 'ptr' itself and then
           print 'info' of right child of 'ptr' recursively */

/*

After executing:

Enter number of elements
5
enter numbers
6 1 5 7 2
1 2 5 6 7......................(output)

*/
```

****

Steps of the Program:

Simply insert all the numbers, which have to be sorted, in a
binary search tree one by one by using 'maketree' function.
And retrieve the numbers in a sorted order by in-order
traversal of this tree.

514

10.12   Address Calculation Sort

In this type of sorting technique, the file, which has to be sorted, is divided into several sorted subfiles. The criteria to place all the elements in several sorted files is shown below:

- Initially, create some number of empty files.
- Apply a function say F on each element of the unsorted list of numbers. This function determines that into which of the several created files, the element has to be inserted.
- After applying this function, insert the element into the specified file, in sorted order.

An item can be placed into a subfile in a correct sequence by using any sorting method, but usually simple insertion method is used to insert an item into a sorted file.

After all the items of the original file have been placed into several sorted subfiles, the sorted list of numbers can be retrieved by concatenating all the subfiles. Sometimes this technique is also called sorting by Hashing.

EXAMPLE:

Consider the following array of unsorted numbers:

92,   86,   15,   38,   16,   25,   45,   51,   26

As this sort places each item of the unsorted array into a sorted subfile, so our task is to create subfiles. For the above array, we will create 10 subfiles, one for each of the ten possible 10's digit, which is the most significant digit in the above mentioned numbers. In this array, largest number is of

2 digits, so, the most significant digit is the 10's digit. And this method will be useful, when total numbers of digits of most of the numbers are equal to the total number of digits of the largest number, as, by using this method, we are going to create 10 subfiles for the 10 possible values of the most significant digit. Initially each of these subfiles is empty. An array of pointers F[10] is declared, where F[i] points to the i_{th} subfile ($0 \leq i \leq 9$), such that 10's digit of every number in the i_{th} subfile is i. And this file is in sorted order. Each of these subfiles is maintained by a sorted linked list of elements, where f[i] contains the starting location of the i_{th} linked list.

F(0) =NULL

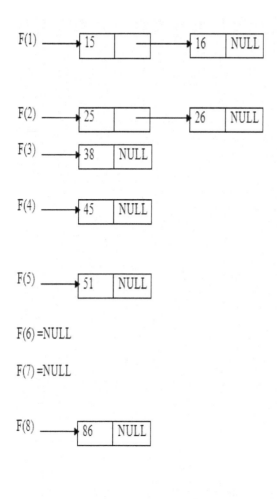

F(1) ───→ | 15 | ─── ──→ | 16 | NULL |

F(2) ───→ | 25 | ─── ──→ | 26 | NULL |

F(3) ───→ | 38 | NULL |

F(4) ───→ | 45 | NULL |

F(5) ───→ | 51 | NULL |

F(6) = NULL

F(7) = NULL

F(8) ───→ | 86 | NULL |

F(9) ───→ | 92 | NULL |

After all the subfiles are produced, sorted file of all the numbers can be retrieved by concatenating all the subfiles through F(0) to F(9).

517

```
************************************************

/*   Implementation of Address Calculation Sort   */

#include<stdio.h>
#include<math.h>
#include<alloc.h>
#define MAX 20

typedef struct node_type
{
       int info;
       struct node_type *next;
}NODE;

void AddressCalSort(int[], int);
int LengthOfLargestNumber(int[], int);

void main()
{
       int Numbers[MAX], N, I;
       printf("Enter number of elements\n");
       scanf("%d", &N);

       if(N>MAX)
       {
           printf("Input size is greater than declared size\n");
            exit();
       }
       printf("Enter numbers\n");
       for(I=0; I<N: I++)
       scanf("%d", &Numbers[I]);

       AddressCalSort(Numbers, N);

       printf("Sorted numbers are\n");
       for(I=0; I<N; I++)
       printf("%d ", Numbers[I]);

}    /* end main */
```

```c
void AddressCalSort(int Numbers[MAX], int N)
{
    NODE *F[10], *PTR, *PREV, *LOC;
    int I, Div, K, Length;

    for(I=0; I<10; I++)
        F[I]=NULL;

    Length=LengthOfLargestNumber(Numbers, N);
                        /* Invoke this function for finding the total number
                           of digits of the largest number in the array */

    Div=pow(10, Length-1);    /* Suppose, largest number in the
                                 array is of 2 digits, then
                                 Div=pow(10,1)=10. So, if we
                                 divide each number by Div,
                                 then we get the 10's digit of
                                 each number */

    for(I=0; I<N; I++)
    {
        K=Numbers[I]/Div;    /* Numbers[I] will be stored in
                                the subfile, pointed by F[K] */

        PTR=(NODE *) malloc(sizeof(NODE));
        if(PTR==NULL)
        {
            printf("No space\n");
            exit();
        }
        PTR->info=Numbers[I];
        PTR->next=NULL;

        if(F[K]==NULL)
        {
            F[K]=PTR;
            continue;
        }
```

519

```
            PREV=NULL;
            LOC=F[K];

        while(LOC != NULL && LOC->info < Numbers[I])
                {
                        PREV=LOC;
                        LOC=LOC->next;

                }  /* Search for the location 'PREV', after which node
                        'PTR' has to be inserted  */

                if(PREV==NULL)
                {
                        PTR->next=F[K];
                        F[K]=PTR;

                }   /* Now 'PTR' will be the starting node of the sublist
                        'F[K]'  */

                else
                {
                        PTR->next=LOC;
                        PREV->next=PTR;

                } /* If 'PREV!=NULL', then insert 'PTR' after node
                        'PREV'  */
        }  /* end for  */

        for(K=0, I=0; K<10; K++)
                for(PTR=F[K]; PTR!=NULL; PTR=PTR->next)
                        Numbers[I++]=PTR->info;
                                        /* Concatenate all the sublists
                                           in array 'Numbers'  */
}  /* end AddressCalSort  */
```

```
int LengthOfLargestNumber(int Numbers[MAX], int N)
{
        int max, I, Length=0;

        max=Numbers[0];

        for(I=0; I<N; I++)
                if(Numbers[I]>max)
                        max=Numbers[I];
        while(max>0)
        {
                max=max/10;
                Length++;
        }

        return Length;

} /* end LengthOfLargestNumber */

/*

After executing:

Enter number of elements
9
Enter numbers
92   86   15   38   16   25   45   51   26
15   16   25   26   38   45   51   86   92................(output)

*/
```

****

Steps of the Program:

Suppose array is:

92   86   15   38   16   25   45   51   26

void AddressCalSort(int Numbers[MAX] int N):

1) Here largest number is 92. The number of digits in this number are 2. So div=pow(10, length-1)=10.

2) For each number I, following statements are executed:

   (a) At first iteration: I=1, Numbers[1]=92 and 'K=Numbers[I]/Div', which is 92/10=9. A new node PTR is created and this number 92 is assigned to PTR->info. After that, it is inserted in the beginning of the linked list, pointed by F[9]. And, after the second iteration, 86 is inserted in the beginning of the linked list pointed by F[8].

   (b) Consider third iteration i.e. at this time I=3 and Numbers[I]=15. Therefore 15 iteration, we encounter 16. So, the proper location of 16 is searched in the linked list that is addressed by pointer F[1], and contains 15 at this moment. Here, '16>15', therefore, 16 is inserted after the first node, and it becomes the last node of the sublist.

   .
   .
   .

   All the sublists are generated accordingly.

3) After that, all these sublists are concatenated in array 'Numbers' and result is printed when control of the program is returned to function 'main'.

www.ingramcontent.com/pod-product-compliance
Lightning Source LLC
LaVergne TN
LVHW022258060326
832902LV00020B/3151